A Father's Diary

Fraser Harrison was born in 1944 at Stackpole, near Pembroke, and educated at Shrewsbury and Trinity Hall, Cambridge. He then worked for a number of publishing houses, including Sidgwick and Jackson where he was the editor for five years. In 1975 he left London to live in Stowlangtoft, Suffolk, and work full-time as a writer. His first book was an anthology of *The Yellow Book*, which was followed by *The Dark Angel*, a study of Victorian sexuality. In 1982 he published *Strange Land – The Countryside: Myth and Reality* and is currently working on a second book about the modern countryside. Last year he contributed to *Second Nature*, an anthology of country writing. He has also published short stories and is a regular contributor to *The Literary Review*. Since the completion of the diary, the Harrison family has moved from Stowlangtoft, but only a few hundred yards up the road to another village.

Fraser Harrison

A Father's Diary

Illustrated by Harriet Dell

FLAMINGO

Published by Fontana Paperbacks

First published in 1985 by Fontana Paperbacks,
8 Grafton Street, London W1X 3LA
Second impression May 1985

Copyright © Fraser Harrison 1985

Set in Linotron Trump
Made and printed in Great Britain by
William Collins Sons & Co. Ltd, Glasgow

To Kath and Brian,
Peg and Doug,
their grandparents,
and to their great friend, Gail

Contents

Introduction

I have called this a *father's* diary because most of its entries are concerned with my children and my own thoughts, feelings and experiences as their father.

I have two children: Tilly (Matilda on her birth certificate, but never called anything but Tilly or variations of it), who is aged four years and eight months when this diary opens, and Jack, who is three and a quarter.

As I began to keep the diary in earnest I made a couple of thumbnail sketches of the children. Tilly, I wrote then, is dark and impish, with grey-blue eyes; she is small for her age and very dainty. She was born with a fine head of hair, which she never lost as a baby; it is now thick and Latin-black and she wears it in a little bouncy pigtail. She is volatile, gay, gregarious, quick to organize others, but no less quick to join in any game that is under way. She is eager for attention and quicksilver in her movements and speech. I think of her as forever skipping and laughing, though recently she has been growing more serious and thoughtful. She goes to a nursery school, as does Jack, and spends half a day a week at 'big school', where she will go full-time next term. She can read simple books, write her name well, and legibly copy almost anything she is given. Her drawings, I would say, are unusually expressive.

Jack, I wrote, is not big for his age either, but he has been endowed with a substantial head, pudding-bowl in shape, and his mother's round face. He has only just left babyhood behind, though he is now unmistakably a little boy. He has a robust and merry look about him and has full-bloodedly entered the stage of benign aggression, which seems to be distinctive of boys' development. He delights in attacking and punching us, but he also frequently asks to be picked up and hugged. He is given to raucous laughter at incomprehensible (to us) jokes. He plays prolonged and elaborate games with his tractors and lorries, muttering to himself all the while. When asked to come here, he automatically runs away, giggling, to hide under his bed. Getting him dressed requires all one's physical and mental strength. (Tilly dresses herself, with a fastidious eye for matching colours.) He freely loses his temper when crossed and lashes out at me with terrible blows. And, like his sister, he is mischievous and affectionate in his dealings with us, and high-spirited with other children.

I have kept some kind of diary since 1971, when I got into the habit of making notes of the laughable incidents, of which I am happy to say there were a great many, punctuating my career as an editor with the publishers Sidgwick and Jackson. After I left London and came to Suffolk to live and write, these jottings swelled into an irregular diary. Then, on the day Jack was born, I decided to start a full-dress journal, which I succeeded in writing up virtually every day throughout the first year of his life. (This decision was not made out of sexist favouritism; on the contrary, my interest was primarily in Tilly's responses to her new, intruding brother. It was many weeks before Jack himself provided much copy.) At that time I had no idea of publication; the text was, in any case, unpublishably intimate, libellous and trite. I reverted to my sporadic jottings.

However, on reading over the journal some time later I felt a very sharp pang of regret that I had not persisted with it. I also realized that a formal journal, made specifically for publication, with no pretensions to being anything other than an account in the year of the life of a father and his children, would be unique, if nothing else. To my knowledge at least, no other book exists which offers a daily record of this relationship.

And so, two years later, with an eye to publication from the start, I set about compiling such a record. The starting date of the fourteenth of May had no particular significance; it was simply the day on which I suddenly felt ready. During the first few weeks I kept alive the notion of adopting the detached, objective point of view of a naturalist noting the behaviour of some rare fauna that had strayed into his house. I think this appealed to me as a defence against the possible charge that the diary was too personal. My plan was to universalize its interest by treating the children as if they were merely representatives of their species. In the way that individual otters, or whatever, are always accepted as embodiments of the essence of otter, I hoped that 'Tilly' and 'Jack' would be understood to be cyphers, typifying a certain phase of human development. Fortunately, I can now find no trace of this nonsense in the diary itself. My nervousness was anyway soon dispelled by the thought that I was striving after a contradiction in terms: after all, who on earth would want to read an *impersonal* diary?

At the outset I was also ambitious to weave into the entries a chronicle of our Suffolk country life, season by season, together with a running commentary on life at large. But I quickly discovered that these three elements did not blend well. I discovered too that, whereas I occasionally had something to say about the countryside or the world beyond our house, I invariably had a great deal to say about the children. And so I happily settled down to writing as complete a log as I could of the children's voyage through a single year.

I made it a duty to write up an entry at least once every two days, whether an obviously reportable event had taken place or not. In the event, this duty was never onerous. Some entries, such as birthdays, Christmas, holidays, first days of term, and so on, virtually wrote themselves, as did those describing the touching little incidents and comic remarks which are the everyday stuff of having small children in a house. But, for the rest, I never found myself scratching my head, wondering how to fill my quota (a page per sitting). Admittedly, I do not think I could have kept up my punctiliousness for much more than a year, though I badly missed the discipline when I stopped. Nor do I think that more than a year's worth would be easily digestible by a reader.

Despite the essentially humdrum nature of our lives here, some new facet of the children's developing selves presented itself almost every day, rendering the diary a pleasure to write, never a chore. Children are undergoing change in some respect all the time. Some changes are achieved by gradual, barely noticeable accretions of ability and perception, some by overnight, quantum leaps. At every level children are both creative and the objects of creativity, for they are literally making themselves and being made at the same time. Parents are therefore constantly being remade as well. By keeping the diary I have been able to preserve the invaluable fine detail of these sequences of change, most of which would otherwise have been irretrievably forgotten – and forgotten by all of us, for the period of the diary precedes the threshold of memory for both children, especially Jack.

I have another, more important reason for not continuing with the diary as a book beyond this summer. Although Jack does not really understand what I have been doing, Tilly has a much clearer idea and has had ever since she learnt to read proficiently. I fear that if I were to go on, they would both begin to feel used, intruded on and even spied on. The diary itself would become an influential, and pernicious, presence in the house, affecting everyone's behaviour.

This is the real charge I have to face, that I have been exploiting the children for my own selfish ends, and it is one to which I have no real defence. I can only plead some mitigating factors. As far as I can tell, neither of the children resents my writing about them or feels badly treated. Tilly accepts the diary as a natural gesture of homage from a fan to a star and she condescendingly refers to it as 'our book', meaning hers and Jack's. She occasionally asks after its progress, but has never shown more than mild curiosity in its contents. Secondly, I have tried to examine myself in the diary as closely as them, and I have not shirked or concealed those aspects of my own behaviour which have made me feel ashamed. Thirdly, I do not believe the appearance of the book will damage them, it may even give them some fun; if I thought they would suffer, I would not publish.

I cannot predict the impact of the diary on them in the future. No doubt, it will provide ammunition for fights to come, especially during the strife of adolescence. However, I hope in time they will recognize that such a book as this can only be written out of love.

The diary contains one very obvious distortion, which I must explain. Sally, my wife and the children's mother, remains a shadowy figure throughout, tending to emerge from the darkness only when her sheep are mentioned. (Among her many other activities, she manages a small flock.) As anyone who has had the slightest acquaintance with her will testify, the insignificant and retiring body depicted here bears no similarity to the original. The reason for her apparent obscurity is, however, simple. My primary objective, apart from making a record of the children's lives, was to give an account of my experiences specifically as a father. When reported on a day-by-day basis, many of them did seem separable from my experiences as a husband, though this is quite untrue of the overall reality of our way of life as a family, which relies far more on Sally than me for its *joie de vivre* and cohesion.

Finally, a word about our home and general situation. We live in a large rented farmhouse in Stowlangtoft, a small village not far from Bury St Edmunds in Suffolk. This is the most important house of my adult life, and the happiest. Sally and I moved here from London in the September of 1975, a move which was the outward sign of my having resigned from publishing and taken a gamble on survival as a freelance. Sally and I held our wedding party here; I have written all but one of my books here; and it was here that we brought both our children home from hospital when they were born.

The house itself was probably built in the eighteenth century for the bailiff of the home farm attached to the Stowlangtoft estate. We can see the old Hall, which is now a nursing home, and most of its parkland from our northward bedroom windows. Unlike so many Suffolk farmhouses, ours cannot really be described as beautiful; on the other hand, it is immensely hospitable, or so it has always been to us. It stands in its own substantial garden, a perfect playground for the children, but the first feature to strike our visitors, through the nose if not the eye, is probably the presence of the pigs, who are our immediate neighbours. On the other side of a low wall opposite our back door is a muddy yard formed by a quadrangle of pens, which are inhabited by a pair of formidable boars and their circulating harems of sows. Pigs wake us in the morning as they scream in anticipation of their breakfast, and their somnolent rumblings soothe us to sleep at night. Both my children pronounced 'piggy' as their first word.

In his memorable, though hardly practicable, 'Advice to a Father', William Cobbett reported, with predictable contempt, that a gentleman in his neighbourhood had recently sued a farmer for allowing a bull to 'perform' in the field in front of his drawing-room window, to the horror of his wife and unmarried daughters. The gentleman lost his case and was obliged to block up the offending window. At some time our house must have been occupied by a man of similar sensitivities, for the window in our drawing-room which overlooks the pig yard was also closed up when we moved in. Acting in the spirit of Cobbett, we unsealed it and now enjoy an unhindered view of pig orgies, such as they are. We were in any event lost to morality, because the bathroom, the children's room and even our own bedroom all face the same way.

Within the house further evidence of early nineteenth-century gentility is to be found. We have a double staircase system, installed at considerable expense of space, which ensured that the family avoided all contact with the servants as they made their way from their sleeping quarters in the attic to their work in the kitchen and sculleries. In every other respect, however, the house is wonderfully adapted to my idea of comfortable living. The rooms are spacious, with high ceilings, and there are enough of them to allow me one for my exclusive use, though the children show scant respect for my closed door. In case an impression of luxury, rather than comfort, has been given, I should add that our only source of heating, aside from an open fire in each room, is provided by a venerable Aga in the kitchen, and that our water is furnished by a pump, which throbs through the house like a sclerotic artery and serves the pigs' tanks before ours.

Working here at home has given me the opportunity, available to very few fathers, to watch and take part in every moment of my children's lives. Nothing in my own life has given me as much pleasure as my family, and nothing has given me as much satisfaction to write about.

Stowlangtoft

A Father's Diary

May

Friday, 14 May

Jack is a man of his times. His customary mode of socializing at the moment is the head-butt, delivered at full tilt. He will sprint round a room, roaring as he goes, and then charge his victim, releasing tremendous exploding noises as he makes contact. This ritual is carried out with a bewildering mixture of good humour and homicidal rage. He reserves his most deadly blows, which hurt, for those he loves most. Sometimes his aggressive energy wells up uncontrollably and he is overtaken by a kind of spasm, during which he roars, explodes, thrashes his arms, shakes his head and runs in tight circles with his eyes shut and teeth gritted. Tilly has never been overwhelmed like him by her own aggression. There is no question that he is killing in earnest when he detonates himself in front of you or blasts you with his 'shooter'. 'You're dead,' he cackles gleefully. No question, either, of the penile character of these weapons: anything he comes across which is remotely phallic is immediately adopted as a gun.

At his age, Tilly often talked about us dying, but she never showed the same murderous feelings. Instead, she would refer to our extinction with hearty matter-of-factness. 'When you're dead' was a common prelude to some speculation about her own future as a grown-up. She believed then that her own adulthood could not properly begin until we had made way for her by dying. Now she never mentions the prospect and it seems to have lost its meaning for her.

Of course, they know next to nothing of the reality of death, although the little experience they have had – the deaths of two lambs – has deeply fascinated them. They were momentarily shocked by the sight of the drowned lamb in the water trough, but had recovered by the time it came to be buried in our garden. They watched its grave being dug, fittingly beneath a yew tree, and involved themselves in the business of its interment, though they needed the reassurance that it would be warm and snug in its sack. Sally has told them that its body will make the flowers above its grave grow big; Tilly predicts daisies will appear there, Jack favours daffodils.

The death of Sparkle, the orphan lamb we all hand-fed, was another matter. They were much more profoundly upset by it and mourn her still. They often say how much they miss her and sometimes mention her name just for the sake of it.

Today we found ourselves following a cortege on its way to the funeral at Badwell Ash of a gypsy. There is a gypsy community living in caravans on a site beside the road that links our village with Badwell Ash. The cortege was very long; indeed, it must have comprised the entire community. Behind the hearse was a tractor pulling a trailer loaded with flowers, which scattered the road every yard of the way. Later, we saw the flowers had been heaped on the grave and all round it in a great square of glowing colour.

Whatever the advantages or otherwise of belonging to a minority culture may be, gypsy children must grow up with an understanding of death that frees them, at least to some degree, from the feelings of repugnance the rest of us have towards the old age and death of others, feelings which in turn only add to the horror each of us feels at the thought of his or her own death.

Sunday, 16 May
Lying in bed with me this morning, the children were comparing my genitals with Jack's.

Tilly said, 'You've got one ball left in case you want to have another baby.'

I said, 'No I haven't, I've got two like Jack.'

Very puzzled, Tilly said, 'But you've had two children already.'

As with all children's fantasies about reproduction, her idea of balls being like bullets in a magazine, ready to be fired off whenever a baby is to be made, is, though mistaken, perfectly logical.

Monday, 17 May
This afternoon I dug up a honeysuckle (*Lonicera flexuosa*, its label informs me) which the hard winter had killed off. To be frank, it had never been much of a plant, and its natural weakness had been aggravated by my inept handling, for I had moved it too often. Originally, it had been planted in a white wooden tub by our back door in the hope it would climb the post supporting the porch and eventually cover it. However, it never grew far enough out of its tub to establish any kind of grasp on its trellis. Each spring it would throw out a cluster of shoots, which would grow a foot or more and then, in May or June, would shrivel and blacken before any flowers appeared.

I moved it to different sites, but it never improved. Ironically, it was probably in its most favourable position when the cold struck it down; last summer, for the first time, it managed to produce a sprinkling of red blossoms, which had a surprisingly sweet and powerful scent.

Looking at its twisted, dried-out skeleton, I could easily reconstruct its calamitous odyssey round the garden: each abortive spurt of growth was registered in a thick, stunted stem, with its own shock of desiccated shoots. Its death, though a good riddance in every practical respect, has saddened me, because I can read in its crippled branches the sequence of our own years here in the house. It is precisely this visible record of the accretion of growth, which many species show very clearly, that makes the presence of plants in our lives so moving – so essential – and eases the over-shadowing knowledge of our own finite passage through time.

Conservation is not only an ecological, but a psychological imperative too.

Tuesday, 18 May
The children's favourite game these days is making houses. Best of all, they like us to throw blankets over a circle of chairs or the climbing frame so they can drag inside their dolls and toys and take up residence. More often than not, Tilly will include a house in her drawings. They also like to make trains with chairs lined up across the kitchen; 'Africa' is their usual destination. However, for Jack, who is generally the driver, the journey is nothing compared with the ritual of embarkation. He becomes completely absorbed in the business of collecting tickets, hitching up carriages, putting on his driver's hat and so on. Although he repeatedly climbs into his engine (the front chair) and shouts 'Off we go' in his loudest voice, his trains rarely leave the station, and if they do they are soon stopped again to be subjected interminably to

his ticket-collecting routine. Tilly, meanwhile, sits patiently through this performance, having got herself organized like some great matriarch, her carriages loaded up with luggage and accompanied by her entire family of dolls, a formidable body when collected *en masse*, each dressed and packed for the journey and equipped with a lunch box.

It might appear that their respective roles in this game conform to classic gender stereotypes, and of course to some extent they do. However, I am sure their game cannot be reduced to a simple prefigurement of the fact that, according to convention, men in adult life are the drivers and women their passengers. Nor do I believe these roles are interchangeable and that only our encouragement, which anyway has never been consciously directive, reinforced by the general cultural environment, makes them choose so distinctively.

It is evident to me that the idea of the train fulfils some phallic fantasy of Jack's, which has no significance for Tilly, but which is quite consistent with the overall theme of his play at the moment. No doubt, one should not act the amateur psychoanalyst, but the analogy strikes me as unmistakable. Through his embarkation ritual, he reassures himself of the train's shape, he identifies himself with it and asserts his command over it.

Tilly, on the other hand, has no real interest in any of this, though she does occasionally like to take the driving seat and actually set off, getting us all to make appropriate 'chuff-chuff' noises. But mostly she sees the train as a vessel, as something to be inside. She organizes her family and its baggage with a powerful gift for logistics. In this, there is a close identification with Sally, and her 'mothering' attention to her dolls and their needs is certainly quite different from the way Jack uses his dolls, which is largely a matter of satisfying his own need for physical comfort. He cuddles them, but seldom looks after them. Also, though it is probably only a question of their difference in age, Tilly brings to the game a depth of forethought and a determination to follow her plan through to the last detail that he never achieves.

To my mind, these very pronounced tendencies in their play do indicate elemental differences in the ontogenesis, the pattern of development, undergone by boys and girls.

Incidentally, I think their game shows as well why the steam train seems so much more romantic than our modern diesel and electric trains. The children have seen plenty of diesels at our local station when we pick up friends and they have made one or two trips on the little three-carriage train that runs between Cambridge and Ipswich. They are very excited by the idea of train journeys, hence the perennial popularity of this game, but they model their imaginary trains on steam ones, which they have only seen on television. When Jack can be persuaded to get them moving, their trains travel in a storm of puffing and whistle-blowing. The children automatically identify with the visible, audible expression of motion in steam trains, and this is surely the key to the widespread nostalgia they attract: they are very readily anthropomorphized. Electric trains glide out of the station and diesel trains trundle out; in neither case does nature stand a chance of winning. But the steam engine can be seen to take the strain and then heave itself into motion with what appears to be a supreme summoning of strength and will, which is registered in the sweat and labour of its steaming boiler and hissing wheels. It makes its effort manifest. To the Victorians, it was the monster of technology personified, but to us it seems more like an animal than a machine, drawing its energy from a source touchingly similar to our own muscles and adrenalin.

Monday, 24 May
One of the children's friends, a little girl aged about three and a half, told us that her hen had got some new baby chickens. I asked her how old they were. She was silent for a long time and then said, very carefully, 'About a year old, I think.'

On Saturday Tilly and Jack were taken to the theatre to see a children's musical. Evidently, they both enjoyed the show, never taking their eyes off the stage, but when they came home neither would tell us anything about it. I am sure all children are alike in this. Later, Jack did tell me about a spider, which had frightened him. He capered about showing me the way it had danced in its web, but then he frightened himself and ran to me, nearly crying. And Tilly told me the theatre was funny because it had sky inside. (The Theatre Royal at Bury St Edmunds, allegedly the oldest Regency theatre still in use, has rococo clouds rolling across a blue sky painted on its ceiling.) This, however, was all we heard about what for them had been an exceptional and thrilling experience.

But then all experience is exceptional to them; everything is new and distinct. The past closes up behind them immediately, while the future is an unimagined blank. They live on an edge of time. Like animals, they are absorbed in the present, in time being, and make no history of their own. Adult notions of the sequence of time and the cyclical ordering of existence have no meaning for them: all meals are 'supper' to Jack. When they are asked to make calculations about time, they mouth a language that has no significance, and the results are crazy or comical.

What makes children tiring to be with is not so much their energy, which is indeed daunting, as the intensity of their involvement in the here and now. They seem to penetrate the present in a way that adults only experience in dreams, or when undergoing extremes of misery and elation, states of mind that are a return to childhood. Adults, having eaten the fruit of knowledge, must protect themselves against being thrust so deeply into experience. Much of life is only bearable because of our capacity to fantasize about a better situation, or to concentrate on the tolerable parts of an intolerable whole. On the other hand, one of the joys of having children is being able to participate for a little while in their Zen-like immersion in play. In fact, that is what defines play. It is not any particular activity, but oblivion within it. If children were burdened with a sense of personal history, if they could recall and reconstruct yesterday, they would be quite unable to achieve their total inherence in the present, and their capacity to continue learning would be shut down. This, presumably, is what happens to severely traumatized children. Having no sense of time, but having been deprived of the childhood gift of forgetfulness, their wound is opened afresh each day. They know too much to learn any more.

Wednesday, 26 May
Every morning we are woken around 7.15 by the screeching of the boars and sows which are kept in the yard just below our bedroom window. They set up their ear-splitting screams at the first throb of the tractor bringing their food. I am told they can distinguish between the engine noises made by the

26

various tractors starting up in the farm each morning, and only begin their chorus of anticipation at the sound of the pig-man's. While shrieking, they also stand with their front trotters on the bars of their pen, grinding their teeth on them and foaming at the mouth.

Once our singular alarm has sounded, we lie dozing in bed. Sooner or later, we hear the thud of footsteps, and the door connecting our room with the children's swings open to bang against the wall. A mysterious pause follows and then Jack appears – in mid-air. Having landed, he totters all the way round our bed on stiff legs, his eyes still bleary. As he makes this journey, he pumps his arms and leans forward as if combating a gale-force wind. Finally he arrives at my side and I slot him into bed beside me where he lies still for a minute or two.

The explanation for the pause and his airborne arrival eluded us until we realized he dislikes walking on the cold strip of bare board that separates the carpet in their room from the one in ours. To avoid it, he first throws open the door, then draws back a pace or two and catapults himself across the icy interval.

Soon enough, however, he is demanding tea and we go downstairs together to switch on the radio, put on the kettle and collect the post and milk from the garage. It has become his job to open the envelopes, which he does by tearing off little strips wherever he can find a loose corner. Though quite dexterous, their hands at this age are relatively very weak. He insists on putting his own sugar in his tea, an excuse really for licking the spoon, which he loads with sugar and barely dips in the cup at all. I take the tea upstairs and he carries up the letters on a separate tray. Meanwhile, Tilly will have crept into our bed with Sally and we usually discover them reading their books.

Lately the morning routine has been got through in a very jolly spirit until it is time for Jack to dress, when he tends to cry and resist. I believe this has something to do with his not wanting to exchange the infantile security of pyjamas for the autonomy that is implied in putting on his clothes. The prospect of facing the day as a self-sufficient identity, isolated from the comforting fetal memories evoked by being in bed and the close physical familiarity we enjoy as we all wake up, still unnerves him. But then, who does not occasionally feel the same way?

Friday, 28 May
Sally is making plans to have her oldest lambs weighed and, if they are heavy enough, slaughtered and butchered. I wonder how the children will react to their disappearance. The experience will probably not be too anguished, for the lambs will not all go at once, and anyway Sally is arranging to buy in a dozen younger ones to fatten up through the summer.

I will never forget the first time, a few weeks ago in March, I saw a lamb being born, and yet I feel no qualms at the thought of their being killed, or even of eating them; indeed, I am looking forward to it.

I remember the lamb slithering to the ground, a red, glistening, shapeless bundle in our torch-light. The membrane had not been ruptured, which gave the lamb inside the gruesome look of already being meat in a butcher's flimsy plastic bag. It lay inert at our feet. Sally, too anxious to wait and let the mother do her job, knelt in the straw and brushed away the mucus from its nose. She blew hard into its mouth. The night was very cold and little clouds of steam rose from the grey, wet, blood-flecked body, which now looked more like a dish-rag just pulled out of hot water.

28

The ewe nosed her lamb and began licking, but it remained motionless. Sally slapped its chest above the heart. 'Come on, little fellow.' She blew into its nose again and pushed it a little, hoping for movement. I put my hand on its coat: it was slimy and much warmer than I had expected. It gave off a sweet, oily smell.

The night was also very clear. I remember the end of the world had been predicted for that week, because all the planets were clustered together in one quarter. I could see Mars glowing fiercely near the moon and Jupiter glimmering below.

Sally slapped the lamb's chest once more. 'Come on. Up you get. Don't die on me.' The membrane in the straw, a mess of tissue and blood, was impossible to recognize as the life-support system it had just been, but the lamb was still only an extruded organ belonging to the ewe. Sally prodded it and splayed out its absurdly long legs. Suddenly we heard a feeble bleat and saw its sides contract. Sally massaged the bony little rib-cage, while the ewe went at her licking with new intensity. The lamb tried to lift its head, which only lolled and rolled, but it bleated again with real strength and its legs twitched and then scrabbled.

Sally switched off our torch and we stood for a moment listening to the unmistakable sound of a ewe cleaning up and grooming her newborn lamb – a deep, throaty, repetitive rumble. She had already licked clean its back and rump, leaving the wool standing up in a neat, curly mat. In the moonlight, we saw the lamb make its first crumbling attempt to gain its legs.

The next day Sally asked the shepherd who works on our neighbour's farm how many lambs he had watched being born that night. Twenty was the answer. Surely, I thought, the phenomenon of life springing into those slippery bags of bones on the freezing grass had long since lost its power to move him? After all, he is the

29

professional, whereas we are merely amateurs, and our priorities are very different. What to us is, we hope, a paying hobby, is to him a livelihood. Not the least of our motives for keeping our flock, if fifteen venerable, nearly toothless Border Leicester matrons can be dignified by the title, is precisely to enjoy its spiritual and other non-commercial rewards. The shepherd, on the other hand, works exhaustingly long hours during lambing, often in severe cold, with six hundred ewes owned by his employer, for relatively low wages. These are conditions of work which presumably leave no place for the kind of middle-class emotionalism we can afford to indulge in.

But it was not so. I have never read of a shepherd nor spoken to one for whom lambing was merely a task to be got through like any other. They all openly declare that their feelings are affected when a lamb achieves life, despite having witnessed it a thousand times before, and that the completion of lambing brings a deep sense of satisfaction.

I know the dangers of thinking this way. For centuries the shepherd has been the object of fantasy and misplaced identification: the queen of France and her ladies did not play at being swineherds. In fact the life of the shepherd was in many ways harder than that of the other farm workers, and much more isolated, though of necessity he was far freer to use his own judgement. This is still true today. Mechanization has turned the ploughman into a tractor driver and while his work is incomparably less laborious, its scope for individualism is likewise diminished. But the shepherd's work has not been so radically changed and the demands on his skill and initiative are as great as ever. However, I am not romanticizing him: the shepherd has by no means escaped from the cultural and social environment the rest of us have to live in, and there are aspects of his job that are no more immune to alienation than any Leyland assembly worker's.

Even so, a shepherd's work clearly does offer satisfactions not to be found in many other occupations. It was only during that moonlit night in March that I understood why people who look after stock are apparently indifferent to the ultimate fate of the very creatures they help into the world with such tender skilfulness.

The explanation for this seeming paradox is not that experience hardens the shepherd, though of course it does, but rather that experience enhances his ability to produce bigger lambs next time, in greater numbers, with fewer difficulties. Lambing and killing are inseparable episodes in a process that does not begin or end with either, but is continous, and whose dynamic is determined by the shepherd. Here is the true source of his satisfaction. Life is made and remade – the fattened lambs are taken to market, the ewes gather their strength and begin to flush, the rams are put with the flock to tup – but the cycle depends at every stage on the shepherd's good management. He is the creator. Next year's lambs have already been born in his imagination.

We cannot all be shepherds and, given the wages and hardships involved, few of us would want it. However, I would argue that as members of a wealthy and technically sophisticated society we can reasonably demand the right to enjoy no less an opportunity than the shepherd to exercise our imaginations in our work. Yet the shepherd, along with a handful of others, most of them in the professions, remains exceptional in being able to fulfil something of his creative potentiality, even though all of us are endowed with it. There is a terrible danger here. We cannot build an improved future until we have first prefigured it in our imaginations, but we will assuredly lose our power to imagine if we cannot use it in our work.

Yesterday in the car Tilly suddenly announced that we were the nicest Mummy and Daddy in the world. I asked her what was the nastiest thing about Mummy.

'Smacking,' was her immediate reply. Jack concurred.

And the nicest?

'Hugging,' she said, after a little thought.

What about Daddy, what was the nastiest thing about him?

'Shouting,' they both said together.

And the nicest thing was hugging too.

When asleep, Tilly lies curled up in the classic fetal position, having tunnelled down her bed, leaving only a wisp of black hair to be seen on the pillow. Jack, by contrast, sleeps flat on his back, his arms thrown out, snoring royally.

Tilly occasionally has nightmares, which are usually about tigers, wolves or monsters chasing her and trying to eat her. Jack sometimes cries out in his sleep and more often than not can be heard moaning, 'No, no, no.' He never wakes, though, and we never know what it is he is protesting against. Last night Sally heard him shouting, 'No, I won't tell you nuffink.'

Of all animals, tigers play the biggest part in their mythology. Wolves are always frightening, but tigers which can be frightening too are very rich in meaning. *Little Black Sambo* is a favourite story with both of them. Yesterday morning Jack made a pen in the bathroom out of pillows for his entirely imaginary baby tigers. He told us he was a 'zoo-man'. Tilly joined in the game and throughout a greatly extended breakfast they solicitously looked after their animals, stroking them and putting them to bed. Sal and I were called on to make many trips upstairs to be shown the baby tigers sleeping, playing, being fed and so on. Jack warned me to be careful because the mummy tiger did not like people looking at her babies, a direct reference to the shepherd's dog which has a litter at the moment and is removed, growling, whenever the children are brought to inspect her puppies.

The sheer hard work they put into these games is remarkable. Jack does everything on the run. But more remarkable is their handling of fantasy: they happily exist for hours in an ambivalent, shifting, melting real — not-real world. They definitely do not become so absorbed in their game that they lose touch with reality and fall into a trance. On the contrary, they are quite conscious of what is real and what is fantasy, but they seem to see no division or qualitative distinction; everything is seamlessly merged and interpenetrating. When one of them holds out an empty hand for you to stroke the baby tiger inside, it is there and not there all at once. And if you go further than they have envisaged, reacting literally, as I tend to do, perhaps by behaving as if it has bitten you, they look both believing and unbelieving, but are not disturbed.

Reality has not yet hardened for them, nor has fantasy been locked up and confined to the head. This two-way permeability, this infinitely labile state of mind, where nothing is disqualified, and everything can be changed into something else or invested with whatever properties you care to choose, is surely the origin not only of art, but of all forms of imaginative transformation, political, scientific and technological. The curse of self-consciousness – the knowledge that we exist and must die – is lifted by this capacity for fantasy.

Monday, 31 May
These last few days have been very hot and sunny, following two days of heavy rain. Its impact has left behind great patches of slicked-down wheat in the fields, but they are slowly lifting as the sun dries them. The neatness of spring, when the crops first cover over the naked spaces between the hedges with all the care of a child filling in a colouring book, is beginning to give way to summer shagginess. Everything is charged with sap, and squirting with growth. The corners of the roads have suddenly been blinded by cow parsley. The trees, however, are already losing their early iridescent gloss and are starting to get their hot-weather dustiness.

Children of course do not grow like this, in big seasonal bursts, nor do they grow steadily along an even trajectory. For long periods they seem not to grow at all and then, overnight, their heads bulge, their legs elongate and they can easily reach things, which only yesterday they could not even see. After one of these sporadic, unpredictable spasms, they settle again to gather strength and learn to use their new powers.

One morning last week, after a night of continuous rain, the sows were let out in the little, weed-ridden yard near our back door. I sat the children on the garden wall to see them and for a long time we watched one particular sow. She had a very concave, wrinkled face and stood right beneath us, delicately picking at the nettles, which were presumably at their sweetest and most succulent after the rain. Even though pigs' snouts are extremely sensitive, she was clearly immune to nettle poison. The children were much impressed by this feat of imperviousness, for they are terrified of nettles. She must have been eating them as a delicacy because, though omnivorous, pigs do not have the digestive equipment for consuming large quantities of fibrous material. I notice they have not touched the nettle beds in the field at the bottom of our garden. She ate very fastidiously, like a gourmet, just tugging gently at the juiciest tops with her lips and tongue. Their huge pickaxe jaws are designed for pulverizing roots rather than chewing leaves, and each stalk took her a long time to deal with, causing her to make loud, liquid smacking noises.

June

Tuesday, 1 June
Yesterday evening, which was warm and humid, I took
the children to see Sally's ten ewes being sheared. A
large crowd had already gathered to watch the show, of
which the shepherd was unquestionably its star.

The ewes and their lambs had been squashed
together in separate pens in the open-fronted shed
attached to the field Sally rents, and the shepherd
stood in the middle of the yard outside wielding
clippers driven by a tiny, throbbing generator at his
feet. His son-in-law, a tall and handsome man with a
black, piratical moustache, had come to assist him,
together with a couple who also keep a few sheep.
Recruited at the last moment was another couple, a
weaver and her husband, who had come to buy a
fleece, but found themselves wrestling with ewes and
lifting up the now corpulent lambs to be weighed.
Leaning along the fence and encouraging the workers
with contradictory advice, amiable abuse and offers of
cider, was an entourage of friends, family and children.
Sally's father was there and he had brought a flagon of
his concussive home-brewed beer to refresh the
shepherd.

Each ewe was dragged out in turn to the shepherd,
who deftly threw her on to her haunches, held her
steady between his knees and thrust his clippers into
her wool. The fleece was peeled off in strips, like
pieces of grey turf, though they were all connected

39

together. To clip her back, the shepherd laid her flat on the ground, kneeling beside her and grasping her by an ear. If she struggled, one of the other men would put his foot on her back legs or her head. In any case, she could only writhe and jerk, because her front legs had been tied together with string. Beneath the matted, greasy outside layer, the wool was a pure white and very thick and soft, like cream cheese. The clippers seemed to scrape it rather than cut it off her pink skin, leaving little tracks of white fluff. The shepherd worked rapidly and accurately, never pausing in his stroke except to turn her over or control her struggles. When the ewe was stripped bare, his son-in-law wound the long strips from her neck into a coil to tie round the rest of the fleece, which was folded and rolled into a tight bundle, the size of a large pillow.

The shorn ewes were taken from the shepherd and pulled on to a deck-chair contraption, specially made for Sally, consisting of a heavy wooden frame with a sacking seat, which was secured to the fence. Once upturned in this, their legs sticking out, the ewes were helplessly immobilized and could only sit grinding their teeth and rolling their eyes while Sal clipped their hooves. Finally they were led back to another pen. Sal has learnt the trick of subduing them by inserting her thumb in their mouths at the point where they have no teeth.

Crammed in their pen, the shaved ewes made a disturbing spectacle. There was something uncomfortably humanoid about their pink, hairless nudity, and there was also something reminiscent of grimmer confinements in their humiliating loss of covering and pathetic exposure to ridicule. They bleated continually to their lambs in the next pen, who answered in their lighter, shriller tones.

When the last ewe had been clipped, a great cheer

went up from the crowd. The shepherd took off his cap and smiled. He came across to the fence in search of a drink, but looked doubtfully at the beer and chose cider instead. The rest of the team put both ewes and lambs through a footbath and the whole flock was released on to the grass, where they immediately put down their heads to crop. Their sudden nakedness, dotted with spots of purple antiseptic where the clippers had nicked them, looked all the more absurd out in the open field.

Everyone congratulated the shepherd on his skill and speed, and everyone congratulated Sal on the size of her fleeces and the condition of her flock. The weaver could not make up her mind which fleece was best to buy. The bottles were passed around and the experts began to speculate on the price Sal would get for her fattest lambs.

Many different elements had combined to make this a splendid and festive event. Foremost was the opportunity to watch a man at close quarters as he practised his skill, a demanding skill, with pride and finesse. The occasion too was itself a cause for celebration: shearing is one of the climaxes of the shepherd's year, being conspicuous proof that he has successfully brought his flock through the rigours of winter and the trials of lambing, as well as a ritual which turns all that work into a commodity.

It was also an event that could only take place on the margins of agricultural life. In cities and industry, one's work is only observed and admired by work-mates or supervisors, but never by families, friends and rivals. Work and private life are entirely segregated. And even on the farm, which as a site of work is unusually exposed to public view, mechanization has effectively isolated the tractor driver in his cab, while the increasing size of fields places him at a distance

41

which forestalls social exchange. But smallholders and small stock-keepers like Sally still cannot survive without mutual cooperation and the support of those around them, whether in the form of loaned equipment, labour, expertise or encouragement. For them, work merges indistinguishably with their family and social life, and all three become interdependent. Their activities are invested with an especially rich local significance, together with a most uncommon opportunity for winning self-esteem, an opportunity not to be found in most ordinary, segregated forms of work. Apart from demolition and construction gangs, who always attract large crowds, it is hard to think of other jobs, even rural ones done out of doors, in which people are able publicly to display their skills. Of course, the moment I write that a clutch of exceptions immediately occurs to me – sportsmen, actors, barristers, bus drivers, nurses, waiters, even window cleaners – but my general point still holds. It is rare to come across work that is as closely and rewardingly integrated with the entirety of a worker's life as the shepherd's.

Saturday, 5 June
Whenever Tilly comes into a room nowadays and hears music, she spontaneously makes dancing motions. These consist of jerky arabesques with her arms and toe-pointing, though they are an attempt to respond expressively to the music. If Jack sees her dancing he will join in, trying to imitate her, but his efforts soon degenerate into clowning and he rushes round the room, caroming off the furniture.

Tilly's movements, which she performs very earnestly and self-consciously, are touchingly comic, but they are saddening too. Her gestures are derived from half-remembered exercises she does at dance class, which she attends for an hour every Wednesday, and they are the sum of her dancing 'language'. Her own impromptu interpretations of music very quickly peter out, largely for lack of steps.

The only dancers she has seen in the flesh are Morris men, but perhaps because of the excitement and hurly-burly of fairs, where we usually encounter them, she has never shown a special interest in their antics. *Top of the Pops*, however, or any dance routine on television delights her, and in her cranky way she will follow them with fair accuracy and great feeling. Watching her as she prances in front of the screen, mimicking the chorus girls, it is impossible to doubt that she finds dancing both exhilarating and satisfying.

Tuesday, 8 June
Poor Tilly is very ill with measles. Yesterday her temperature was more than 102° and her face was inflamed by an incarnadine blotch, stretching from her neck to her temples, which burned so fiercely she was almost luminous. Today, when she woke, the inflammation on her face had eased a little, but appeared to have scattered in little spots all over her body. Not an inch of her skin was unmarked; even the soles of her feet and the skin beneath her nails were spotted. Her eyes have been sunk in her head and she has hardly been able to open them. She has been listless, in fact inert for nearly two days, and has done nothing but sleep and sit pathetically still on our laps. However, though helplessly compliant in every other respect, she has insisted throughout on wearing her hair in an absurd tufted topknot, which gives her the look of a boozy pineapple.

Signs of recovery came just before lunch today. For

43

nearly the first time in twenty-four hours, she sat up and demanded, of all things, frozen peas. Not cooked, but straight from the bag, which as a matter of fact is how I like them best. She also watched with great interest the extraordinary ceremonials leading up to Reagan's speech at Westminster. She was most impressed by Hailsham's Lord High Chancellor's wig; she could not be convinced that it was not his own hair and remarked, rather enviously, that it would make very nice plaits.

Meanwhile, Jack, by way of demonstrating his own firm grasp on health and his annoyance at the disproportionate attention lavished on Tilly, has been impossible. This evening, among many other explosive incidents, he persisted in kicking me again and again. I kept pushing him away, but at last Sally smacked him. He was of course outraged and cried passionately. I then took him to another room and invited him to hit me as hard as he could, in the hope of getting some of his feeling out of his system. He proceeded to take a mighty, haymaker swing at me, missed, spun right round and fell on the floor, banging his head. Instantly, his mortal enemy was called on to be his comforter.

'Rub my head,' he cried pitifully.

These episodes are very difficult. Apart from anything else, one is always hovering between rage and hysterical laughter at his infuriating, yet preposterous behaviour. Tilly has never engaged in these doomed challenges to our patience. Except for riding them out and exercising superhuman self-control, which neither of us possesses, I cannot think what to do.

Wednesday, 9 June
I took Jack to the pub on his own this evening. Tilly was still too ill to come, though she is almost re-

covered now. Her spots have merged together in a faint blush and I am sure by tomorrow they will have disappeared altogether. One thing to be said for children's illnesses is that they go as suddenly as they strike.

At the pub, which has a large garden with a seesaw and a tyre to swing on tied by a long rope to a tree branch, Jack was excellent company. He generously shared his crisps, used up four straws on his bottle of coke and told me an interminable story that never got beyond its opening line – 'Once upon a time, there was a little boy called Jack . . .'

Later, at home, however, the demon in him reasserted itself. I took them up to bed to read them their stories and he put me through his most aggravating routine, kicking the book out of my hands, getting off my knee to run away and hide, covering the page with his hand, covering my eyes, putting his hand in my mouth and so on. Despite my glowering at him with what I intended to be my most forbidding expression, he continued to taunt me until I felt real anger rising inside me. Finally, in a fury, I threw him on his bed, which he loved.

The emotions aroused in me by my children are more intense and overpowering than any I have felt outside the keenest moments of sexual infatuation, and they have been infrequent, whereas my feelings for Tilly and Jack are continually sharpened.

This presumably is what bonding is all about. Actually, I think even the tremendous rage which must occasionally overwhelm every parent is absorbed by, and does not impair, the bonding process, providing the child is not hurt or badly frightened, for the greater one's anger, the more complete one's guilt afterwards. As far as I can tell, our children are not traumatized by my displays of rage, or Sal's, they merely wish they were not happening and wait for them to pass. Not long ago, Sal was reduced to smacking Jack because he would not go to bed; the following morning she asked him what he remembered of the incident and, after some thought, he rather puzzlingly said, 'You cuddled me.' I believe that, within the context of loving one's children as best one can, it is infinitely better to release one's bad feelings than to strive to disguise or suppress them. Successful suppression must result in their being perniciously displaced into some other part of the relationship. Nevertheless, I hope this particular aspect of Jack's development is short-lived.

Tuesday, 15 June

At his own request, we have made Jack a punch-bag out of a cushion cover stuffed with newspaper and hung it in their playroom. He hits at it with his great, swiping, do-or-die punches, his teeth audibly gritted and a murderous look in his eye. Despite the fact that it frequently swings back and knocks him flat, he obviously finds it satisfying, for he can easily be diverted from shrieking with rage or hitting us by a request to go and bash his 'boxing bag'.

When we were setting this up for him, Tilly asked if she could have a cradle hung up for her dolls. Not that one is allowed to call them dolls; there is hardly a greater crime in this house. They are Sophie and Emma, her babies. Sally has accordingly fixed up an elaborate system of strings and cushions, making an excellent hammock, which is complete with a mobile dangling above it. Tilly dutifully swings her babies to and fro with a special rope, crooning lullabies to them in her toneless 'singing' voice.

It is quite unfair to represent Jack as some kind of blood-crazed bruiser. Though he certainly delights in kicking, punching, head-butting and detonating in a

46

way that has not the remotest parallel in Tilly's behaviour, he is also as capable as her of sustained and fully absorbed play, or nearly so. Last night he took into the bath one of his dolls, a hideous, plastic gremlin with shocking pink hair made of some artificial angora-like material, and gave it a very thorough wash, including its hair which was shampooed, rinsed, combed and blow-dried. The entire operation took the best part of half an hour. Alas, although he has not yet noticed, his tender care has reduced its hair to the consistency of uncooked spaghetti. He more often plays in this concentrated, persistent way with his toy garage and collection of lorries.

What he does not show in his play is the constancy of attention Tilly gives to her dolls. She scarcely lets a day go by without changing their clothes, washing them, brushing their hair and putting them to bed. This morning she was especially quick to get them up and see how they had spent their first night in the new cradle.

When she was much younger her games with her dolls pretty well consisted of doing to them what was done to her. In those days she spent so much of her life being up-ended and generally tossed about, mostly to have her nappy changed, it is not surprising she took every opportunity of passing on the treatment and, in the process, of restoring her sense of autonomy. The game has not really changed much, except now she is concerned to dominate an entire family structure. Power is the name of her game.

Incidentally, Jack is not at all pugnacious with his contemporaries. I have never seen him punch or kick one of his friends. He occasionally explodes them, but only in the most cheery and affectionate spirit.

Thursday, 17 June
We have both noticed that Jack has gone through a sudden eruption of growth during the last few days. He seems to have grown stockier, more barrel-chested, more solidly planted on his legs. Now the weather has turned sunny again he has been wearing shorts and they seem to have conferred on him a classic boyhood look of incorrigible dishevelment: socks forever concertinaed round sturdy legs, shoelaces trailing, shirt sleeves dangling from his arms, a shirt tail hanging out of the back of his shorts, his vest hanging out at the front, his hair matted and his face permanently smudged.

Tilly, by contrast, seems to become more dainty as she grows: her legs are like little twigs. ·

Saturday, 19 June
This morning, not for the first time, Jack trapped himself – and me – in a Catch-22 situation. We were in a shop with four other children, including Tilly, all of them girls except Jack as it happened. He picked up a bag of crisps and I agreed that all the children could choose a bag each. Jack decided he wanted to change his and, after a prolonged search, reappeared with a large bag of mints. I insisted that he could only have crisps, since they had all been bought sweets earlier, and anyway crisps were what had been agreed on. He resisted. I returned the mints to the shelf and told him to choose his crisps. He refused and by now was crying.

The shopkeeper said, 'He's just like my Jack. A little bugger.'

'Belt up,' he said to Jack, in what he intended to be a jovial tone, 'or I'll set the dog on you.'

I gave him another chance to get himself a bag and then paid for the others. Before we left the shop I took him back to the crisps shelf and told him he could still have some, but he refused again.

As soon as we closed the door of the shop he demanded his crisps. I said he was too late and we were not going back. He began to cry in earnest and to shout, 'I want one, I want one.' He cried throughout the journey home, shrieking in my ear as I drove. He was too upset for reason or even the promise of crisps later to make any impression. The girls were easily persuaded to offer him some of theirs, but, predictably, that only made him cry the harder. I was only able to soothe and distract him when we got out of the car, though it was twenty minutes before he stopped forlornly muttering, 'I want one.'

These situations are sometimes forced on children, when they are made to rush their decisions, for example, but on this occasion I was sure I had given him every opportunity of choosing what he wanted, though not of course the mints. Brooding on it later, I could think of only one way, which had occurred to me in the shop, whereby I might have forestalled the scene outside, and that would have been to buy him a packet of crisps while he was not looking and present him with it as soon as he changed his mind. That would have saved him, and the rest of us, much distress, but on the other hand it would just have been another way of giving in to his intolerable demands, which was the real issue and not the mints at all.

These confrontations, and the minutiae of their coming about, are the stuff of every parent's life. My own view is that although such clashes of will, from which the parent emerges the victor, may well be beneficial to the formation of the child's character, they are best avoided, and that there are subtler, gentler, more productive means of teaching your child the necessary lessons of modifying his wishes and compromising with authority. Actually, in our particular case, I think there was only one lesson to be learnt, and I knew it already: Jack occasionally feels some compulsive need to impose on events this kind of neither-nor, double-bind alternative, and once he has done so negotiation, persuasion, insistence, bribery and all other stratagems are quite useless. Nothing can be done, except wait him out. Tilly has never behaved this way and I do not know why he does.

Monday, 21 June

Princess Diana has had a son, yet to be named. Charles was in the hospital throughout her sixteen-hour labour and attended the birth.

It was reported on the radio that the Duke of Edinburgh had been playing squash while his last son was being born; not out of indifference, but because that was the fashion among his generation. My own father spent the night on a sofa in the sitting-room of my grandparents' house while my mother was in labour upstairs, and had to be woken to be told of my arrival.

This is one of the great generational divides. I remember when Sally was pregnant the subject of fathers attending delivery was most controversial and the cause of heated discussions between ourselves and our parents and their contemporaries. It is certainly strange that the fashion has swung round so completely in the last few years, though nothing seems to be more prone to wild oscillations in taste than infant care. I suppose every generation tends, however irrationally, to defend its own experience, but I can only say that I count watching the birth of my two children among the most moving experiences of my life, and the most decisive. In fact, I have only heard one of the many fathers we know with small children say he did not feel the same way.

When Tilly was born I had a brief taste of what it would have been like to be the classic chain-smoking, floor-pacing father, for I was put in a waiting-room as soon as we arrived at the delivery suite while Sally was examined. Sure enough, I paced and smoked in the time-honoured manner, even though I knew there was no chance of anything happening for a long time, and I was very glad to be taken through after an hour to join Sally in the delivery room. While I was there I shared the waiting-room with another father, but he had made a bed for himself out of two armchairs and was sound asleep. At one point a nurse came in and tapped him on the shoulder.

'Your wife's had her baby,' she told him, 'it's a little girl.'

He opened his eyes for a moment. 'Not another fucking woman in the house,' he said disgustedly, and went back to sleep.

I said it was a decisive experience. Perhaps I already had the kind of psychology that goes to make a child-oriented father, but, if so, I am sure that this potential was galvanized immediately and to the full by the sight of my children being born. That sudden, slithering dive into oxygen and daylight which the newly expelled infant makes, back arched and chin forward, its waxy, matted, bloody scalp, its purple, clenched face, its shrivelled body and bent-up limbs, produced in me, even before I knew its sex, a jolting charge of love that was so powerful and intense I felt I had virtually been born again myself. There was no pause while I opened myself to feeling, no interval of gradually swelling emotion, just an instantaneous onslaught of grabbing, all-consuming love.

No parallel or precedent for this had occurred in my

life. Falling in love with women, no matter how deep a feeling it had led to, no matter with what romantic immediacy it had taken place, had nonetheless always been a process involving some measure of discrimination, and not a little attention to self-interest. But my love for my children sprang into life fully formed and screaming lustily for nourishment, as if it too had been gestating all those weeks along with them.

Saturday, 26 June
Yesterday I bought the children a pair of scissors each, with which they were very pleased. As soon as we were home, they plunged into an orgy of cutting up. Nothing was safe. They even cut up a bowl of assorted nuts, systematically splitting each one. Later, while I was entertaining some people in the kitchen, they played for a long time on their own and then Jack came running through, a mixture of glee and apprehension on his face.

'He's cut his hair,' said Tilly, who was clearly impressed.

And so he had. At considerable risk to himself, he had chopped down to suede-head level a jagged triangle of hair, its base at his right temple and its apex buried somewhere on the top of his skull. Everyone laughed at him. I picked him up and told him, rather wetly, that it looked very nice. However, he did not seem to care what any of us thought, for he went straight back and slashed away another clump. Sally, who was out at the time, and did not get to see his tonsure until this morning, has just tried to soften the damage by graduating the edges of his original strokes. The result is that the whole right-hand side of his head now looks as if it is recovering from some unspeakable disease, or a terrible wound. He himself has not commented on his actions, but gives every sign of being quietly satisfied.

Sunday, 27 June
Open day at the Redgrave fen nature reserve. We decided to go. Sally had been told there was a possibility of her using some of the overgrown grazing land beside the fen and, anyway, we all wanted to see the reserve. The warden took her to look at the grass, while I set off down the nature trail with the children. It was a hot, close morning, with thunder clouds blackening the sky.

Jack is usually impossible on walks, begging to be carried as soon as we start. If I make him walk, he stumbles along directly in front of me and facing me, his arms outstretched, shouting, 'Up, up.' On this occasion, however, he soon became absorbed in discovering the different plants along the trail, which were indicated by little explanatory signs, and plodded stolidly for more than a mile, only holding my hand.

The trail brought us across a sort of causeway running between a chain of peat cuttings – small, waterlogged pits cut out of the fen – and leading towards the river Waveney, which rises here. The children insisted on having every word of every sign read out to them, and never lost their suspicion that I was short-changing them. Consequently, we progressed very slowly, stopping at each sign for me to intone the particulars of *Potentilla erecta*, *Juncus subnodulosus* and the like. Actually, the common names of these plants that like poor, wet ground are rather splendid: butterwort, grass of Parnassus, petty whin, marsh helleborine, lousewort, black bog rush and so on. The children inspected all of them minutely, but

53

did not understand why they were not allowed to pick any flowers. I could see that in the end they put this prohibition down to some autocratic whim of mine, since the profusion of flowers wherever they looked made it obvious that my argument about rarity was wilful nonsense.

Further down the path we came to some newer peat cuttings, which according to one of our excellent notices had been cut in the hope that they would be colonized by the large raft spider. This, the biggest native British spider, was only discovered in 1956 and at present is known nowhere else in the country. One of the wardens told us that it had in fact moved into these new pits, which suggested that its numbers were on the increase. He also told us to look for it along the edges of the ponds, among the reeds and rushes, but despite a prolonged and earnest search, and many false sightings, we did not find one. We did, however, see innumerable water boatmen as well as dragonflies, which seemed to be at their most brilliant and iridescent in that lowering light. They hover so motionlessly they appear to be resting on invisible landing stages, and they do not fly so much as hop from one aerial perch to another.

Next we came across a stretch of path that was infested with tiny froglets, none bigger than a bracelet charm. The children were able to catch them without my help and hold them in their cupped hands to inspect them. We also saw handfuls of black tortoiseshell caterpillars, which were clustered so densely on their nettle leaves they looked like single, exotic blooms.

Back at the start of the trail, we were shown a raft spider in a glass tank. It turned out to be a male, with large, swollen 'boxing glove' palpi in front, and a plain white stripe running along the edge of its grey-black abdomen. It was not yet fully grown and still smaller than the huge household spiders (*Tegeneria gigantea*) which have built their bridgeheads of web in all four corners of my study ceiling and occasionally stalk the picture rails late at night. With one long, elegant leg secured to a piece of reed, the raft spider was standing on the surface of the water, its other seven legs splayed out. Contrary to its name, it does not build a raft, nor any kind of web or trap, but relies on the extreme sensitivity of its feet to detect vibrations below. It will grab and consume anything smaller than itself, including fish. There were a few sticklebacks swimming in the tank and for some perverse reason they had collected just beneath the spider, but it made no move to attack, quite ignoring Jack's taps of encouragement on its tank wall.

Giving far better value was a diving beetle, which had been put into a tall preserving jar along with some debris from its pond bottom. One particular piece of decayed wood had registered as prey. Stealthily man-oeuvring its cumbersome body, it placed itself just beneath the surface, but immediately above its victim, and very slowly dropped to within an inch of it. Then, with a ferocious lunge, it overpowered the twig and shot back to the surface, clutching its futile prey and sending clouds of mud swirling round the jar. Presumably, it operates on the same principle as the submarine, and is able to exercise so delicate a control over its movements and generate the necessary thrust for these sudden ascents by forcing water in and out of little chambers under its carapace. The beetle turned the twig over and over, looking for the soft edible parts it should have possessed, and finally dropped it, only to start the performance again, much to the delight of the children, when the twig had settled and the water had cleared.

This savage aggression inflicted on a completely un-resisting victim reminded me, quite unfairly, of a Red Indian I once saw near Miami who allegedly wrestled with a man-eating alligator, though the animal in question was sedated to the point of helpless inertia. He would sneak up on his prone adversary, throw himself on it with a blood-curdling cry, wrap its front legs round his own neck, struggle with it as if for his life and at last throw it contemptuously to the ground. He would then stand with one foot on its still-motionless form, his hands clasped above his head like a champion. Throughout the entire show, the alligator never even opened its eyes.

Meanwhile, Sally had been offered the chance of grazing sheep over an enormous acreage, more than three hundred acres, which the Suffolk Trust wants to see cropped and returned to grass. However, although they want no rent for the land, this would mean turning her present hobby into something approaching big busi-ness. And, in any case, there is some doubt as to whether the land is dry enough for sheep.

The value of our visit to the children was immediately manifested by Jack, who spent the rest of the afternoon searching our garden for 'creatures'. He was successful too, for among many other exciting captures he hunted down a little spider, coloured a lurid orange, which appeared to live by lying in wait for ants and the like in a hole beneath a cobblestone outside our back door. He brought it in to show us on a leaf and proposed to give it a bath. I think this plan derived from some mistaken, but perfectly logical, idea that spiders inhabit baths, where we do indeed often discover them. Tilly responded in her way as well by producing a series of drawings of creatures and plants, the most spectacular of which showed a pair of clearly recognizable sheep sheltering in a hut from a truly apocalyptic flash of lightning.

The fen has been designated a Grade 1 Site of Special Scientific Interest; unlike many Sites, its future is reasonably secure, for some of it is owned by the Suffolk Trust and the rest has been acquired by them on long leases. It represents a classic case of a natural phenomenon in need of rigorous protection if it is to retain its unusual features. In order that the surrounding farmland should be efficiently drained, the river Waveney has been 'canalized' – straightened in places and dredged – and the ditches in the fen area have been dug out, but now there is a danger that the water level in the fen itself will drop. However, maintaining this water level is critical to the survival of the fen's present, unique ecology. Were it allowed to fall so low that peat development ceased, alder and willow trees would start to invade, cutting off light from the small, rare plants below and causing the whole area to revert to woodland. On the other hand, water must not be brought back off the nearby farmland to raise the level, because it would be too rich in nutrients for the existing flora. The balance is delicate and has to be constantly monitored, but the Trust, with the cooperation of the East Anglian Water Authority, appears to be doing the job very successfully.

The case for conservation is self-evident when one is actually walking round the fen. The sheer wealth of natural variety that confronts one at every step is a sudden and shocking reminder of what has been lost from the countryside at large, the unprotected, agricultural countryside. Also, in this rather weird land- and waterscape of banks and ditches, peat pits, marsh and river, it is impossible not to be aware of the extreme precariousness of the ecological equilibrium.

I have always been sure that it is ultimately pointless to attempt to justify the need for conservation on any but what might be called spiritual grounds. Conservation is bound to be a national luxury, though commercial side-benefits may ensue, and will certainly involve a deprivation for agriculture: to conserve an environment is, by and large, to restrict, if not foreclose, its capacity to produce food. Failure to acknowledge this puts the argument for conservation in a false and vulnerable position. The real vindication is only debatable in terms of *human* nature, since we now live on an earth whose bio-structure, old-fashioned Nature, is effectively at the mercy of human will – and folly. Our species requires, as a matter of cultural and psychological necessity, a relatively enduring and prolific landscape, if we are to preserve our own precarious equilibrium. An environment reduced to desolate uniformity, even though fertile beyond the wildest dreams of agribusiness, would, I am convinced, finally tip us into collective madness.

July

Sunday, 4 July

Nowadays, at bedtime, Jack usually falls asleep without a struggle as their story is being read, but this is only a recent, and very welcome, breakthrough. Just a few weeks ago, he would regularly climb out of his bed after we had left them and run round the corridors screaming and giggling until one of us would have to go upstairs and force him to lie down. As soon as we were downstairs, he would set off again. These incidents, though not without their comical side, were extremely trying and often culminated in ugly outbursts of anger, at least from me. Throughout, Tilly would lie in her bed, saucer-eyed with exhaustion, complaining that Jack was keeping her awake.

However, now it seems to be Tilly's turn to resist. The other night she got out of bed, but there was no mischief in her, for she only lay on the landing, crumpled in a corner and crying. I tried to get her to go back, but she climbed out again and began to cry even more pitifully. She told me something had frightened her; I believed her and let her stay up for half an hour, after which she willingly returned and was asleep almost immediately. The next night she behaved the same way, only this time she would not go back even after I had let her stay up for a while. In the end I left her in bed crying, which I did not like doing, though I could tell that she was now very close to sleep. Her sobbing did not last longer than five minutes.

61

She never did tell what had frightened her. Sally was suspicious, but I was sure that she was genuinely frightened and not saying so as a ploy to stay up late. Perhaps she had heard a noise, or seen something, or just imagined she had. After all, they are very prone to misinterpreting the physical world, which for them does not yet conform to the laws in which we place our faith, but is as volatile and mysterious as their own bodies. Nor do they possess any concept of future in which to plant hope during their barren seasons of despair.

I remember once, when she was much younger, she walked into the woodshed with me only to leap back, clinging to my legs in terror, because she had mistaken a large log in the shadows for a pig.

I suspect that in fact she had been overpowered by a sense of unease, by a rush of anxiety. This seemed to be borne out by her saying she did not like being on her own, despite Jack's being there and our quite audible presence downstairs. It is easy as a parent to be deluded into thinking that their minds are wholly exposed and fully legible, but it is not so. Their minds do not develop like flowers, slowly unfurling from bud to bloom, with every moment of unfolding open to the observation and comprehension of the all-seeing parental eye. To some extent, of course, it is like this, but beneath all the openly visible growth there remain potholes, deep rifts that are impenetrable and will only become more fathomless, at least for parents.

As a way of trying to divert her from whatever had disturbed her and giving her something to look forward to, on the second occasion I suggested we might write and draw a story together the next day. She did not respond, so I left it. However, in the morning, as soon as she woke, she reminded me and repeatedly mentioned the scheme at breakfast. While she was out at school I stapled together a little book and we set to work the minute she returned. Without a moment's hesitation, she picked up her felt-tip pen and drew a perfectly recognizable bear of the Pooh genre.

'Here is a bear,' I was instructed to write on the opposite page, 'walking in the long grass and having a lovely time.'

She could hardly wait for me to finish and snatched the book back to draw the bear again, together with a house.

'Here the teddy bear comes to a little house. He opens the door and there stood a little girl and boy,' she told me to write.

She grabbed the book a second time, but wavered a little and had evidently come to the end of her preconceived ideas. Spontaneous invention took over and she drew a boy and a girl, whom I knew to be Jack and herself.

She found it harder to devise a caption and fell back on explaining the lack of continuity: 'Here are the clowns by the teddy bear, but the bear is sitting on the other side, so you can't see him.'

I proposed that we should stop and take up the story when she was ready to do some more. She agreed.

To anyone who has ever attempted to shape an idea in a form capable of artistic articulation, her blithe confidence and instantaneous execution are truly enviable. I, at any rate, can seldom 'write' a sentence without first drafting it three or four times, and on bad days the process is far more laborious.

Neither these drawings nor the story seemed to have any connection with her fears of the previous night, but the following day, after having gone to sleep unprotestingly that night, she brought home from nursery school a drawing that clearly had a direct bearing on her experience, though I could not unravel its precise meaning. It showed a row of five identical girls, all of whom were sad, as shown by their down-turned mouths. At the end of the row was a sixth girl, who was happy, with an up-turned mouth, and also distinguished by different coloured clothes. Above each was a green streak leading upwards to a large blue cloud that overhung them all. The happy girl's streak was differently coloured too. In one corner shone the sun. We were told that these were little girls and their dreams. She would not say what their dreams were, but informed us later that the happy one had a diamond ring, although it did not in fact appear in the picture.

I believe her drawings are more expressive than most. Also, she has now reached the stage where she is able to make a recognizable likeness of her subject, and no longer confines herself to the archetypal figures and symbols which, evidently, are common to the drawings of all young children, irrespective of their cultural backgrounds. Yesterday, she did a drawing of Peter, a great friend of ours whom we see most weekends, and myself, easily identifiable by my grey hair. Peter was not so distinctively visualized as me, but then she had drawn a friendship, rather than two individuals, for our separate bodies were to be seen emerging from a single pair of trousers.

Thursday, 8 July
Tilly has been getting out of bed again, but the problem seems to have been solved by an imaginative mother of one of her friends, who has given her an allegedly magical teddy bear, named Andrea, and told her that its powers include being able to 'magic' little girls to sleep. Tilly is very pleased with her new bear and is never without it, completely neglecting her

other children Andrea has been solemnly placed on the pillow beside her and she has indeed gone to sleep without a murmur of resistance for two nights running.

I do not know what goes on in their minds when they accept these fanciful propositions. (Earlier this year, Jack was quite content to abandon his bottle, to which he had been fanatically attached, in favour of an ordinary cup, after being told that the birds had stolen it to feed their babies with.) Of course, Tilly loves getting new dolls and perhaps her anxiety, or whatever it was, has dispelled itself, but there is no question that she has given some credit to Andrea's magical properties and that they have had a soothing effect.

Saturday, 10 July
Very distressing news in the post today. For a moment I was overwhelmed by despair and panic. I reached out for the children, who were opening the letters for me. They hugged me and clung to me, which was very consoling, but soon enough they began to look disturbed themselves. They cannot bear any sign of weakness or confusion in either of us, for they have a ruthless and unerring sense of where their own interests lie, and they know these are not going to be served by a parent who shows an inclination to give up or succumb to fear.

Monday, 12 July
This morning we took two of Sally's lambs to Bury St Edmunds to be butchered. They had to be delivered early, so we all went together; Sally sat in the back with the children and watched over the lambs, which we had loaded into the hatchback compartment of our

Renault. The whole operation went very peacefully: the lambs did not struggle when we put them in and lay down during the journey, some eight miles. They put up no resistance when they were carried into the slaughterhouse. Although one of them, named Rosemary by Tilly, had been hand-fed by all of us, the children were not too upset by this experience. We did not, of course, let them see the inside of the abattoir, which even when not in use is horrific: I just caught a glimpse of a row of heavy chopping blocks, each scrubbed pure white with its own set of knives, saws and choppers neatly racked beside it, also huge metal basins for catching fat and blood, and the stands where the offal is hung up to be inspected for disease before the carcase is jointed and dressed for sale.

Tilly said she thought it was sad that Rosemary was going to be 'cut up', but she said so in a resigned, realistic tone that betrayed no distress. I believe she is aware of the continuity that Sally's sheep-keeping involves: some of our original spring lambs are still on the field and, meanwhile, more have been bought in to fatten, so there has been no absolute break with the spring lambs she saw born, despite these now regular disappearances. Also, Sally has recently bought her own ram, a disreputable-looking Hampshire Down with a broken horn, and the children know that his function is to make next year's lambs. The cycle proceeds and they understand that.

Jack too was sad about Rosemary. He said very little, but during our journey he repeatedly turned round to stare at the lambs. After we left the abattoir, he announced he had seen the 'cooker'. In fact, he had seen the cold storage chamber. While he knows there is a connection between lambs on the hoof and food on our plates, he has no conception of the intervening stages, but he had apparently explained this disturbing transformation reasonably enough as cooking. The white cold storage chamber had presumably looked to him like the Aga in our own kitchen, and I think he had fixed on it as an object of reassurance, for he would associate the Aga not only with our hot meals, but with its comforting warmth. During the winter, they often play near it, and perhaps he had remembered as well the newborn orphan lambs being put next to it in their cardboard box. All these pleasant connotations no doubt offered him a way of discounting the lambs' suffering, and probably even a way of denying their death altogether.

He is very keen on chopping and slashing in his games, and often amputates my hands or feet with a grisly sawing action while laughing fiendishly, but the gruesome reality of Tilly's 'cutting up' was just frightening.

Wednesday, 14 July
A bad day for me. I came home feeling humiliated and angry with myself, having muffed an interview for a job. Even though I could see it coming and badly wanted to avoid it, I lost my temper with the children at bedtime and made them cry.

Thursday, 15 July
On Monday evening I took the children to a little fair that travels round our villages throughout the summer. We are by way of being fair-groupies, for we have faithfully followed it to every site in the district three years running. Our visits are by now deeply ritualized: without fail, and in this precise order, the children ride on a geriatric roundabout, dutifully 'steering' their trains and cars and waving royally to

me on each revolution; they bounce joyfully on an inflatable plastic castle; we all climb aboard a terrifying gondola-type swing and Tilly decorously pulls the rope to make it go back and forth; they each have a candy floss which encrusts their faces and arms with pink birdlime; and finally, I give them ten pence apiece to put into the 'Mystery Gift Train', a little engine that trundles round a track, disappearing into a tunnel and reappearing with a little box, which it tips down a chute for the child to pick up. These trash presents – plastic rings, bracelets, watches and so on – are surprisingly successful and almost always make it possible for us to leave without tears.

We are plagued with flies at the moment, and will be until as late as October, if it turns out to be a mild autumn. This is the price of living near a pig farm. On a hot day we can expect to have to squirt our kitchen with insecticide four or five times a day and to sweep up a kill of two hundred and more on each spraying. All our paintwork, pictures, shelves and lampshades are thickly speckled with their dotted droppings, which harden and stick fast, requiring a heavy scrubbing brush to clean them off. Our meals are eaten in a frenzy of buzzing, as they cluster round every unprotected crumb: a couple of grains of sugar lying unwiped on the tablecloth will attract a crowd of half a dozen, blacking out an area as large as an old penny. At night it is impossible to read in bed because they are attracted to the light and cluster on the inside of the shade, making sudden, agitated sorties on to your book and face. I can only work in my room by keeping the windows and door permanently shut, whatever the temperature. Otherwise, I am continually disturbed by their crawling over my arms and papers.

The other day, someone told me that the troops who fought in the trenches during the Gallipoli campaign in 1915 managed to uphold their morale, despite terrible casualties inflicted by disease no less than the Turks, until at the height of summer the flies began to breed, laying their eggs on the ideal material provided by the abundance of putrefying flesh. Then, at last, the men began to lose their minds as fast as their lives.

Delirium tremens is supposed to be accompanied by hallucinations of flies crawling all over the victim, as if he were already a corpse. I can think of no greater inducement to temperance. These hallucinations are, presumably, an extreme form of paranoid delusions of persecution, for nobody touches our bodies unless by accident or invitation; nobody, that is, except an aggressor. In this respect, flies are mercilessly aggressive.

They come from nowhere, in irresistible numbers, relentlessly reproducing themselves. On a sunny day, even a sealed room will be infested. Their seemingly pointless, incessant restlessness has the effect, on me at least, of convulsing and crumbling up the physical world: the very walls appear to cringe and shudder in an effort to shake off their foul and internal intimacy.

None of this is made any easier to tolerate by the knowledge of their disgusting eating habits. Their mouths take the form of short, flexible tubes, through which they suck up their food. In order to soften and moisten it, they first spit out saliva which contains digestive acids as well as a residue from their last meal. Given their partiality for excrement and every sort of rotting matter, this makes them very efficient vectors of disease.

Saturday, 17 July
At breakfast the children spread on their toast a combination of lemon curd, marmalade, Marmite and honey. For once, they consumed every crumb.

During the last two days they have spent every available hour making houses for their dolls and teddy bears. These are like nomadic encampments set down in the wastes of corridors or in the shelter of doorways. They gather up all our cushions and pillows and construct a kind of primitive long-house, in which they put their huge families to bed. The game involves a complex interaction between the children and their dolls, between themselves and between them and our invisible presence.

These games always have an imitative dimension, in that they do to their dolls what we do to them, but they also become elaborated in other ways. Nine times out of ten the children build a closed compound or cell from which we are excluded or have to get permission to enter, and whose borders demarcate their sovereign territory. Within this reserved area they seem to give their fantasies an even freer rein than usual and they also seem to collude together in making a secret world, sometimes using a private gobbledegook, which for them is still a rare activity. As it happens, their recent game has been quite accessible to an outsider, for they have decided to go on an expedition. This is a new and thrilling concept, open to the loosest interpretation, but mostly consisting of endless preparations, which are never disappointed by actual travel. Today, they have been getting their family ready by cleaning every member's teeth.

All this is in great contrast with a game I used to play over and over again when I was Tilly's age. I remember playing it very clearly; indeed, it is one of the most vivid memories of my early childhood. I used to arrange my sizeable collection of Dinky vehicles in a long line and load them with my soldiers and model animals. The object was to organize a fully connected caravan, which could be moved as a single body. I played this game in an interminably repetitive way, which no doubt was typical of an only child, or anyway of an obsessionally inclined only child. I used to play in a state of barely contained hysteria, for the game was, I remember, fraught with unfocused anxiety. It could never be brought to perfection: lorries became unhooked or animals spilled out. Even when everything went to plan, it still yielded no satisfaction and I was compelled to begin again.

Tilly and Jack's games have their repetitive side, of course, but none of the obsessively ritualized quality that mine had. Within the basic formula of housebuilding or putting their dolls to bed, their games are spontaneous and free-flowing, and new variations easily accrete to them. Nor do they find it difficult to accommodate other children in their games, something I was incapable of at their age, at least in my own room.

I remember a little boy who was regularly brought to tea to play with me. I dreaded his visits, though I rather liked him. During the winter, we were sent up to my room and I would watch with horror as he methodically went through my drawers and cupboards, gleefully tipping out my toys and muddling them up. He would then happily settle down to play amidst the rubble, while I would stand against the wall, stupefied by the maelstrom unleashed on my fastidious, fussy little world.

To this day, I could not work if my desk were not immaculately tidy, with everything in its appointed place.

Monday, 19 July
This morning we took two more lambs, much bigger ones, to be butchered. Tilly asked if they were going to be cut up and I told her they were. Jack immediately

asked me the same question and I gave him the same answer. I know they do this when they are feeling anxious about something. They are only satisfied with an answer given in direct response to their own question, even if the exact exchange has just taken place. However, they did not refer to the lambs again and seemed less disturbed by the experience than last time.

Wednesday, 21 July
Both of them, but especially Jack, have kept up their interest in insects and spiders aroused by our trip to Redgrave fen. Currently, a very special treat is to be picked up, holding a torch, to examine a corner below one of the upper shelves in our kitchen dresser, where a female daddy-long-legs spider (*Pholcus phalangiodes*) has successfully hatched a large brood of spiderlets. The mother, whose enormously elongated front feeler legs must be nearly five centimetres in length, is quite visible in daylight, but the torch is needed to pick out the young ones, as they hang, like their mother, motionless and upside down, among the upper strands of her sprawling, dishevelled web.

The children feel a particular affinity for her because some weeks ago they brought her to show me and we released her in the kitchen, hoping she would take up residence there. They are fascinated by the pholcus and hunt for them everywhere. Our outside lavatory used to boast a large colony, but it is deserted this year. The children have learnt that if the spider is lightly touched it will instantly vibrate its body at tremendous speed, without moving its feet, and will keep this up for as long as a quarter of a minute.

According to Ronald Lockley's delightful account of the pholcus in his book *Orielton*, this is a device for shaking out of the snare any insect too large to be consumed, such as a wasp or a bumblebee. But I wonder if he is right, for I have noticed that though these gyrations are spectacular, reducing the creature to a blur, they do not in fact agitate the web very much. Perhaps, instead, it is a method of deterring predators. On the other hand, I have also noticed that the mother in our kitchen will not do her trick at the moment, presumably for fear of tipping her brood out of the web.

Fortunately, the children are too interested in the 'baby' spiders, of which there must be a dozen or more, to be disappointed by her refusal to perform. They do not vibrate either when touched, but simply run away. I suppose they will not take up their species behaviour until they have spun their own webs, which they will be doing soon, for they have already completed their first moult. The desiccated husks of their original skins dangle like little ghost spiders among the threads and tremble eerily under the children's breath. Evidently, they will set up their first webs close to their birthplace, so we can look forward shortly to having the entire dresser infested with them.

Jack often brings me beetles and spiders and demands that I look them up in my insect book; we then try to find a picture to correspond with what he has found. Tilly does the same with flowers, though she has her own book, *The Observer Book of Wild Flowers*, which Sally's father gave her last birthday, and she likes to report her finds to him.

With any luck, they will both grow up having an instinctive feel for natural history and will discover they possess a considerable body of knowledge, all effortlessly acquired. Even though I was born on a farm and spent many holidays there as a small child, I learnt nothing about wildlife and animal behaviour, and not much more, incidentally, about farming. Paradoxically, however, it was at home, in Liverpool, that I did become keen to learn about animals, largely as a result of being taken to Bertram Mills's Circus, which pitched its big top every summer in Sefton Park and, in those days, allowed the public to look at the animals in their cages when they were not performing. I clearly remember deciding to become a lion-tamer, an ambition that subsequently evolved into wanting to be a naturalist-explorer in the style of Armand and Michaela Denis, whose books I read avidly. Indeed, this desire must have endured into early adolescence, because I can also remember, with equal clarity, my naturalist aspirations being complicated by wilder, more urgent fantasies relating to the voluptuous Michaela, as I suddenly discovered her to be. Yet, despite the attractions of the delightful strawberry blonde and her quaint accent, my interest in nature atrophied, and by the time I came to live here, on this farm, I found I knew nothing. So I set out laboriously to teach myself about the countryside.

But it was too late. Surrounded by very beautiful landscape, with the calls of innumerable birds echoing in my ears and the scent of flowers teasing my nostrils, I could only close my study window and hunch up my shoulders to block out these distractions. By dint of much reading, I now have a reasonable grasp of the principles of evolution and ecology; I have been able to write at length about rural history and the cultural importance of our beleaguered, wasted countryside; and I have even written about the behaviour of pigs without being challenged. But, for all that, I cannot put a name to a single one of the moths that dash into my lamp at night, nor can I identify half the flowers in our garden. Tilly knows the names of many more flowers than I do, and she has absorbed the information casually, during the everyday course of her life. Not that I am deprecating my own efforts. We all have to tackle existence from our own singular contingency, held back by our particular handicaps and pushed forward by our gifts, such as they are. However artificial, my methods produced results and not only on the printed page, for I have drawn more satisfaction from my peculiar, partial and oblique way of looking at the countryside than anything else that has materialized from my work.

I know too that the occasional bouts of being unable to see meaning anywhere, which used to drop over me, blackening everything out, like a torturer's hood, that the compulsive desire to possess something which can never be found, far less bought, that the frenzied questing which drove me into book shops and record shops in search of a particle of truth, some scrap of spiritual nourishment to throw into the raging void, I know that all this, to a significant degree, was the result of feeling that I had no solid footing in the living, natural world, no understanding of its working and no role to play in it, except that of parasite. However, I can testify that since I began to study the countryside, to say nothing of living here and bringing my children into a rural world, these very powerful negative emotions, which used to rule my life, or long passages of it, have largely abated. They have not disappeared, and never will, but nowadays I am no longer overwhelmed by the old sensation of hauling myself up a black ladder in a black hole with no top or bottom.

In my city days, I became addicted to the very rootlessness that I most dreaded in my depression. In effect, I tried to walk myself out of it. Every lunch hour, every evening on my way home, every spare, solitary moment, I would take to the streets, restlessly wandering, adding another stretch to my pointless marathon, unable to stop, unable to fix on a goal. Most of my friends loathed the empty fury of city streets and did everything they could to escape at weekends. The wealthy ones bought their own country cottages. But I loathed the countryside. I loathed that great vault of green and mud, in which I had no place and could find no pleasure. But then the countryside, like the stars or the ocean, like music and other phenomena that speak more profoundly to the emotions than the intellect, is closed off from those whose souls are too dry and tight to surrender themselves to being engulfed by feeling.

Actually, as a child on my grandfather's farm in what is now Dyfed, I did respond feelingly to the spectacular Stackpole coastline, with its jagged, sea-bound rocks, like the spires of submerged churches, and its castellated cliffs through whose dungeons and subterranean passages the tide boomed and surged, destroying, so it seemed to me, the foundations of the earth itself. For the farm, however, and its lovely setting among woodland and lily-ponds, for its steep fields and little writhing lanes, folded between shaggy hedgerows, for the seabirds and seals that ride the Gulf Stream and breed their young among its inaccessible crags, and for the cliff-top warrens and rolling pastures which make that corner of Wales so striking to look at and so fertile to farm, I felt next to nothing.

To this day I am not completely certain what it was in 1975, apart from Sally's hatred of London and my commitment to her, that drove me unhesitatingly to take up the chance of living here, in remotest Suffolk. But clearly some sound, life-loving instinct was triumphing over the sterile forces that had hitherto determined my life.

Whatever neuroses we are implanting in them, and whatever unhappinesses life inflicts on them later, our children will not, I believe, suffer from the crippling

76

sense of estrangement which I have experienced. Furthermore, in their affinity with the countryside, they will have a resource with which to combat the sense of alienation embedded in human consciousness and impinging on every one of us, to a greater or lesser extent. Our efforts to reconcile the meaning we vest in our work and relationships, our chosen place in existence, with our knowledge of the transience of life and the inevitability of death can never be wholly successful, and will always be threatened by intimations of cosmic absurdity. Hanging over all of us is the fear that our lives are no more than meaningless intervals in a system whose only significance is biological. This apprehension of futility is bound to be especially acute and pressing in a godless culture that lacks a commonly shared belief in a supernatural explanation of human destiny. However, anyone who possesses a strong sense of involvement and attachment in relation to the countryside, or to some specialized branch of natural history, will never entirely give way to the sensation of being unintelligibly thrust in and out of existence. Few things give more confidence to one's sense of belonging than an interest in other forms of life. This confidence is magnified a hundredfold if one is able to follow closely the natural and cultivated life of a locality which is somehow special to oneself. And if, in addition, one's spirits exult at the sight of a horse chestnut in the full splendour of its mushroom-pink flowering, and one can perceive the sublime in the action of a spider binding up its struggling victim in chains of silk, one will always be able, at the very least, to repel despair.

Wednesday, 28 July

During this week, the first of the school holidays, the weather has been perfect for harvesting and children's play. Every morning we have watched the combine harvesters rumble out of the yards towards the fields, and every evening we have waited for the trailers to return with their towering loads of straw bales. At night, the heat makes it difficult to sleep, and we are kept awake too by the noise of the grain dryer at work on the glistening black rape seeds, which lie like a mountain of caviar in the barn opposite our bedroom window.

The children have been in the garden almost permanently. This week they have been joined by Sylvia, the daughter of our friend Peter; she is nine months older than Tilly and as blonde as she is dark. They play together in a way that I think must be extraordinary. Since they like to sleep together, alternating houses each night, they have been in each other's company, with hardly a break, for four days running. During the course of these thirteen- or fourteen-hour stretches, they never seem to quarrel and hardly ever appeal for adult intervention.

Their games are most elaborate and involve a considerable degree of forward planning. Yesterday they arranged a party for their dolls and the scope of their catering, and its attention to detail, would put a professional to shame. Their guests, of whom there must have been twenty or more assorted dolls, bears and other soft toys, were all carefully seated according to some very complex scheme of interrelations, and each was given its own paper crown to wear. These had all been cut out, decorated with felt-tip pens and Sellotaped to fit the individual heads. The table was laid in full and food and drink were served. Underlying the game, which today has been transported to the garage where another banquet has been organized, is a constantly articulated fantasy of families: the dolls are of course their babies; sometimes they are the eldest sisters of a large family of siblings; sometimes they are sisters again, but with their own separate families.

Jack tends to fit rather uneasily into these structures. He is usually called on to play a subhuman role, somewhere between a doll and a real baby. He certainly never qualifies in their eyes for full parental status, and his claims to being the father of his own family are indulged, but not really respected. Nonetheless, though he comes to us much more often for attention and reassurance, he plays contentedly with them for remarkably long periods.

Today, another boy, a little older than Jack, was brought round to play, and the two of them soon peeled off from the girls to pursue their own, very different kinds of amusement. For a while they played with Jack's toy cars and garage, and especially his dumper truck, but their games had none of the settled, evolving, constructive character of the girls'. Mostly they spent the afternoon roving the garden, kicking over the molehills, slashing nettles with their sticks, and engaging in mock battles, not with each other, but with phantom enemies.

I have just caught a glimpse of the two pairs through the gap in my curtains, which, ridiculously, I have to draw shut through the summer months to keep the sun out of my eyes, thus giving myself the feel of a toad, or some such low creature that can only subsist in shady, concealed places. First, the girls were framed, like a little vignette, in my peephole: each was pushing a hugely overloaded pram, freighted with innumerable dolls, blankets and provisions, and as they struggled over the bumpy grass, they were earnestly conversing, their heads nodding in unison. Next I spied the boys, who strutted past, whooping; they paused for a moment to unsheath their stick-swords and mutilate the climbing frame.

Later, I met Jack in the corridor. Usually, if he sees me out of my room, he demands my attention and only reluctantly lets me go back to work. On this occasion, however, he just said, 'Hi, Dad. Nick's here,' in a most businesslike tone and roared away, after detonating me in his friendliest fashion. By a quirk of fate, the preponderance of children we know are girls and so Jack often finds himself the odd man out in every sense. When he does get the chance to play with another boy, this archetypal boyish behaviour immediately emerges, and the contrast with the girls' play becomes very pronounced. On both sides, however, their games have an unmistakably primitive quality, for in their various ways they play out the most elemental human activities. Lately, Jack has taken to pounding and smashing pebbles with a big flint on the doorstep, for all the world like some Stone Age man chipping his spearhead into shape.

Saturday, 31 July
Jack's drawings strike me as being very peculiar. They are not nearly as sophisticated as Tilly's were at his age, but they have an unpredictable, upside-down logic all of their own. Today he made a drawing of me, which began quite conventionally with an ovoid head, filled out with circular eyes and nose and a straight line for the mouth, to which he added a pair of long, spiderish legs only. Next he drew Sally in much the same way, but larger and placed at ninety degrees to me. Then he drew Tilly between us, standing, as it were, on her head, with her legs pointing in precisely the opposite direction to Sally's. Finally he drew

80

himself, oriented at yet another angle. The four figures now appeared to be floating in a gravity-free space, randomly distributed. But, suddenly, he extended all the legs and added a profusion of arms, with the effect that we were connected up to each other, forming a unified group. And so, in the end, he produced an affecting account of us as a family.

This may well have been prompted by the fact that, today, we have actually split up, for Sally and they have gone to stay in a holiday cottage in Norfolk with her mother and her sister's children, while I have stayed behind to work. Although they have only been gone a few hours, I am already regretting this arrangement and have virtually decided to join them, at least for the second week of their holiday. Life without them seems quite meaningless, no matter how much I may get done in their absence.

Soon after they left, I was wandering disconsolately round the garden when I noticed something very odd, which had never occurred to me before. By way of marking Jack's birth I planted a tree on the same day near our sitting-room window and, like him, it thrives. Nothing odd about that. However, the tree I chose is known as a twisted or tortured nut, for its branches grow in corkscrews and knotted coils, as if the plant were continually subjected to terrible pain. Hardly a fitting symbol of one's son and heir.

August

Monday, 2 August

Armageddon. The final battle between the kings of the earth rages and the end of the world has come. The seven angels are pouring out the vials of the wrath of God upon the earth. Men are scorched and gnaw their tongues in pain, but repent not. The homely Suffolk countryside is consumed in fire, and devils with forks in their hands cavort among the flames; smoke reeks up to heaven, blacking out the very sun.

The end of the world comes every summer as farmers all over the district burn off their stubble. In very hot weather, such as we have had today, the straw burns fiercely and its crackling is terrifyingly loud. The men only have to put a match to a couple of stalks and the whole field seems to be alight. No fuel is needed to spread the flames: the men just drag their forks along the drifts of straw left behind by the combine harvester and the fire follows like a pack of infernal dogs.

My thoughts turn on these lurid scenes as I sit here, alone, working in my empty house. Life seems quite meaningless without my family. I have discovered in my solitary self the most unattractive traits. Within only three days of being on my own, I have become crabbed, finicky and orderly to the point of obsession. I can easily imagine what I would be like as an old man, living alone. I would be skeletal, because eating by oneself destroys the appetite, but my brain would be corroded with alcohol, because the solitary life places no restraint on drinking, yet ceaselessly induces it. When I did eat, I would do so revoltingly, having no care for the stuff except to push it in as quickly as possible and wash up the debris. I would be ferociously inhospitable, fearing that visitors would disrupt my beloved systems; and, of course, I would be deservedly lonely too.

Tuesday, 3 August

Yesterday evening, seeking a little company after a gruelling day at the typewriter, I walked through our garden, noting with that lurch of pride every true gardener experiences when nature does his bidding, that after a mere three years' gestation my vine is going to yield its first grapes. This magnificent crop comprises exactly one bunch, which in turn comprises exactly eight fruit, eight minuscule, green nodules swelling nicely in the very hot sun we have had over the last week and more.

There are pigs at the bottom of our garden. What used to be the vegetable department has been clipped off by a wire fence to form a pig paddock. It is now rife with nettles and docks, which have grown to a height of five feet, turning it into a kind of mini-safari park. Only a few sows seem to be released on to this patch, otherwise it would not be so overgrown, for they will quickly reduce any field to a battleground of trenches and holes, allowing nothing but grass to grow and that only in patches.

When I arrived at the fence, a pair of them were still out, enjoying the late evening warmth; usually they retire early to their pen, as soon as the temperature begins to drop. They have made a wallow right next to the wire and one or two of them are generally stretched out, their sides bulging through the squares in the netting, as I put out the ash from our Aga each morning. They respond positively to a human presence, never failing to acknowledge you with a grunt and a swivelling stare of their pink-lashed eyes; if you stand at the fence for a moment, and if it is not too hot, they will lumber to their feet and roll towards you, their mobile snouts wrinkling and snuffling with curiosity.

Last night, I found one of them had coated its left side in mud, which had blackened and hardened into a kind of armour, for it had dried in a series of interlocking plates. On the other side, she was an innocent pink. They look very primitive, reminiscent in fact of rhinoceros, as they lurch on their strangely pointed trotters, following their tunnels through vegetation twice their height, and pausing here and there to crop the juicier fronds of nettle, and dock leaves that have not grown too leathery. Conditions in this field are perfect for them: plenty of shade from trees and weeds, sufficient moisture in the hollows for the soil to be churned into cooling mud, which also serves, when dry and crusted, as a sun-shield; more than enough lush plants to take the edge off an appetite that is anyway satisfied twice a day by concentrate feed. I grunted at them and they grunted in reply, letting me scratch the tops of their heads and their necks, where their skin has an elephantoid scaliness.

Despite their great bulk, their air of formidable matronliness, their twin banks of pendulous udders sweeping close to the ground, these animals are in fact mere adolescents and will barely attain maturity before being killed off. Very few are kept after they have produced their fifth or sixth litter, at which point their phenomenal fecundity begins to decline. Their potential life span is probably not really known, since so few survive to die naturally of old age.

In his *Natural History of Selborne*, Gilbert White recorded that a neighbour of his kept a sow for seventeen years, by which time she was far from senile, for though she had lost a few teeth, she was still raising litters. For ten years of her life she had produced two litters every year, averaging ten piglets a time. He calculated that she must have been responsible for the existences of at least three hundred offspring. Not only that, but when she was at last slaughtered, having been fattened up beforehand, she made 'good bacon, juicy and tender'.

Tuesday, 10 August

Back yesterday from Burnham Market, where Sally and the children are staying. I miss them, but not as wretchedly as before because now I know what a splendid time they are having.

Under the matriarchal authority of their joint Granny, Sally's mother, our two children and their two boy cousins, together with another little girl of exactly Tilly's age (her mother and Sally were in next-door beds in the maternity ward), are being given a classic seaside holiday. Sadly, I suppose they will not remember it, but I am certain they will grow up with a love for the sea and beaches and all the everlastingly infantile pleasures they have to offer.

I stayed with them for four days and I can hardly distinguish one from another in my memory, for they were rigorously ritualized, which is of the essence of happiness. Every morning the children would wake at a brutally early hour, dress themselves and rush about the house until breakfast. Meals were supervised with unanswerable discipline by Peg, their Granny, who insisted on the children remaining in their places, emptying their plates and not leaving the table without asking. This unaccustomed regimen induced gourmandizing appetites in all of them, especially our two, who appear to derive their energy from the air when they are at home. Once the adults had eaten, a trip would be made across the Green to collect the newspapers from the newsagent. This was a popular event, which none of the children missed, for it held the possibility of their being bought toys. When I was in charge of these expeditions I warded off their clamouring by allowing them to choose postcards to send to their various relatives.

John, the eldest of the cousins, who has just turned six, showed a problematic taste for rude seaside cards in the McGill vein. With an elderly maiden aunt in mind, he chose one which showed a man wearing pyjamas and sitting on the edge of a hospital bed, clutching his hands between his legs. His face was contorted in agony, and his pain was further emphasized by puffs of smoke emitting from his ears. A doctor, identifiable by his stethoscope, was up-braiding a grotesquely buxom nurse, who was holding a steaming kettle. 'No nurse,' he was saying, 'I said *prick* his *boil*!' I have no idea what appealed to him in these cards, whose jokes he certainly did not under-stand; indeed, I am not sure he even realized they were jokes, but every morning, without fail, he made di-rectly for them and unerringly picked out the crudest.

Soon after, we would set off for one of the innumer-able beaches and resorts which compose that coastline. Laden with all the traditional equipment, buckets, spades, beach balls, fishing nets, rugs, picnics, books for the adults, waterwings for the children, towels, changes of clothing, bottles of squash, cans of beer, sunhats and so on, we would surge from the car to set off on the longish trek which has to be made to reach most of these beaches. Since my walking pace is equivalent to that of a slow three-year-old, Jack and I would bring up the rear, with him trudging gamely beside me, firmly holding my hand and seldom asking to be carried. Because he considered himself the more experienced of the two of us, having been in the district a few days before me, he helped me along, solicitously pointing out obstacles and potholes, and buoying up my morale by telling me the kind of half-lies adults use to soothe children on journeys − 'Not far to go now, Dad,' 'We'll soon be there,' and the like.

I think I most enjoyed our trip to Overy Staithe, which calls for an arduous, but spectacular, trudge across a dried mud causeway running above a perilous mud marsh. This leads into a narrow-necked bay, bounded by sand dunes, which in turn opens on to a seemingly limitless beach that allows the tide to recede to the very horizon, where it glints like a sliver of hardened sky, leaving the ribbed sand shimmering with silver scales as the light is caught in the pools and tiny rivulets of draining water.

Once on the beach, despite these long excursions, the children would immediately start playing, and remain completely absorbed for many hours, demanding next to no adult attention. Though my own memories of days on the beach are mixed, I do remember being very happy while playing with my father among the pools left behind by the tide. He had a genius, or so I thought at the time, for mechanical engineering, and under his direction we would build vast and complex systems of dams, lakes and canals, tirelessly battling against the continual silting up of our channels and the erosion of our barriers and dam walls, until at last the tide returned to destroy all our work beneath the shattering push-pull force of two or three powerful waves. At Overy Staithe, Jack and I, following this great family tradition, set about damming up a marina where he could sail the fleet of navy blue mussel shells he had collected on our 'yomp' to the bay. He had never done such a thing before and was hugely excited by the project, working at it with fiendish energy and maintaining an unbroken commentary on our progress and setbacks.

Tilly was keener on swimming and playing in the water. Once equipped with her inflatable armbands, she is fearless and swims, or rather rampages through the water, with the exuberance of a dog, her eyes wide open, a permanent grin on her submerged face, and making tremendous blowing noises as the water sluices in and out of her mouth. At Brancaster she played for a long time knee-deep in a rock pool where, with a single mighty scoop of her bucket, she captured a jelly fish, showing both courage and decisiveness, for she knew it could sting her. We all watched as it propelled itself round and round the bucket, contracting and dilating its mushroom-shaped body so as to thrust back jets of water and push itself forward. It swam holding itself at quite a sharp incline, with its tentacles bunching and trailing in turn. At each pulsation, its body clenched into a little dome and momentarily acquired a series of vivid, electric-blue translucent bands, which then faded and gave way to a glassier, colourless transparency at the end of the stroke. We considered taking it home, but, largely on the grounds of being unable to think of a suitable name for it, we decided in the end to pour it back into its pool.

During these four days, we also managed to pack in many other activities proper to a traditional seaside holiday. We took the children to the fairground at Hunstanton where the high point proved to be smashing into Granny on the dodgems, which my children had not ridden on before. In the harbour at Wells-next-the-Sea, we watched a small freighter having its cargo of soya beans unloaded by a crane wielding a huge grab. We bought prawns and two species of shrimp from a celebrated fish stall in Burnham Overy. We even marched through the woods at Holkham in the hope of spying nudists.

Nor did Jack's interest in insects go unrewarded. At Holcomb we discovered that the ragwort was being eaten to the stalk by black and yellow striped caterpillars of the cinnabar moth. I have never seen the moth myself, but when we looked it up later in Jack's book it turned out to have a very pretty and unusual coloration. The lower half of its wings is coral pink, while the upper half is brown with streaks and spots of cardinal. This colour combination, had it been put together by human hand, would be said to clash nastily, but, for some reason very difficult to explain, we never think nature's 'taste' vulgar.

The children soon learnt that almost every one of these numberless plants, which were easily detectable by their bright yellow flowers, was loaded with caterpillars. They went on the hunt and brought them back to me by the handful, to the horror of a lady sitting nearby, who declared herself to be a conservationist. However, she did not understand the problem I really faced. The wish to conserve is, after all, seldom the result of a purely rational calculation, and is much more often part of a deeper, emotional involvement. But, for a child, to feel interested by something is inseparable from wanting to keep it, collect it, touch and poke it about and show it to your friends and parents. These practices may be regrettable from a conservationist point of view, yet stifling them would be fatal to the children's incipient enthusiasm, and might deprive the world of a couple of nature lovers, a loss it can ill afford in these days of accelerating rates of extinction and enduring indifference.

On the other hand, there was clearly no excuse for missing an excellent opportunity of impressing on them the rudiments of good conservationist behaviour. Accordingly, I told them they would have to return their captives to the ragwort before we left the beach, because otherwise there would be no moths next year for us and everyone else to look at. This argument carried very little weight, since the concept of next year has barely any meaning for them, and, as at Redgrave fen, what I was saying was exposed as patent nonsense by the countless numbers of caterpillars infesting the whole length of the bay. Even so, they indulged me and laboriously put back the little tiger-striped creatures, which crawled off their fingers and began chewing the leaves as soon as they touched them. In all, I would guess we diminished the population by no more than ten, though we must have handled more than a hundred. Only Jack refused to part with every one of his collection; he insisted on taking home a single specimen to check it in his book.

At the end of these expeditions, we would drive home to our cottage, where Peg would preside over the children's supper. These were gargantuan affairs of sausages and eggs, or fish fingers and chips, or scrambled eggs on toast, always supplemented by two vegetables and bread and butter, with pudding and cheese afterwards. The children were then bathed in turn and put to bed. Two stories was all it took to put the entire group to sleep.

With the little energy remaining to them, the adults gorged themselves on their own feast and after blinking at the television news staggered off to bed. My bedroom in the attic faced the church tower, whose clock was at the same level as my window. During the day I often heard it solemnly sounding the hour with its clanging strokes and whirring intervals, but at night I never once heard it.

Friday, 13 August
This black date turns out to be propitious for me, because Sally and the children have come home a day early. My rate of production has slumped and all my precious systems have been trampled over and buried beneath the refuse of the holiday. But there is no sound so uplifting as that of children pounding and shrieking round the house while they rediscover their old haunts, their favourite books and toys, their special places and forgotten treasures.

Though I can see many effects of the holiday in their behaviour, they themselves have already put it out of their minds. It is not a question of short or defective memories, for if you interrogate them closely enough you can gouge out of them a series of intensely visualized incidents and scenes, all separately recollected, each a tiny, discrete unit of autobiography. The point is that the direction of their thinking, the flow of their minds, is downstream from the present towards the future; for them to think back into the past is difficult because it is unnatural, like swimming upstream against the current, and they are soon fatigued.

Sunday, 15 August
Earlier in the year I built the children a pair of little gardens in the shape of a heart, with a rockery at the top made of piled-up flints. In the centre I sunk an old porcelain kitchen sink, which was to serve as a goldfish pond. But, to my present annoyance and

94

shame, I never planted them out properly; nor did I make much effort to look after the few plants that were put in. The pond was never cleaned and filled, the fish was never bought, the rockery pockets were left empty and the weeds were allowed to invade and occupy.

This may sound maudlin, but I am sure every parent must at some time curse himself for having missed or neglected opportunities of enriching his child's world, for having deprived him by omission. Unlike gardens, children cannot be dug over, cleansed of weeds and pests, refertilized, reseeded and cultivated with more care than last time. There is no going back, no new season when last year's bungled experiment can be corrected, no dormant period when defective growth can be pruned back to ensure next year's healthy crop.

With Jack's help, I weeded and dug over the whole plot, leaving it immaculately tidy, though at this time of year there is nothing much worth planting. To his delight, we lit a bonfire and he took on the job of stoker, sending fearsome streaks of flame high into the air by piling on dead grass. For some reason, throughout the afternoon he repeatedly demanded that I praise him, saying over and over again, 'I've done this well, haven't I, Dad?' Each time I told him he had done well, but my assurances did not satisfy him for long. I think the explanation must be connected with our recent separation: in effect, he was asking me to confirm that I still loved him. In any event, I swore that next year they would both have flourishing, cared-for gardens, complete with ornamental pond and glittering fish.

This is a week of great resolves. For the hundredth time, I have decided to give up smoking. Today is the fourth day without tobacco. I certainly feel more determined than usual, but, contrary to cliché, I find the earliest days, the days of cold turkey, the easiest, for I am always puffed up with self-righteousness and moral superiority. However, this period of conspicuous triumph over the weaker self soon passes and is succeeded by the real trial. Before long other people are taking for granted your victory over temptation and already think of you as a reformed smoker. You no longer impress them with behaviour they have never had the slightest difficulty achieving. You no longer feel so self-satisfied over your own choice of abstinence. Then you are truly on your own and suddenly the thought of smoke gently suffusing your head, the memory of all those familiar, reassuring little tricks and habits that make up a smoker's life, the idea, in short, of sticking a cigarette between your lips, becomes irresistibly attractive. The physiological addiction to nicotine may well pass, but nothing seems to take away the psychological longing that is deeply, incomparably satisfied by smoking cigarettes. When I last gave up for any significant length of time – two years – the desire remained as sharp as ever, though it made itself felt only sporadically. I was once bemoaning this at a party in front of a woman whom I took to be a non-smoker, but she cut me short by saying, 'Don't be so self-pitying. I can assure you, the ninth year is the worst.'

The children hate my smoking. Coached by Sally, an ardent anti-smoker, they tell, 'It's naughty to smoke. You'll die.' Peter and I have made a non-smoking pact.

Wednesday, 18 August
First intimations of autumn. It has been cold and wet, and last night a ferocious easterly gale blew, reminding us of the only truly terrifying feature of the weather we suffer here. Fortunately, the children were asleep be-

fore yesterday's wind gathered its full force. We heard it outside through the evening, as it whiplashed the trees and blew across the chimney tops, making them resonate like bottles, but sometime during the night it seemed to breach the house. Like an infuriated gaoler searching for an escaped prisoner, it stomped up and down the corridors, banging the doors and rattling the windows.

The first autumn we lived here, in 1975, we were devastated by gales of a power I had never experienced before and never want to again. They reached their climax one particularly black night, when it also rained so densely we felt as if an inverted sea were pouring down on us. At that time we were in the middle of an intensive house-training programme with two mongrel puppies, both bitches. Despite the fact that the end of the world was taking place outside and the house was lunging at its moorings, I was determined that no compromise should be allowed and so I duly put them out for their final pee of the night. Pushing into the storm like wing forwards, they made stout progress round the side of the house. The wind was doubly powerful when they reached the corner to get to the grass, but they were not daunted and only crouched lower, leaning their shoulders more forcibly into the gale. Alas, they were defeated in the end, for as soon as they squatted down, the wind spun them over and bowled them like hoops across the lawn. They finally lodged beneath a wall and I had to carry them in; they were exhausted, sodden and unsatisfied.

However, there was more drama to come. Later, I went out again to check that the car was unharmed. Though there had been no thunder – this was a very different kind of storm – I heard two or three very close rolls and crashes. I threw my torch-beam around our little yard and suddenly saw a sheet of corrugated iron, which had been torn from the roofs of the pig pens opposite, as it whirled through the howling storm towards me. I ran.

The following morning, which was bright, clear and peaceful, we found half a dozen of these lethal projectiles encircling the back of the house.

The whole estate was littered with dismembered and uprooted trees. Sadly, the beautiful avenue of limes and elms, oaks and beech, leading from the village's main street up the slight incline, which in Suffolk qualifies as a hill, past the old Hall and its parkland, towards the little outcrop of cottages near the water tower, one of them now occupied by Peter, had received the brunt of the gale's destructiveness. The road had been made impassable by barricades of torn-off branches. Three or four entire trees had simply been ripped from their beds and now lay in a rubble of smashed wood, their roots poking out of the ground and standing higher than many of the smaller trees in the hedgerows. These victims were probably already weakened by Dutch Elm disease, but nevertheless they were a melancholy spectacle. The gaps they left have only recently been filled and our children will be in their old age before they will be able to see the avenue restored to its original grandeur.

Thursday, 19 August
Sally's sheep share their field with a goose, a creature of incalculable antiquity, but undiminished aggression. Prior to the sheep's arrival, this cantankerous bird had enjoyed the run of the field and was able to retire at nights to its own, well-appointed quarters. Understandable enough reason, one might have thought, for resenting the intruders and punishing them. Not a bit of it. Ever since the sheep's

occupation, the goose has inseparably attached itself to the flock. Whenever the electric fencing is moved and the sheep are pastured on a fresh section of grass, the goose makes sure it is confined with them. If by some accident it is left outside, it struggles and protests until allowed to rejoin its charges; for that, I think, is how it conceives of the sheep. So now it passes every day and night with them, contentedly imprisoned, eating the same food as them and suffering with them the discomforts of the weather.

When the sheep are being herded, the goose follows behind, swinging its outstretched neck threateningly, like a cop's night stick, its feet flattening the grass in clumpy, rolling strides, as it chases them up with its hoarse, asthmatic hiss. Clearly, there is a potentiality here that domestication has failed to exploit; though they are sometimes used as sentinels, this capacity for herding seems to have gone neglected.

Its aggression is reserved for some unfortunate fattening lambs, which Sally bought recently. Its behaviour reminded me of my schooldays, for it bullies them with a persistence and cruelty that can only flourish among closed populations. This morning Sally had the whole flock penned up in a small shed and the goose had of course crammed itself in as well. It strutted haughtily beneath the bellies of the ewes, who were unconcerned, until it came up against a lamb, when it would instantly spread its wings, as far as it could, and stab viciously with its beak. The lambs were obviously frightened, but had no way of escaping its persecution.

This goose used to have a companion of its own species. Earlier in the year, Sally asked their owner if he was planning to kill them for Easter.

'Kill them?' he exploded. 'Not likely. We've kept those geese for fifteen years.'

99

But the word had been spoken and one did in fact die a few weeks later, though of senility and not by the axe.

Saturday, 21 August
Driving in the car this morning, the children and I were discussing something that had happened a long while ago, at least by their reckoning.

'You were in Mummy's tummy then,' Tilly informed Jack.

I asked him if he could remember being there.

'Yes,' he said doubtfully, 'it was lovely.'

'It *was* lovely,' Tilly confirmed. 'When I was there I hugged Jack's egg and kept it warm.'

This extraordinary remark revealed two things. The first was another of the comical, but resourceful and practical, fantasies she works out to explain the gaps in her understanding of the reproductive process. Evidently, she envisages the eggs of prospective children piled up in the womb, like eggs in a nest, waiting for their turn to grow and be born.

It also showed how she refuses to contemplate an era of time prior to her own existence. She does accept the idea of the 'olden times', as she has learnt to call history, a period which predates everyone and everything she knows and which is really fiction as far as she is concerned. What she cannot accept is that there was a period immediately preceding her existence when her whole world was already assembled, but was lacking her and even the thought of her. This fantasy of the egg bank provides excellent compensation in the form of a kind of retrospective immortality, for it allows her to have been with us all along, as an egg.

Sunday, 22 August

I have lit my fire. The first time since April, I do this every year absurdly early as a shamanistic way of precipitating autumn, which I love above all the other seasons.

Twice last week we arranged for Jack to go on special visits by himself to play with other boys. On both occasions he greeted the plan with rip-roaring enthusiasm and could not wait to be taken. On both occasions too he returned fizzing with his own brand of affable pugnacity and spoiling for any kind of physical encounter. Accordingly, we have devised a form of boxing match for him. This involves his adult opponent sitting on the floor to present a target, while he charges with his fists upraised and his face distorted by a horribly menacing expression, which is mostly the result of his thrusting out his bottom jaw to the point of unhinging it. After withstanding a flurry of charges and putting up a suitable show of resistance, his doomed adversary is supposed to collapse backwards, lying prone and utterly vanquished. Jack then makes a bell-ringing noise to signify the end of the contest and raises his arms above his head in a champion's salute.

His aggression, which is quite free of malice and cruelty, is generally contained or frustrated when, as is frequently the case, he is the only boy playing among a crowd of girls, but if it is given the chance to discharge itself in the company of another boy it will do so with irrepressible gusto. In terms of fantasy, he is a committed militarist. I asked them recently what presents they would like their Granny, my mother, to bring them on her forthcoming visit. Both replied instantly and without vacillation. Tilly demanded a high chair for her doll and Jack said he wanted, 'Army men, army vans, a gun that really fires and all sorts of army things.'

Having watched my children develop these very distinct tastes, I am now convinced that, insofar as they are typical representatives of their sexes, there is a substantive difference in the forms of fantasy and play, and in the modes of expressing aggression, between the genders, a difference that is not the product of conditioning. It is always difficult to judge one's own behaviour objectively, but as far as I am aware their completely divergent interests were not elicited by us, though of course they have not been discouraged in any way. I am equally convinced that Jack's present fascination with guns and soldiers does not remotely prefigure an adult life of violence and homicide. On the contrary, his games and fantasies are themselves the means, and very effective ones too, of gaining control over what is manifestly a very powerful impulse. They are the beginning of the process whereby we harness and make creative use of this elemental force, which furnishes the necessary dynamic to overcome difficulties in work, or any other activity, and compensate for one's handicaps. If aggression is repressed and denied an outlet, it can only turn inwards to fester and corrode; at its most extreme, this ingestion of hostility can result, so we are told, in the drive to commit suicide. If, on the other hand, it is left to run riot and is never harnessed in play, it will not develop beyond the raw, primitive, infantile state, and in adolescence will find expression in mugging, soccer hooliganism and so on. Soldiers are presumably recruited from those who did not learn to refine their aggression and canalize it into harmless jobs or sports, but learnt enough to need some outside authority to sanction the relief of their anger. There is no evidence, at least none I have read, to suggest that little boys who play with toy soldiers and cowboy pistols turn out to be more aggressive and violent in adult life than those who were forbidden them. Holding the views I do on disarmament, I would hardly allow Jack to indulge his murderous fantasies if I thought there were the slightest chance of nurturing a warmonger.

None of this, however, is to suggest that Tilly does not have her own mode of aggressive behaviour. She certainly does. The crucial difference is that she does not seem to experience the prompting of her aggression as a physical sensation, as Jack clearly does. I do not believe she feels within her the same explosive release of an energy that will not be discharged without combative physical exertion. Unlike him, she is not overwhelmed by the urge to punch, kick, batter, slash, detonate and generally assault her immediate environment. Nonetheless, she does pursue and satisfy her wishes with a determined forcefulness that can only be described as aggression, though it is confined to manipulating her relationships by means of strategy, tenacity and guile. He cannot match her in this, and I am sure her greater sophistication is not just a question of her being a little older. Presumably, the explanation for the difference between her organized and largely cerebral aggression, if that is really the word for it, and his spontaneous outbursts of bellicosity lies at bottom in the discrepancy between the relative physical strength possessed by the two sexes. Each gender has adapted its behaviour in order to optimize their respective powers.

These patterns of behaviour are of course also partly based on imitation and identification. Ironically, it is Sal, far more than me, whom they see exercising physical strength, for they almost always 'help' her when she rebuilds her sheep pens or moves their fencing. However, there is one form of direct identification with me on which Jack is very keen at the moment – shaving. I have given him an old razor, without a blade, of course, which he keeps next to mine, and every morning he asks to be put up on the little tiled shelf beside the basin so he can scrape the soap off one side of my face while I attend to the other. This he does with methodical care and will not let me wash until every last bubble has been removed. When I have finished, he takes my brush, loads it with soap and lathers his arm, which he then shaves, scrupulously inspecting it afterwards for stray hairs. Next he takes off his pyjama top and starts on his chest and stomach. Finally, if I let him, he will take off all his clothes and seat himself in the basin, soaped all over and looking like a melting icecream.

As I write this, I can see him walking across the lawn in his comical trudging way. Recently, he has become obsessed with space rockets and now wherever he goes he imitates the action of a rocket, as he understands it, muttering 'Blast-off' to himself every few paces and making his exploding noise as he flings open his arms. His aggression, though expressed through the imagery of carnage and destruction, is nevertheless touchingly amiable and somehow not at all at odds with his gentle and thoughtful personality; in him, threats of homicidal mayhem seem no more than an aspect of his sweet-tempered exuberance.

Walking to the church with them today, Peter reminded me of one of the great moments in Jack's life. Last Christmas we took them to a special children's service held here at our village church. At the end the vicar gave them a talk, which he illustrated with drawings attached to pieces of cardboard with little doors in front designed to be opened dramatically at the appropriate moment. He opened one set of doors to reveal a picture clearly intended to represent the throne of God.

'Now,' he said, beaming round his diminutive congregation, 'which little boy or girl can tell me what this shows?' He held up the card and pointed to it.

'Toilet,' shouted out Jack.

Sunday, 29 August

The high point of last week was our visit to the sheep sale at Ingham, a village lying a few miles outside Bury St Edmunds. These sales are held on each last Friday of the summer months. Driving along the road, one is suddenly confronted by an extraordinary sight, for the sheep are so densely packed in their pens and are so numerous that the side of the hill where they stand looks as if it has grown a crop of wool.

Though Suffolks preponderate, many other breeds are to be seen, including exotics like the St Kilda, which is a black-wooled miniature, with long, straight, wickedly pointed horns. There was a pen of Ryelands, which have long sideboards drooping from their cheeks reminiscent of Victorian Dundrearies, or 'buggers' grips', as they were known. A splendid Dorset ram was for sale too; it had perfectly coiled horns, each culminating in a delicate prong, which could almost have served as a corkscrew. The spirals unfolded on a precisely regular basis, conforming to some mathematical principle.

This is more than can be said for the prices prevailing at these auctions, which do not seem to be determined by any economic or other discernible rational factor. But though they are affected by the mood and whim of the public, they must nevertheless obey some darker, more mysterious law whose workings are only understood by the auctioneer, for he never looks downhearted or elated, but simply satisfied, as if the outcome of the proceedings had never been other than transparently predictable to him. On this occasion, prices were very low, but Sally was only there to look and talk, not to buy. She has now been keeping sheep for a year and is already an institution at such sheep events.

The rams are auctioned one by one in a little circular

tent made shadowy by the crowd gathered densely around a crumbling amphitheatre of straw bales, some sitting, some sprawling on the upper tiers and more still clogging the doorway. Those interested in bidding squeeze their way to the front and lean on the ring of hurdles enclosing a penny-sized arena, where the drovers prod and urge on the rams so they can be seen to their best advantage. The auctioneer allows plenty of time for reflection before bidding and speaks in a soft, almost deferential tone. The ewes, in contrast, are sold by the pen, out in the open, in a raucous, fairground style.

The children and I watched some of the vans being unloaded and were shocked to see a group of aged, skeletal creatures, their coats green with their own dung, totter out of one vehicle which, to judge from the address on its side, had driven two hundred miles that day. They all stumbled awkwardly down the steel ramp, being driven far too fast by a pair of children. Last came a very decrepit ewe, which only reached the bottom with great difficulty, falling down twice and walking with obvious discomfort. At the bottom it refused to move further and the children had to call their father. By now a considerable crowd had assembled, most of whom where muttering in disapproval, but he gave no sign of embarrassment. He pushed the ewe, lifting it slightly by the tail, but it sank to its knees and lay upright, its hollow sides heaving. Sheep's faces are very inexpressive, but this frenetic breathing pattern was a sure indication of fear and pain. He forced it to stand and shoved it forward a pace or two. It collapsed again. In this way he laboriously impelled it down the aisle between the pens until he reached the one allotted to his broken-down flock.

I went back later to look again at his wretched beast,

but the flock was packed in so tightly it was impossible to identify any individual, though I am sure that
more than one was only being kept upright by sheer
pressure of numbers. I could not understand who
would wish to buy such a flock, for the animals at this
sale were being bought for breeding, not slaughter.

September

Monday, 6 September
My father's birthday today; he is sixty-four. Sally's
thirty-fourth birthday was on Friday and Tilly will be
five this Thursday. The last days of August and first of
September are clustered with birthdays: we have
celebrated four others, including Peter's, during the
previous few days.

Time is snapping at our heels.

An era is at an end, along with the holidays, for
tomorrow Tilly starts full-time schooling. Her friend
Sylvia, Peter's daughter, goes back to school (in
London) tomorrow as well, and I have just left them at
our local station, bound for Ipswich and Liverpool
Street. They have been here in their Stowlangtoft
cottage most of the summer and the village seems
quite empty without them. This morning has been
altogether devoted to goodbyes, because my parents
are also now on their way home after a four-day visit.

As if in mockery of my maudlin anthropomorphism,
the swallows and house martins have today begun to
prepare in earnest for their mass departure. We always
notice them as we wake in the morning, for they con-
gregate on the wires immediately outside our bedroom
window. As yet they are impossible to count, but later
in the month they will crush together, shoulder to
shoulder, occupying all five strands and making it easy
to take a useful census. At the moment they are only
pausing to gather in tens and dozens for a few seconds

at a time before scattering to wheel and dart above the roofs of the pig pens. The martins far outnumber the swallows. Actually, despite their name, they disdain our house, but favour instead the farm office, which is lower and perhaps more sheltered. The eaves all along its west-facing front are festooned with their little mud pouches, while below, the gravel and doorsteps are streaked with white where their droppings have fallen. However, the rain will soon clean up after them, though their nests remain intact from year to year and some must be of a great age.

The children seem to feel only the briefest twinge of sadness when the end of things is reached. Their minds are forward-looking: they greet the future with eagerness, assured that it has nothing but bounty and pleasure to bring them, and they leave the past behind as casually as they drop their sweet-wrappings.

Standing at the door this morning waving goodbye to my parents, Tilly shouted at the retreating car, 'See you soon.' Jack, on the other hand, threw himself into the farewell ceremony with his usual gusto, which on this occasion was somewhat misplaced. He still makes no distinction in his tone and manner between a goodbye applied to a parting of a few hours and one, like this, of many months. Tilly, however, has begun to nuance her gestures. She has acquired a greater understanding of the extensiveness of time and its calibrations; hence her remark about seeing them soon, which was a way of contracting the unde-termined gap between now and then. She also has more understanding of the other person's feelings and tries to make her sorrow explicit in her farewells, though she has not yet learnt to act out, as we do, the feelings we believe the other would like to see us show.

Wednesday, 8 September

Yesterday was Tilly's first day at school, which is in Badwell Ash, a village two miles from here. She was already very familiar with it, having gone there for half a day each week throughout the summer term. We all went with her in the morning and she strode into her classroom with great confidence to look for the peg with her name and hang up her new birthday satchel. If anything, she felt more comfortable with the place and the routine than her teacher, who is new to the job. We left her, happily greeting old friends from last term.

Jack, incidentally, was deeply fascinated by everything he saw. He made me take him round all the displays in the assembly room, which he inspected with care, commenting on the work. When called on to make a critical judgement, he is always complimentary. Sylvia and Tilly, though older, are the same in this respect and will stay silent rather than pronounce negatively.

Tilly was still in her ebullient mood when I picked her up in the afternoon. She emerged among the throng of other children, eagerly scanning the crowds of parents for one of us, and started to run as soon as she saw me. I picked her up and asked her if she had had a nice day; she said yes, very firmly. I asked her what she had done and she told me she had worked and played. It appeared that she had definitely enjoyed her first day, though she said little else about it on our way home. She did add, in her earnestly expressive way, that it had been 'a very exhausting day'.

Stupidly, we had agreed to go out that night and had arranged to leave the children to sleep with friends. When we told her, she began to cry and was not consoled by my telling her that we would collect them later and put them back in their own beds, something they have often done before. In the end she went will-

113

ingly enough and we got them home and to sleep again without incident, but early this morning she came into our bed, crying. She fell asleep almost immediately and before telling us what had upset her, but when she woke she began to cry again. Between heaving sobs she announced she did not want to go to school. She offered no reason, except that it would be a long day and that we had picked her up late yesterday. (Not true.) She calmed down at last and was suddenly content to go; by the time she actually departed, she appeared quite carefree.

It is hard to say what such outbursts truly and fully signify. I am sure she likes her school and teacher, and I am equally sure that most children put up similar protests during the first few days of going to school, without being unhappy once they are there. Nevertheless, she had made a specific complaint, albeit an apparently unfounded one. No doubt, the day did seem arduously prolonged to her and tiredness probably allowed whatever feelings of confusion and homesickness she experienced to prod at her painfully. I think she realistically comforted herself throughout the day with the thought of seeing us at the end, but during these momentary stabs of distress she became annoyed with us for not being instantly accessible, a fact she had been able to rely on, after all, for the entire preceding period of her life. Her annoyance was then translated into the accusation that we were late, as indeed, by this logic, we had been.

Even long-lasting episodes of intense emotion tend to be reported and described by means of single, gnomic comments, and, because they are so densely charged, it is often very difficult to decipher these utterances and connect up all their meanings. I never know whether or not I have hit the truth. Sometimes I ask her if my interpretation is right, but usually I refrain, for by the time I have worked it out her mood has passed and I don't like to revive it. However, these situations generally recur and the truth slowly unearths itself, like a stone coming to the surface of a field.

In any event, when we collected her this afternoon she was on fine form and made no mention of being tired. This was just as well, for although we did not know it we had a strenuous evening ahead of us. One of Sal's oldest ewes has been suffering from a septic ear for the last couple of weeks, and has been dubbed 'banana ear' on account of the unfortunate organ's swollen, elongated shape and the disgusting similarity the matter which Sal scrapes out of it bears to banana flesh. But today, when we went to inspect the sheep after school, she found that not only had the infection become dangerously severe, but that the flies had eaten patches of her face raw. We instantly loaded her into the hatchback compartment of the car and drove her to a vet in Bury St Edmunds. On the way, Jack complained that the smell from the ewe's suppurating ear was 'sgusting', which it certainly was, and proceeded to hang his head out of the window, like a dog. The sheep herself struggled a little at first and then resigned herself to the journey, visibly losing condition over even this short distance, in the disconcerting way sheep do when they give up the will to live.

The vet gave her a sedative and we had to wait twenty minutes or so for it to take effect. The children played in the yard outside, where the car was parked, watching the procession of cats, terrified in their basket prisons, and dogs, mostly repellent miniatures or quivering, spindle-shanked mongrels, being carried or dragged in and out of the surgery. Tilly sometimes declares that she wants 'a puppy of her very own', but this longing is not so often or so passionately expressed

115

now that Sally has her sheep. Jack has never been as keen on owning a pet, though he was very interested in the pair of gerbils we recently looked after for friends who were on holiday. He could not be prevented from putting his hand in their cage and churning them round, as one might stir goldfish in a bowl; his idea was either to catch one, or to encourage them to perform on their wheel, which in fact they would do without any urging.

The children, who were running to and fro on the asphalt, suddenly ran into each other and fell down in a gruesome tangle. After a brief, ominous silence, there were shrieks of pain and shock. I picked up Tilly and found that she was not badly scratched. We inspected her legs and saw only abrasions, but no cuts. Then she looked down again and noticed two tiny oozing rubies of blood, one on each neat knee. Like Othello, she roared, 'Blood, blood, blood,' pointing at her pin-prick wound with a shaking finger as if her entire leg had been shot off.

Jack too was spotted with blood, so I took them to the surgery where, to their secret delight, I was allowed to sit them on the table used by the vet to examine the animals and wash their cuts. I dread to think what unspeakable infections they were exposed to.

I have observed before that whereas they will watch with equanimity, even a ghoulish relish, as the farm vet opens up the corpses of sheep and pigs to perform post-mortems, the sight of so much as a droplet of their own blood reduces them to hysterics. This must be a very primitive reaction. Adults cannot look at any blood, whether human or animal, without repulsion and horror, for blood is so closely identified with death that its most innocuous manifestation is still enough to arouse the most acute apprehension of our 'unshunnable destiny', to borrow again from Othello. But to children death is a joke, a rumour, something that happens to adults. Not that they never think about death; they do, and do so often, I believe. The concept interests and worries them, but without causing them to acknowledge that their own selves are perishable. They are protected from the idea of death, or rather their own death, by a blithe assurance in the security of their own existence that is virtually biological in its strength and blindness to any contradictory evidence. By the same token, however, their instinct for self-preservation is exceedingly well developed and the slightest threat to life, even a minute bobble of blood on a much-scarred knee, provokes a violent response. Since their lives are dependent on the initiative of others, they make their needs known with the utmost vehemence, regardless of how serious the threat really is. This is the difference, surely, between the two reactions? To children, blood means that life itself is menaced, while to an adult blood is a reminder of death, a premonition of the inescapable.

Meanwhile, the ewe had succumbed to the sedative and was lolling on the floor of the car. We carried her in a blanket to the surgery and the vet told Sally that he had no choice but to amputate her ear. We were welcome, he said, to stay and watch if we were interested. I was, but lacked the courage.

It did not take him long to finish the operation and soon enough we were carrying her back to the car, her ear now no more than a neatly sewn stump. We took her back to the stable yard Sally has the use of, and put her under cover.

Sally has just been to look at her (11 p.m.) and reports that she is already on her feet and showing no signs of discomfort.

Thursday, 9 September

Tilly is five today. A party after school has been arranged, but unfortunately I had to be out most of the afternoon. When I returned I found a dozen children rushing round the garden – we are presently enjoying the most glorious Indian summer – taking part in a kind of gymkhana of jumps and exercises Sally had set up for them. The lawn was littered with scraps of present paper, squashed paper hats, and the rather revolting, damp rubber shreds of burst balloons. The remains of Tilly's cake were melting and crumbling in the sunshine. It is a tradition that they can have their birthday cake made up as a model of whatever they choose. This year Tilly had requested a hedgehog cake, and Sally had ingeniously represented its spines with chocolate finger biscuits.

Tilly is very conscious of having achieved real maturity with this birthday. Brooding on her new seniority, she cheerily informed me, 'You'll be dead soon, now I'm five, Dad.' More than Jack, she has always seen growing up as a process of competition for a fixed number of places: she cannot become an adult without my giving up my incumbency. (Sally does not seem to present the same obstacle.) This gesture of solidarity led to a discussion concerning whom they would marry. Jack, as usual, opted for Tilly, but for the first time she resisted, saying, 'Don't be silly, you can't marry one of us.' However, she did wistfully say that she would like to marry me, though in the end she named someone else, one of the boys at her school. I told them that, in any case, I was already married to Sally. In a burst of pure Oedipal fervour, Jack scoffed at this ridiculous claim, pointing out that I could not be married to her because she was a Mummy; in other words, that she belonged to him.

118

Friday, 10 September

A curious footnote to Wednesday's incident. During the First World War, it seems that doctors working in hospitals behind the trenches were amazed and puzzled to find that the wounds of soldiers that had been left unattended and were infested with the maggots of blowflies, which are notorious for spreading infection, were healing more quickly than those that had received immediate attention. But then they discovered that the maggots were in fact eating away the festering flesh, thus preventing the infection from worsening and allowing the flesh to heal. This was in the days before penicillin, when even slight injuries could prove fatal, and so it was decided to have maggots specially bred in sterile conditions in order to plant them in suppurating wounds.

However, none of this makes me the slightest bit more tolerant of the flies which continue to plague us, in ever greater numbers. They have been so vile this summer that I have begun seriously to think about finding another house, something it has not crossed my mind to do since the first day I moved in here.

Tuesday, 14 September

Yesterday, a friend of ours who works for an agro-chemical company, specializing in insecticides, assured us that the insects were winning the war. We did not disbelieve him, and now we have further proof of it, for poor Tilly's scalp is infested with lice and her hair is powdered with their eggs. This is, presumably, part of her initiation into full-time education.

Sally had seen the lice on the back of Tilly's neck a couple of days ago, but because she had been playing in the sand-pit had mistaken them for grains of sand. I too had seen one on her, but had thought it was a little

119

scab. In fact, they are easily confused with either. However, Sally became suspicious yesterday when she saw an angry rash on the nape of Tilly's neck. We picked off one of the 'scabs' and looked at it under my powerful, x 8 glass, which instantly revealed it to be an actively mobile creature of some kind. Recourse to Jack's insect book soon enabled us positively to identify it as *Pediculus humanus capitis*, a squat, slightly bulbous, fawn-coloured insect, whose rear two sets of legs are equipped with relatively enormous and reddened claws. These enable it to cling tenaciously to its host's hair.

Tilly did not go to school and spent the day with her hair tied up in a scarf until the 'nit nurse' called. She told us that head lice are nowadays a virtually inescapable feature of primary education. Furthermore, in certain parts of the country, not East Anglia fortunately, a species of super louse has evolved, which is immune to the insecticide shampoos, indeed it actually thrives on them. She gave us some lotion to apply before the shampoo and I rubbed it into Tilly's scalp. It turned out to have a powerful base of alcohol and although I put it on as carefully as I could, without splashing it into her eyes, the fumes were so strong that her eyes became inflamed. She shrieked with pain. I gave her a damp flannel to bathe her eyes, but it was a long time before she stopped crying.

Later, she said to me, 'Jack hasn't got bugs,' in a tone that implied there was no justice in the world.

'You wouldn't wish them on Jack though, would you?' I replied, rather pompously.

'I *wish* I hadn't got them,' she said forcefully.

She did not appear to be revolted by her experience, taking it all in her stride, and peering at the gathering collection of specimens under the glass with interest, but she has told Sally that she does not want anyone else to know.

I am not surprised these vermin have achieved their pandemic distribution, for their hold on life is as tenacious as their grasp on hair. We removed the first one from her head around nine in the morning. I put it on a dark surface to inspect it, but had to turn it over on its back to prevent it from crawling away. At two in the afternoon it was still twitching vigorously. By the evening it appeared to be dead, but when I prodded it with my penknife it responded with a wriggling of its lobster claws. As I went to bed, around midnight, I poked it again and only elicited a feeble, barely visible movement. By morning it was not only dead, but had already desiccated into a crumb of chitin.

Monday, 20 September
For most of yesterday Tilly played with her friend from London, Sylvia. Perhaps because they only see each other at weekends, but more I think because they are both very resourceful, their way of playing together is unusually intensive and quite self-sufficient.

Entirely on their own initiative, they set up a fully equipped household in our garage – not the most salubrious location they could have chosen. On the oily floor and in amongst piles of rotting sacks and abandoned lumber, they made up beds, complete with blankets and pillows, they arranged a dining area with table and chairs, they laid the table, putting out elaborate place-settings, and, having furnished these quarters with toys and books, they installed a vast community of dolls. Throughout, they overcame formidable logistical problems, supplying and carting the whole establishment without any help, except from Jack.

Once the household had been settled, they turned to its washing. Every one of Tilly's enormous collection of 'baby' clothes, some fifty items at least, was first methodically soaked in a high concentration of washing-up liquid and then, still slippery and glistening, hung out to dry on a makeshift line. This operation took the best part of two hours and involved them in gruelling and concentrated labour. Apart from asking to have taps turned on, extra clothes pegs found, and so on, thay had no communication or contact with adults during the entire afternoon.

The sheer hard work they dedicate to these self-appointed tasks is very striking, and suggestive too, for it is clear that the exertion of effort is in itself deeply satisfying; they take pleasure in the process and act of work.

Jack drops out of these games after a while. The girls are not nasty to him, as far as I can tell, nor do they actively exclude him. However, he simply does not bring to their complex and arduous activities the same degree of commitment, to say nothing of stamina.

Although it is laughable to confess it, I too felt left out by them yesterday. Both Sally and I are feeling a little estranged from Tilly since she started school. For the first time in her life, she is regularly spending long stretches of time away from us, which we can only sketchily reconstruct in our imaginations by using the little that Tilly tells us and adding to it our memories of our own early schooldays. This is very different from the days when she was at playschool, as Jack still is. Here presides the splendid Mrs Moyle, who will graphically account for almost every minute the children are in her charge. Also, both of us have helped at playschool and know its routines well. But school represents the first sphere of their lives to which parents have no casual access, no automatic, unconsidered right of entry. These initial days at school are therefore a sad intimation of the distances and

122

silences, the tabooed areas, that will inevitably expand between us all as she grows up.

We were bemoaning this at lunch to our friend Mo. She briskly dismissed our regrets as maudlin twaddle, verging on dangerous possessiveness. School, she admonished us, is the first place where, after five years' continual exposure to their parents, children at last have the chance to win some autonomy and gain a liberating perspective on them and all their elders. We bowed our heads beneath the gale of her criticism, knowing from our own experience that what she said was true, though we were hardly able to rejoice in it.

In any event, my sense of separation from Tilly was allayed in the best possible way. After school this afternoon I took her shopping in Bury St Edmunds and during the journey there she talked to me, with hardly a pause, about school. Evidently, some breakthrough has taken place, suddenly allowing her to talk about her experiences at school in a new, carefree way.

She told me about the work they had done. They had been asked to suggest words beginning with 'B', which were then written up on the blackboard. I asked her if she remembered any.

'Yes,' she said solemnly, 'beetles, bath, baby, bum.'

A distinct, if small, change has come over Jack since Tilly started school. While she is out, he is of course the king and rules alone. This has had the effect of giving his play an extra dimension, which is hard to describe, although it is unmistakable. His solitary games are noticeably more imaginative and he calls for less adult assistance. Alone, he plays with the same kind of impermeable concentration as the girls when they are together; however, when he is with another boy, as he was this afternoon, he is utterly absorbed in the pure fun of going on the rampage, but the games are short-lived and undeveloped, mostly consisting of digging and detonating. Whereas the girls are forever setting up house, he is forever laying siege.

There is one, rather curious game they both love. After their bath, they beg to be wrapped in towels as they lie on the floor. I then have to say, 'What's this revolting-looking bundle of smelly old laundry doing here? It must be thrown away right now, before it stinks out the whole house and makes us all sick.' I pick up the offending heap and pretend to hurl it into the bath. The wording originated with some forgotten joke of mine, but it has since become inflexibly ritualized. If I fail to express sufficient disgust, I am made to go through the routine again, emphasizing my repulsion for 'these reeking rags'. Tilly has recently introduced a variant, whereby I have to describe her as 'a lovely sweet' and unwrap it by taking off the paper, i.e. the towel, but I still have to pretend to throw her in the bath. Jack will permit no deviation from the smelly laundry formula and asks for it over and over again, rolling himself up in his towel and remaining quite motionless until I give in and oblige him.

Wednesday, 22 September
School is dominating our lives at the moment. Last night, on the way to their bath, which we try to get under way thirty minutes or so before their official bedtime of seven-thirty, Tilly made a great speech as she dragged herself up the long haul of our staircase.

'I'm not going to go to bed. I'm not tired, not a *bit* tired. I'm not going to go to school tomorrow. If you make me go to bed now, I'll come downstairs and I'll stay down for a long, long time.'

All this was said in a hysterically tearful voice, between yawns. She looked haggard with fatigue and of course went to sleep as soon as I had finished reading their story.

In the morning, she once more protested against school, producing half a dozen reasons why she did not want to go, only one of which carried any conviction and that was her familiar complaint that the day was too long.

Later, as she was leaving, I called after her, 'Have a nice time.'

She immediately replied, 'No, I'm going to have a horrible time at horrible school.' But this was chanted in a self-mocking, sing-song voice, while she skipped along the corridor to the front door.

She certainly cries very easily at the moment, especially in the evenings, and it is a desperate sort of crying we have not often seen before. But for all that I do not think she actively dislikes school when she is there, though it is clearly putting no small strain on her. The truth is probably simple enough: she really does get very tired, and in the process she experiences more bad feelings, over a longer stretch of time, than she has been used to. We hear in her protests the echoes of the much stronger, blacker voices that have been shouting in her head on and off throughout the day.

We have all had our hair cut today. We enjoy a pleasantly decadent arrangement, whereby our hairdresser comes here to the house. She is always dressed à la mode, and makes a delightfully incongruous figure as she steps out of her sports car and picks her way through the puddles in our driveway, sniffing daintily at the pungent odours wafting across from the pigsties. Once in our kitchen, she washes each head at the sink and shears us in turn, while a drift of multi-coloured snippings gathers on the red tiles at our feet. Collected together, our hair completes an abbreviated spectrum, from Tilly's pure ebony, through Sally's sable and Jack's lighter brown, to my own grey, which gets whiter at each cutting.

125

Ever since Jack cut his own hair in June and had to be nearly scalped in order to disguise the damage, we have kept it very short. This suits the cuboid shape of his head, though it is made to look all the more massive by his little stalk of a neck. We sit him on the kitchen table to be barbered. Slowly, his head sinks into his shoulders and his chin settles on his chest. Then he remains quite motionless, falling into a sensual trance and, as often as not, he is asleep before the job is finished.

Tilly's hair is cut in a kind of Cleopatra style, but for school she has it arranged by Sally in plaits, braids, bunches or coils, as the whim takes her. These confections are generally modelled on styles she has seen on television and they test Sally's ingenuity to the utmost. There was some talk of her having it cut close to her head after the louse attack, but I am glad she has prevailed and been allowed to keep it long, because it is very beautiful.

Even as she was born her hair was her distinctive feature, for although it was waxily matted and stuck to her skull, it was conspicuously long. The following day it was washed for the first time, whereupon it rose vertically from the top of her head and stood with irrepressible springiness in a magnificent, black, furry nimbus. It was a great source of pride to her parents that she was used as the demonstration baby when the other mothers were taught how to wash their infants' hair. This was a needless exercise for the great majority, whose bald polls were nevertheless lovingly shampooed and combed.

Friday, 24 September
Last night and the one before Jack woke out of a nightmare, shrieking. Both times he said a 'beekle' was trying to touch him, which is very odd because he is fascinated

by beetles, indeed all 'creatures', as he calls insects, and does not hesitate to pick them up and play with them. At his age Tilly used to have nightmares too, but they were mostly about large, aggressive and, to her, semi-mythical animals, such as tigers and crocodiles, which would chase and threaten to eat her.

After both his dreams, Jack could not be consoled and finally Sally left him with me, while she went to his bed. As soon as he found himself beside me, he took my arm, muttered, 'Nice Daddy,' and began to snore. To be loved like this, and to be able to soothe someone else merely by being oneself, making no other effort, is of course profoundly gratifying, and I am always secretly a little pleased when we are forced to this last resort of letting them into our bed. However, by the morning I usually regret it, for although he sleeps beside me in his characteristic position – flat on his back, chin in the air, arms flung out – he nevertheless contrives to kick me in the kidneys with unerring accuracy no matter what position I take up, and to do so with unfailing regularity once every half hour, effectively murdering sleep.

Tuesday, 28 September
On Sunday, we all watched a version of *Ivanhoe*, which had been specially made for television and was quite undistinguished, except for its spectacular jousting sequences. The children literally gaped with astonishment as they watched, and afterwards, on the way to bed, they insisted on mounting us and re-enacting the tournament up and down the landing.

Yesterday, while I was in Bury, I bought Jack a pair of toy knights, mounted on chargers and wielding lances. Though made of plastic, they are very handsome, with ornate helmets and luridly coloured tabards over their armour. They lack the finish and detail which I associate, perhaps quite falsely out of nostalgic delusion, with the lead toys of my childhood, but they are certainly cast in much more dramatic positions. As I recall, my knights sat stoically in their saddles, facing frontwards, their horses plodding beneath them. Jack's, by contrast, are unmistakably engaged in bloody, if one-sided, combat, and their mounts are charging at full tilt, their manes flying with their plumes.

Jack has no sense of history. The concept simply has not dawned on him, not even to the extent of Tilly's idea of the 'olden days', and so, to him, there is no incongruity in sending his armoured knights to war against tanks and artillery. On the other hand, his knights have elicited an unexpected response, because for the first time he seems to be treasuring toys for their aesthetic properties. Usually his attitude, even to brand-new toys, is strictly functional and he shows no interest in the paintwork or other decorative features. However, for his knights he has demanded a special box, which he now carries round the house as if it were the repository of holy relics. Occasionally, he unveils his treasures, carefully placing them on a flat surface and not tumbling them out on the floor as he would ordinarily do; once he has situated them to his satisfaction, he leans back, his chin on his hand, to contemplate them. I have heard him putting them through their combat routine, but only once or twice, and then very gently: he makes soft galloping clicks with his tongue and moves them towards each other with a rocking motion, while releasing muffled explosions to indicate the clangour of battle in the background. He treats them as dolls, to be put to bed in their stable-box and fed with wisps of hay, but he also venerates them as *objets d'art*.

I bought Tilly a little bank in the shape of a pillar-box, which she seemed very pleased to have, for she was given a five pound note by Sally's mother for her birthday and has been wanting to convert it into an official saving. Nevertheless, I wondered if she would have preferred a pair of knights instead, but when I asked her, she said, 'No,' very firmly and in a way that suggested to me she had already considered this question. She plays with Jack's soldiers now and again, ranging them in orderly lines, but she does not get a big thrill out of them, any more than he does from dressing her dolls.

One recently discovered source of thrills, which they both crave with equal fervour, is the crumbling cellar that runs beneath our staircase and extends below their playroom. A huge door in the hall, with a suitably gothic squeal in its hinges, opens on to a steep set of steps leading down to what was once a large underground room, but is now a black, shallow space, no higher than a couple of feet, because the room above has been lowered. On either side of the steps are cavernous store-cupboards, ghostly with peeling whitewash, where I store my homemade wine. Hitherto, the children have been too frightened to come down with me, but now, providing I equip them with a torch apiece, they will gingerly follow me, whispering to each other and shivering with apprehension. At the bottom of the steps they sit in the dust to probe the darkness with their torch-beams. Although there is nothing down there except rubble and smashed jam-jars, this dreary household tip holds a fascination for them, perhaps because it is transformed into a magical grotto by the presence of a thousand spider webs shimmering and palpitating as the light exposes them. Every corner glistens with silvery-grey filaments, which seem to emit a faint, tremulous light of their own. Some webs hang from the bricks and joists in sheer, shimmering wisps, like items of *outré* underwear, and I always think of our dungeon as an abandoned warehouse, chock-full of bizarre fabrics nobody will ever order.

The question is, however, what does this enormous population of industrious spiders live off? Except for the mummified corpse of a rat, which the children have not yet noticed, no evidence of any other form of life is to be seen. Certainly, flies cannot penetrate the gothic door, and even if they could, there would be nothing down there for them. The cellar appears to be the site of a self-sufficient, cannibalistic ecology, for the spiders have nothing to eat but each other. Perhaps a balance is struck between the different species. Or maybe, and more probably, the denizens of our oubliette just spin their webs and wait for victims to stumble in from other parts of the house by routes only accessible to spiders. I am at least sure that they do eat each other: while we were down this time we discovered a *pholcus* frantically binding with chains of silk an ordinary house spider, which had become tangled in its ragged web. By the time we caught sight of it, right above our heads, the prisoner was completely cocooned and could only feebly flutter a single leg.

The children are convinced that this predator is one of the spiderlets, now grown up, which we found in July strung out below a shelf in our kitchen dresser. They may be right.

Thursday, 30 September
Autumn has definitively arrived. These mornings, when Jack and I go to collect the post from our garage, are chill and misty (or, as he calls it, 'dusty'), though

130

the afternoons are still bright. The virginia creeper, which hangs in jungly fronds round the porch at our back door, has begun to turn blood red. Soon it will shed its leaves, leaving a stubble of pink stalks across the face of the house. The swallows and swifts have gone, and though a residue of martins still remains, they whirl in agitated clouds and are fewer each day. Their place outside our bedroom window has been taken by a single robin (the gender of robins is almost impossible to identify), which perches on top of the telegraph pole. Each morning and evening it takes up its position here and trills belligerently, undoubtedly staking out its territory for the winter, which they spend alone.

I do not think the children are really influenced by the seasons, which change too slowly for them to perceive. In Jack's case at least, a day is long enough to have its own seasons. Their year is not divided up by natural events, but the great annual festivals, notably birthdays and Christmas. Next to these in importance, and unrivalled by anything else in their calendar, is the coming of the fairs to our villages in the summer. Poor Tilly, however, has developed a poignant awareness of the weekend and its significance. Every morning, as we lie in bed, she counts off the days until Saturday, and also the weeks until 'the long holiday'.

October

Tuesday, 5 October

Children inhabit a world of starker, fiercer contrasts than ours, ringed by unintelligible forces, a world where emotions always threaten to overpower and every situation is fraught with chaos. They exist in a psychological state which, to an adult, would be at the limit of tolerable extremity, and would indeed be supportable only for a short moment of crisis. The strain of living, as they do, on the outer edge of feeling would rapidly induce breakdown. By the same token, their exposure to sensation, unshielded by any real sense of either precedent or expectation, also allows them to achieve an absorption in pleasure which is utterly forbidden to adults, though this infantile purity of misery and joy survives as the medium of dreams.

Wednesday, 6 October

Last night Jack refused to go to sleep, or rather to lie down and listen to their bedtime story, which for weeks now has been the almost invariable prelude to their falling asleep. Instead, he kicked off his blankets and began to cavort on his bed, grinning at me with a particular, flirtatious expression he has when he is being provocative. I was feeling very tired and knew that if I were to take up his challenge I would only lose my temper, so I put down the book and left them to their own devices. This was not fair on Tilly, who was willing to listen.

135

It was hardly fair on Jack either, for their routine has been much disrupted these last few days, owing to the redecoration of our kitchen, a major operation that has involved moving most of our possessions from their familiar places. A side-effect of these manoeuvres has been that the children have requested a new room for themselves, somewhere they can use as both bedroom and playroom. Consequently, they have been installed, on an experimental basis, in one of the huge spare rooms which lie on the opposite side of the house to our own. Yesterday night was in fact only the second they had spent there, and this, as I knew full well, was enough to make getting to sleep difficult for them.

In any event, I came downstairs and began to help Sally with the painting. We both heard a scrabbling noise outside the door, and there was Jack, naked, except for a streak of white gloss on his bottom, and giggling with fear and mischief. Sally took him upstairs, became angry with him and ended up by smacking him. I hate it when she does this, but then I had abdicated from the situation and effectively delivered him over to her.

These incidents are so sad because we find ourselves turning all his good humour and high spirits into pain and tears. Later I went up to see them. He was still crying and looked very confused. Tilly, who looked tired and anxious, told me that she had taken him into her bed to hold him and stroke his head, something which has always soothed him. He had got into his own bed when they heard my footsteps on the landing, but she was still holding his hand. I made him comfortable and stroked his head some more. He was soon asleep, though his even breathing was occasionally broken by shuddering sobs. I was moved by Tilly's solicitude and told her she was a very nice girl. Usually, she squirms with pleasure at compliments and returns them, word for word, but this time she just looked at me thoughtfully.

In the morning neither made any reference to the incident. Jack was as ebullient as ever and asked if he could collect the post on his own. I agreed, but watched him from the sitting-room window as he forged his way through the potholes in our drive, which have been turned into small ponds by the persistent rain we have had these last days. This inconvenient arrangement, whereby our post and milk are left in the garage twenty yards from our back door, is a hangover from the days when we owned a dog. Nell was her name and I was passionately fond of her. She was, however, the product of an enterprising liaison between the shepherd's collie bitch and an Alsatian, a lethal mix of breeds which, in her case, made for sweetness and charm inside the house, but vicious ferocity at the gate. As dog-owners do, we used to describe her habit of attacking the legs of postmen and the like as 'nipping', though 'savaging' would have been closer to the mark. Finally, she drew blood and had to be killed. In any event, Jack successfully completed his trip, despite having to hobble most of the way, as if in a chain gang, because his pyjama trousers had fallen to his ankles and he had no free hand to haul them up.

Meanwhile, Tilly had woken early and from the moment her eyes were open had talked incessantly about school; she continued to do so while we got dressed and had breakfast, and was still talking as she left the house to go to school. Evidently, some barrier in her mind had been breached, but we could not guess what had done it. We heard all about her teachers and the children in her class, their foibles and crimes. She seemed to be announcing her acceptance of her new world, to be acknowledging that she had taken her place in the hierarchy, a social phenomenon she had not met before. At one point during her enthusiastic account, Sally said that it sounded as if she were having fun, after all. This she would not agree to, but came up with the new formulation that 'School is horrible fun,' which was no small concession.

When we ask her to tell us why school is 'horrible', her invariable epithet, she generally says she dislikes the work. We were surprised the first time she said this, because one of her most striking characteristics has always been her willingness to settle down to a job and give it all her energy and attention. For example, if you ask her to draw a birthday card, she will readily compose one and will not be satisfied until it is properly drawn and coloured in, with the lettering neatly added. She is able to concentrate for as long as twenty minutes or half an hour, a long stretch by the standards of her age. As yet, Jack has not shown anything like the same capacity for sustained effort.

One of their favourite expeditions is to visit our church here in Stowlangtoft and in the summer months we must go at least once a fortnight, a practice which, presumably, has invested us with a quite misplaced reputation for piety. In fact, we make our visits in order to draw the carvings on the misericords and bench ends. Suffolk churches are renowned for their medieval carvings and, as it happens, our church has an unusually rich and well preserved collection; I have even seen it described in a guidebook as 'one of the places of pilgrimage for any connoisseur of woodcarving'. Its benches, which are thought to have been installed around 1470, have beautiful traceried ends and buttressed armrests. Each of these is topped by a carving of a bird, animal or mythological creature, including griffins, unicorns, pelicans, a cockatrice, a squirrel gnawing a nut held in its paws, a cat with a bird in its mouth, two pigs, one with human feet and one playing a harp, a mermaid and a portrait of Gossip, dipping his pen in an inkwell. They are naturalistically rendered, and all share a blunt, and often humorous, vigour. The children certainly enjoy looking at them and feeling them. I think they appeal to children in the way cartoons do, for they have the same clarity of outline and simplicity of character. Of course, they are also fanciful and mysterious.

Tilly and Jack have notebooks specially reserved for church visits and other sketching trips. Once inside a church, Tilly scurries from bench to bench until she finds a subject that attracts her, then she sits on the bench, legs crossed, notebook on her knee, pencil in her mouth, and studies her carving. After looking at it for some time, she sets about her drawing with her customary deft and enviable confidence. When she has finished, she brings her book to me and I write in the title, date and church. Ever since she has been able to hold a pencil she has displayed unusual powers of concentration and I do not know many children who observe so closely when they draw.

Tilly's great friend Sylvia is here again after a break of nearly three weeks, and they have been playing together with their usual absorption; in fact, they immersed themselves in some game the moment they met at the station and have hardly had a word for anyone else since. Sylvia did not want to go back with Peter to their cottage yesterday evening for fear of missing a minute's play, and so she stayed the night.

A very welcome innovation has come into their games. Whereas in the past almost all their games were elaborated round building a home and setting up a household, today, for the first time, their game is a more or less direct reconstruction of school. This has perhaps been made easier by the fact that, as part of the recent reshuffle of rooms and their uses, their old playroom, which leads off the kitchen, has been converted by Sally into an office for herself and a workroom for them, in contrast with their new bedroom, which doubles as a playroom. She has provided them with a large table and a bench where they can sit and write, or draw or do their jigsaw puzzles, to which they are addicted. (Tilly told us she is the best in her class at puzzles.)

As soon as they woke this morning, they ran downstairs in their pyjamas and knuckled down to their self-imposed homework with all the frantic diligence of students revising for their finals. When I came down, I discovered all three sucking their pencils as they pored over some exercise set by Sylvia. This is another excellent feature of their new game – that Jack is incorporated. Without actively pushing him out, the girls do not generally take much trouble to keep him involved, but what use is a school without pupils, even disruptive and impertinent ones?

I do not say all this is welcome out of any premature desire to see Tilly working hard, but because I believe – I hope – it indicates that she is beginning to enjoy being at school.

Monday, 11 October
We are obviously wrong. Tilly came home from school this afternoon and cried repeatedly until she went to bed. These bouts of crying have their own cycle and when she is in the middle of one she is inconsolable. Nor will she say why she is crying, except that she is unhappy.

The idea of a child being unhappy, being continually unhappy, being unhappy as a matter of course in the way an adult might claim to be, is not only distressing, but an offence against nature. Not that I am so naive as to imagine that childhood ought to be passed on a cloud of bliss, unpunctured by nothing more upsetting than the odd bloody knee. But it is surely a condition of childhood that the surrounding adult environment contrives to prevent misery from pressing too hard or long, and sees to it that anxiety never becomes chronic?

These days Tilly's crying has a terrible intensity I have not seen before. In an adult, crying is a sign of giving in to some overwhelming emotion, though, paradoxically, 'breaking down' often heralds the discovery of new strength to endure. In a child, however, unless it is simply caused by physical pain, crying may well be a sign of having exhausted his or her limited verbal resources, but not necessarily of surrender. But then children's crying contains so many emotional elements: rage, outrage, frustration, fatigue, defiance, shock and so on. At the moment Tilly's crying seems to be made up only of misery and despair. She does not sniffle or sob, but opens her mouth in a great O, like a theatrical mask of Tragedy, and releases a howl of anguish.

Thursday, 14 October
This evening I was very short-tempered. Sally had to go out and when I put them to bed the inevitable clash with Jack took place. Tilly usually finds these incidents upsetting, but this evening she was on excellent form and managed to weather the storm, which in the event was mild and brief, without distress.

She had been to a gymnastics class in the afternoon

141

to see if she preferred it to her ballet class. Clearly, she had greatly preferred it. As they undressed for their bath, she demonstrated some of the excrcises they had been put through. Her exhibition was poignantly comic. She wears the smallest size of leotard manufactured, but though she is at last beginning to fill it out, it still hangs baggily around her legs. Having stripped down to this quaint garment in the most professional manner, she proceeded to twist and knot herself in improbable shapes, her little face emerging now and then from a tangle of limbs as she asked me, 'That's clever, isn't it, Dad?'

Later, when they were lying peacefully in their beds, I asked her if she was feeling more cheerful than she had at the beginning of the week.

'Yes,' she said, most emphatically, 'I'm not at all unhappy at gym.'

I asked her if she was a bit happier at school too. She said yes again, a little less certainly, but without hesitation.

Sunday, 17 October
Tonight Sal and I played pelmanism with them. Admittedly, we used a small pack of Animal Snap cards, containing such characters as Dr Bunfuz the rabbit, Humphry Goggle the frog, Mr Cunningleigh-Sligh the fox, and Nubby Tope the mole, but I was amazed at how well even Jack could remember where they were placed.

Of course, this only goes to show that the development of their faculties is very uneven and does not take place along a plane of gradual accretion, but by quantum leaps, to use a fashionable phrase. It also shows that parents are almost bound to underestimate their children's abilities, since they tend to judge by the results of the leap before last. Adults too sometimes change in the same sudden way, but their catastrophes are very seldom credited.

The children play games keenly, but without bloodthirsty competitiveness. However, neither can bear to lose for too long, so a certain amount of judicious management has to be applied. Tilly brings her habitual concentration to bear on pelmanism, with predictable results, but Jack employs a very odd style of play. He appears hardly to look at the cards as they are exposed, and fiddles about in the most infuriating way while others are choosing, yet when his turn comes he seizes his cards at once, showing no hesitation, and is able to pick out pairs with bewildering precision.

Tonight he did something very endearing. Just after supper, Sally accidentally pushed her elbow into Tilly's eye. She shrieked with pain. He immediately responded by kneeling down and banging his head, quite hard, on the floor. This was unquestionably a gesture of solidarity with Tilly: he wanted to share her suffering and perhaps to attract some of it to himself. It was done instinctively and, like much of his behaviour, looked very primitive. Next, he rushed off to collect a doll for Tilly. As it happened, he lighted on one that has a defective eye, for its rolling mechanism has jammed, fixing its left eye in a permanent wink. I was not sure whether he did this by chance or deliberately, as a further effort to disperse her pain.

In another respect he has been much less endearing. He has begun to make a habit of obstinately and suicidally persisting when he is asked to stop doing something. For instance, this morning he appeared in our bedroom with an armful of socks, rolled in pairs, which he had taken from a pile of clean washing.

143

These he fired off round the room as if they were hand-grenades. We asked him to put them back, but to no avail, and soon our tone had escalated to one of rage, for each request only incited him to hurl another missile. Even when the outcome of these crazy confrontations is not only predictable, but imminent, he continues to provoke, his look of hilarious mischief completely unaffected by our threats and glowering. But when at last I shout at him in my most enraged voice, which does frighten him, or Sally slaps his hand, as she did this morning, he appears to be amazed that such a thing should happen and screams with shock and indignation at the injustice of his treatment.

Their cousins – Sally's sister's two boys, with whom we went on holiday – were here this afternoon. Our children are always astounded, and excited, by the boys' rumbustiousness. Jack, in particular, follows John's wilder escapades with rapt admiration, for it would never cross his mind to do such splendid things as pull the vital log out of the pile in our woodshed and bring it down in an avalanche, or throw mud pies at the car until the windows were blocked up. These feats are very interesting to Tilly too, though she worries more about what we will think and she shies away from their roughness.

We walked all the children down Kiln Lane, which leads to Peter's cottage and is beginning to take on a new beauty as the trees turn. Near the old Hall we filled our pockets with sweet chestnuts, but when we came to roast them they proved very disappointing: most shrivelled to nothing and the remainder were tasteless.

Last night Jack woke us up, crying. When I went into their room, I found him struggling out of his blankets and shouting something, which I could not make out. I put him on my knee and asked him to repeat it, but he was crying too hysterically to be intelligible. It was some minutes before I got him calm enough to speak more clearly.

'Tilly's always first upstairs,' he sobbed, bitterly.

I told him that she was not and that, anyway, next time we went upstairs I would see that he went first, but despite these assurances and my stroking his head throughout he was not to be consoled, and in the end I had to put him in our bed.

Why this idea of not being first upstairs should be so distressing, I do not know. Tilly herself has more than once collapsed in tears, quite unpredictably, at the bottom of the stairs when Jack has been ahead of her, using exactly the same formulation, and so I don't think Jack's outcry can be put down to just a bad dream. Nor does the problem appear to be merely thwarted competitiveness, for in Tilly's case if I offer to hold Jack and let her take the lead, she will always refuse and will indeed cry all the more.

Usually, they like to bound up the stairs as fast as they can go, but perhaps when they are feeling tired or anxious they suddenly become overwhelmed by the sheer height of the staircase, which is considerable – sixteen deep steps. Children of their age are so much smaller than us that it is difficult to identify with their sense of scale. They are of course much weaker too; in fact, they are even weaker than they are small. While surface area increases only as the square of length (length x length), volume increases as the cube of length (length x length x length) and therefore grows more rapidly than surface. I am about twice as tall as

Jack, but I am also nearly six times as heavy, and for this reason, though I can't think of any way of measuring it precisely, I suspect the differential between our relative muscular strength is much greater than between our relative heights.

Saturday, 23 October
My birthday. We were woken in the middle of the night by Tilly and Sylvia creeping downstairs to get my presents ready. They were doing everything by the book: they had made their beds, put on their slippers and cardigans and were speaking only in whispers. I gave them a shock when I came out and confronted them in the corridor. Tilly's face was white as flour and her eyes were starting out of her head, but she did not drop her whisper. I made them go back to their bedroom and then looked at my watch to find it was six o'clock, which was not really so early. Sally took pity on them and led them downstairs. They soon reappeared with parcels and cards they had drawn themselves. I was not allowed to open anything myself, though I did get them to keep something for Jack to open when he woke up.

Yesterday, as we drove to the station to collect Peter and Sylvia, Tilly asked me about the Hall in the village, which is now a nursing home.

'That's where the old people go, isn't it?'

'Some old people,' I said. 'You have to be rich to go there.'

'They go there when they're ill.' Then, after a little thought, she said, 'That's where they die.'

'They shoot them,' added Jack, grimly.

He brooded on this for a while.

'Are you going to die?'

'We all die sometime,' I told him, rather ploddingly.

146

'Not us,' said Tilly very firmly and indignantly. 'Well, not until a long time after you. You'll be dead quite soon, won't you?'

Jack is not so heartily reconciled to my imminent decease and always looks a little worried during these conversations. Neither of them has the vaguest clue about relative ages. I asked Jack how old he thought I was going to be on my birthday.

He obviously had no idea, but making a shrewd guess, he said, 'Five?'

I told them I was to be thirty-eight and this morning, as the girls were opening the parcels, I asked Tilly if she could remember my age.

'Eighty-three,' she said promptly, and did not really understand why her answer was so ludicrous and made me laugh.

Although they are extremely conscious of the calibration of age differentials among their peer group, they lump adults together in a single mass; white hair, wrinkles, infirmities and so on seem to register with them merely as distinguishing features and not as the badges and indicators of age. They rightly insist on having their own ages calculated in both years and months, which are of course critical gauges of their development. Jack is 'free and free-quarters' and will not accept anything more imprecise.

Despite having passed the decisive half-way milestone of thirty-five, and therefore being closer to the grave than the cradle, I do not find my birthdays depressing occasions; on the contrary, I rather enjoy them and even derive some sense of complacency from them, for I can truly say that I like my life more, not less, as it goes on. Though I am no richer, and am indeed poorer, than I was a decade ago, I had none of the things then that I most value now: I had not met Sally, I had no children, I was not a writer and did not live in the countryside.

147

Tilly has recently discovered the joys of scatology. Jack also enjoys conversations about poo-poo, but he does not yet bring to them the sniggering, secretive hilarity that Tilly and her schoolfriends are just beginning to enjoy. They are both enormously fascinated by our drains and often beg me to lift up the covers of the inspection pits, which lie in our drive and can be levered off to reveal the culverts leading down to the main sewerage system in the street. They peer into these with a sort of reverential amazement. I think they are impressed by the vastness and complexity of the system required to dispose of something they unload so casually. They are not yet disgusted by excrement: I try to explain the dangers of infection and get them to wash their hands after going to the loo, but they are not at all convinced and only go through with the ritual in order to satisfy what they clearly regard as another of my crazy whims.

Tilly has, however, acquired a new self-consciousness about her body. When she was in her bath last night, she devised a makeshift swimming costume out of a flannel and Sally's plastic bath-hat.

'Look,' she said to me, prancing about in this absurd garment, 'you can't see my fanny or my bottom.'

'Fanny' is not a word we have used much, but it is presumably current among her schoolmates, from whom she has picked up these notions of modesty. She has not developed any sense of shame, as far as I can tell, but rather has found a heightened awareness of the special and very interesting nature of these parts of herself and other people. To see someone else's knickers has suddenly become a great source of amusement to her.

She has always thought my own penis an object of entertainment; whenever she sees it, she makes a grab

148

for it and tickles me with painful vigour. These assaults are accompanied by much giggling and shrieks of 'tickly-tickly', which with them is more of a war-cry than a shout of playful glee. For that matter, she takes a keen interest in all adult penises she gets the opportunity to see. Any man who comes to stay, and is foolish enough to let her into the bathroom while he is having a bath, finds himself subjected to close examination and is the victim of usually invidious comparisons. She regards it as an impressive feat when Jack has an erection, which for some bizarre reason he often does when watching television. We were all watching the other night, the children still in their towels after their bath, and Tilly suddenly shouted out, 'Look, Mummy, Jack's willy's gone all stiff!' He then arched his back and pulled on it to make the spectacle all the more awesome, and we all duly expressed our amazement.

'Willy', incidentally, is another word in common currency at school and in fact among most families around here. We started, when Tilly was much younger, by referring to 'penises' in our rather pedantic way, but this was soon corrupted by Tilly to 'peeny', which passed into our vernacular, along with 'giny' for vagina.

Tuesday, 26 October

Jack has lately developed a trick of behaviour which is both pathetic and rather irritating. If he is admonished, even in the mildest, most reasonable tone, he will immediately rush away and crumple up in a corner somewhere, apparently destroyed by shame. Nothing will mollify him, and it is often many minutes before he shakes off his mortification and the look of pitiable humiliation fades from his face. His present extreme

149

sensitivity to any form of reproach makes one conscious of just how much monotonous scolding children endure without protest or resistance during the course of their ordinary day, scolding which for the most part is dispensed automatically and unthinkingly. I speak for myself. Of course, his tenderness to rebukes that were really meant as pleading requests, and would have been received as such by Tilly, also imposes an absurd inhibition on us, but I do not believe he is taking advantage of it.

Along with this, he has developed the habit of running into my room, wearing the same wretched, mortified look, to tell me that someone has been nasty to him. He makes his complaints with such an appearance of misery and shock at the other person's vileness that I always find it hard not to take his part, even though I know that it is virtually impossible to get to the truth in a dispute among children and make a just ruling.

On the other hand, his new vulnerability is being matched by a deepening of his bedtime devilment. If he is in the mood, and he certainly was tonight, he will squirm and giggle and make faces at me, instead of sitting quietly on my knee and going to sleep, as he usually does, while I read them their story. Although I recognize that these tricks are generally prompted by a combination of fatigue and high spirits, fortified by a touch of hysteria, and represent only the most innocuous and good-natured challenge to my authority, I find it very difficult nonetheless to keep my temper. I find it even harder when he jumps down and runs round the corridors. He will shriek with delight and terror if I make the slightest move to chase him. I try using my most fearsome voice, lamely alternating my shouting with wheedling pleas to be nice to us, but this only excites him the more. It is difficult to believe

150

that he is the same hypersensitive boy who melted with shame an hour ago at the softest word of censure.

When I reach the stage of shouting, I am not only angry but desperate, because I know I am reaching the end of my meagre arsenal of threats and bribes. I never smack him, but I do grasp him very firmly and thump him down on my knee, gritting my teeth violently and placing no restraint on my voice, which sounds as if my throat is full of blood. I become red in the face and I am sure I look quite demented, though not frightening, for he very rarely shows any sign of submission. These are dreadful scenes, and if I am sensible I give up and ask Sally to take over. A change of person is often all it takes to throw cold water on his rampaging and then he is asleep almost instantaneously.

Tonight, as Jack was sprinting out of the room for the sixth time and I was on the point of hurling down their book and storming off to my study, Tilly, who always remains motionless and detached, though very apprehensive, during these clashes, looked sharply at me and said, 'It's fair on Jack, but not fair on you, Daddy.' I asked her to explain, but she turned away and would say no more. Actually, I knew what she meant, and she was right too. She was saying that Jack's behaviour was not so wicked and intolerable as to justify my response, but that, on the other hand, he was not taking any notice of the fact that he was driving me mad.

The book I was about to throw down, incidentally, was Dodie Smith's *The Hundred and One Dalmatians*, which is the first full-length novel we have read to them. Most nights, it puts Jack to sleep very quickly, though he claims to be enjoying it. Tilly, however, really is loving every page and can reproduce the story with fair accuracy and an abundance of incidental detail. Last weekend I heard her giving Sylvia a précis of the plot, to bring her up to date before the evening's reading, and this included an impassioned denunciation of the villainess, Cruella de Vil, who might well have stolen dogs of ours from her tone.

Sunday, 31 October

Sadly, the children seem to be taking less interest than they used to in the sheep. I think this dates from the evening when we had to drive the ewe with a suppurating ear into Bury. Ever since, they have expressed intense disgust at any smell or sign of sheep having been in the car. No doubt, their interest will revive when the lambs are born in the spring. That, however, will be later than planned, because the ram which Sally put among her flock, a handsome and conscientious Texel, with a squeeze-box muzzle characteristic of the breed, has proved too short in the leg for her rangy Border Leicester ewes. He showed no lack of enthusiasm for the job, and was marking their backs with the chalk on his belly, but, as the shepherd confirmed the other night, he was failing to penetrate them. She has now put in her other ram, the one-horned Dorset she bought some time ago and has been renting out. He is not only big enough, but keen to the point of debauchery, for he gave Sally herself one of the vigorous shoves with his head which excite the ewes. Unfortunately, he cracked skulls with her and succeeded in giving her mild concussion.

She took some lambs to the butcher in Bury during the week and a friend who was staying taunted Jack, saying, 'Don't you want to go and see the lambs being killed and chopped up? I thought you were a soldier and liked killing.' Jack looked appalled. Nothing could be further from his fantasies of bullets, bombs, tanks, soldiers and so on, than actual butchery and blood.

152

Last night, we all went out to see some people, among whom was a couple with their first baby, a little girl, about six months old, and just able to sit up providing her legs were splayed out first and her body was bent a little in the middle, like a bag of sugar, to balance her head. She reminded us of Tilly as a baby, because she had a shock of thick, black hair and was petite. As things turned out, the evening was not a social success, and at one point even turned quite nasty, but I noticed that this couple were in that delirious state I remember well from the days when Tilly was first born, in which one is simply oblivious or indifferent to such trivialities, for nothing can match the momentous significance of a tiny baby's every smile and gurgle.

Tilly responded to the magic of a baby and sat beside this one, devotedly looking after its needs and amusements for nearly an hour. Jack too was very attentive, but not for so long.

Tilly has at last discovered that I am writing about them. Now she is able to read simple words, and is keen to improve her reading, she peers at what I am typing, hunting for words she can recognize, and of course she recognizes none faster than her own name. I have told her I am writing a book about her and Jack. As a result, she often comes to ask me, in the most affably patronizing way, as a great person would enquire of her hack biographer, how the book is going.

November

Monday, 1 November
Yesterday was Halloween, and for the first time the
children were fascinated by it. Sally had got hold of an
enormous pumpkin, and in the afternoon she cut a lid
out of its top, scooped out the flesh and carved the
conventional round eyes, triangular nose and jagged,
sawtooth mouth in its skin. When it was dark, she
gave the children sheets to wear and they pranced
round the garden making ghostly moaning noises.
Meanwhile, I had lit a candle inside the pumpkin and
set off in the opposite direction round the house,
holding the mask high above my head and swinging it
from side to side. When they finally caught sight of it,
they were not at all frightened, on the contrary, they
were enchanted, for it gave off a warm light and its
expression, though apparitional, was friendly.

Jack told everyone he met about Halloween and
claimed to have seen it, mistaking the event for a
person, like Father Christmas.

Later, when I brought the children back from having
tea with some friends, we discovered the pumpkin
apparently floating in the porch. Sally had put it on top
of the stepladder. I turned off the car lights and we saw
a white, eerie shape moving silently above the shrubs
behind the woodshed.

'Look! A ghost,' I screamed, but the children were
not fooled.

'It's Mummy,' they both said, scathingly.

And indeed it was Sally, fluttering a tablecloth at the end of a stick. This was altogether a splendid effort on her part, for we were much later than expected and she had been lurking among the bushes, in the dark, for more than fifteen minutes.

They have a very selective belief in magical beings. Ghosts, they have both separately assured me, are people dressed up in sheets. Fairies, however, are a very different matter. Tilly gave me a detailed account of them: 'They wear gold dresses and gold hats and silver socks. They're quite small and they live under my bed. I gave them a big crumb to eat. At night they come out and sometimes I hear them jumping about.'

Tuesday, 2 November
Poor Jack is ill today. He woke with a temperature of 102°. We sponged him down and gave him some paracetamol. For this we needed a teaspoon and asked Tilly to get one from the kitchen. After some time, she reappeared with a handful of teaspoons, as well as the cake tin and two plates.

'I thought he would like some chocolate cake.'

This sweet gesture was not entirely disinterested, for though he ate nothing, and in fact ate nothing all day, she promptly tucked into a large slice. He went to sleep again before the rest of us were dressed and apart from a brief recovery in the middle of the morning, when he laid out his train set, he has languished on the sofa ever since. So far, no symptoms have developed apart from extreme lethargy.

As if to demonstrate her firm grasp on life, Tilly has been very good-humoured and exuberant. She is on excellent form anyway at the moment, having at last reconciled herself to going to school. Rather to our surprise, she went back after the half-term holiday with only a token protest. Her official line on school these days is that it is 'quite nice', though this is said in a grudging voice to show that she is still reserving her position.

Two things seem to have contributed to her change of attitude. One undoubtedly is that she is now working effectively and to her own satisfaction. She was given top marks for a writing exercise yesterday and came home feeling extremely proud. For some reason, she confides her triumphs as well as her anxieties to Sally, but without putting any embargo on my being told afterwards. The second factor is harder to be precise about. She has made a friend, Madelaine, and although we were never worried that she lacked friends, for she has always been sociable and affectionate, it is clear that she is very pleased with her new relationship, which is all of her own making.

Last week she brought Madelaine home to play for the first time and Jack behaved abominably Tilly played hostess perfectly, showing Madelaine round the house, letting her play with all her favourite toys and generally being attentive, but Jack did everything in his power to render the visit a failure. He threw their cards off the table as Tilly was explaining how to play pelmanism, he repeatedly switched off the television, and made himself obnoxious in a hundred other ways. Fortunately, Madelaine turned out to be a tolerant, kindly girl and she put up with his antics. In any case, nothing could cloud Tilly's delight at having her special friend to entertain, and in the end Jack left them alone, choosing instead to persecute me. He moodily cut up a piece of paper into little pieces and littered them over my study floor, but this too palled after a while and he went back to the girls.

Thursday, 4 November

Jack made a complete recovery yesterday and has been back at his nursery school today. During Tuesday night he climbed into our bed. He still had his temperature then, for I could feel him burning next to me like a hot-water bottle and I had to throw off one of my blankets. But the first thing I knew in the morning was when he sat bolt upright and announced that he had to go downstairs. This he did and returned to make it obvious he had undergone a change of Jekyll and Hyde-like decisiveness. The limp, wan, silent wraith of yesterday was gone, and in his place stood, or rather discombobulated, the old familiar Jack.

'Look, Daddy,' he shouted in my ear. 'I'm a charging knight.'

This activity not only involved running round the room in a lolloping gait, slapping his backside, but also making anachronistic exploding noises.

As the day wore on, he showed no sign of having been ill; on the contrary, he showed exceptional vigour, bringing to an unprecedented pitch of irritation a number of newly developed tricks. One of these, and perhaps the most irritating, is his spitting. Fortunately, this consists more of noise than spray, but it is nonetheless unpleasant. Another of his present specialities is to emit a high-toned screech, which he has refined to the point where it makes one feel as if one's skull were being trepanned with a blunt corkscrew. He has now acquired sufficient motor skill to run round the room very fast, pulling everything within his reach to the floor as he goes. One of his favourite targets is the long oak settle which stands in a corner of the kitchen and has three large cushions and a foam-rubber seat. These he can sweep to the ground while on the run, making four successive deft movements and never breaking his pace. In fact, he will be homing in on his next target before you realize he has struck. And lately he has also taken simply to hitting one or other of us as hard as he can. He cannot hit hard, and anyway does not seem to want to punch us out of personal malice, but rather precisely because we are the best available unbreakable objects on which to vent his rumbustious aggression. On the other hand, it is his obstinate, foolhardy, manic refusal to desist, or respond in the slightest way to our pleas, reasoning, threats and even forcible resistance, that finally inflames one's wildest anger.

Our response is always out of all proportion to his crime, if it can be called that, but although he is merely being mischievous and provocative, he often reaches a state where he cannot be stopped except by making him cry. I have discovered only one sure way of diverting him and that is to take him outside, put him on Tilly's bike, which he has just learnt to ride, and lead him on a brisk expedition down the village street. This has yet to fail, though it is hardly practical at night or in bad weather.

When he is rushing about, bent on one of his suicidal confrontations, I am always aware of his massive head, which he lowers and pushes forward, as if he were a bull. He has cut his hair once again and, though the effects are not as disfiguring as before, his foreshortened fringe does make him look all the more thuggish. And yet when he looks up from his charging, the face beneath the great mace of his skull is sweet and touchingly merry.

Monday, 8 November
When Sally and I row, which thankfully is not often, the children immediately intervene, telling us to shut up. They are relentless and do not stop protesting until

161

we fall quiet. They will even put their hands over our mouths. This of course is another example of the ruthless way in which they protect their own interests.

Wednesday, 10 November
More than a year ago we were given a book specially written for small children which describes the facts of reproduction – *A Baby in the Family* by Althea. It has long been a favourite with our children and many is the time we have intoned such deathless passages as, 'When a man and a woman make love they cuddle up close to each other and the man sometimes puts his penis, which has become stiff, into the woman's vagina.' They have always appeared to derive some inkling of understanding from the book, and have bandied the jargon around in the most sophisticated way. But yesterday, as Sally was reading it to them, Jack interrupted her to ask, in a tone of mixed astonishment and disgust, 'Do you and Daddy cuddle like that?'

'Yes.'

'Does Daddy put his penis into you?' he asked, still more amazed.

'Yes.'

'Ugh,' said Tilly. 'That's rude.'

'Do you still do it?' persisted Jack. 'Are you going to have any more babies?'

'We still do it, but we're not going to have any more babies.'

He looked very puzzled at this and she tried to explain the rudiments of contraception.

'Have you any more babies inside you?' he asked, not having understood a word.

Neither of them can understand that fertility is a potential, which is voluntarily realized. He has some idea that each mother's complement of babies is stacked up inside her, like missiles in a bomb bay, each fully formed and awaiting her decision to drop them.

They have both acquired this notion of 'rudeness' at the same time, presumably as a result of Tilly's being at school. The other day, Jack announced that he did not want to take his trousers off in the garden to have a pee, something he has done a thousand times before and always in the most carefree manner. 'People will see my willy,' he told me, darkly. And I heard Tilly telling him that it was rude to let people see your knickers. On the other hand, it would not be true to say that their lives had suddenly been clouded with shamefulness. Discussions about the relative rudeness of willies, bottoms, knickers and so on are conducted with high-spirited gusto, and almost always collapse into choruses of 'poo-poo'. This magical expression never seems to lose its power to induce joyous giggles, no matter how interminably it is repeated.

Yesterday, while driving our two children and Jenny, a great friend of Jack's, I asked them each to tell a joke. Jenny produced a very polished one, which involved reciting Humpty Dumpty, but finishing with the lines, 'And all the king's horses and all the king's men had scrambled egg for breakfast again.'

Tilly invariably tells the same joke when asked and, to me at least, it is incomprehensible. 'When is an elephant fat?' she will demand with great archness, and before you can answer, she will say, 'Because it's thin,' and shriek with slightly unconvincing laughter. She will then tell it the other way round, when apparently it becomes even funnier. I think the answer to this riddle is probably simple: she wants to tell a joke, but like me can never remember one and so has fixed on this incantation, which has the form of a joke and, with indulgent adults, will even pass as a joke. In fact, she has a very sharp eye – much sharper than Jack's – for the absurd in people's behaviour, including her own, and she is often endearingly funny at her own expense.

Jack's way of contributing to joke sessions is to reel off a line of nonsense, very quickly, and interrupt it with a thunderous guffaw. Unless stopped, he will continue to do this, the nonsense gradually evolving into the inevitable 'poo-poo', until his voice begins to give out.

Friday, 12 November
Yesterday evening we all went to Tilly's school to watch their Christmas show, which was brought forward because so many people were kept away by the bad weather last December.

It was all most impressive. Each of the three classes performed a separate piece and did so with style and gusto. Tilly's class, the youngest, of course, sang, with the appropriate actions, a song about rabbits, 'Powder Puffs and Curly Whiskers', a song about a jack-in-the-box, and finally 'The Wheels on the Bus Go Round and Round', a song with which playschool has made us all very familiar. Along with a little boy, Tilly had been given the responsibility of holding up a huge cardboard profile of a bus, complete with drawn-in passengers and driver, while the others sang and acted out the words. She looked very pretty and was dressed in her favourite party dress, as well as her black patent party shoes. Unfortunately, she must have been tired, for she yawned once or twice and leaned heavily on her end of the bus, which nonetheless held up.

As is sometimes the case on these occasions, there was, regrettably, a rowdy element among the audience, which did its best to put the performers off their stroke. Sitting on the floor at the very front was a knot of hardened, cynical playgroup members, who noisily barracked the bus song, jeering whenever the words differed from the ones they had been taught. Most vocal among these hooligans were Jack and his accomplice Jenny.

'It doesn't go like that,' Jenny could be heard sneering, while Jack scoffed with his most derisive laugh. In the event, the song did persist for perhaps a couple of verses more than was ideal, and Jenny's patience was tested beyond its limit. 'I can't stand this any longer,' she announced.

Christmas is beginning to loom large. If asked, both children will recite, at great speed, an interminable list of things they hope to receive from Father Christmas. He is a figure in whom they believe implicitly, though they conceive of him more as a force than a single, actual individual. In fact, to them he is rather like the Holy Ghost: his spirit can enter into people, even ordinary, familiar people, and temporarily endow them with his own magical powers.

One very hot day during the summer, in August I think, we drove to Diss and parked near a bowls club where, as it happened, a fancy dress party was being held to raise funds. One of the members, a large, jovial man, had chosen to wear a Father Christmas costume, which suited his personality, if not the sweltering weather. However, the children's faith in Father Christmas was not shaken in the slightest by this anachronistic and patently secular person. Much to our relief, they both laughed, and Jack, in deepest astonishment at the man's ignorance, said scathingly, 'It's not Christmas today, is it?' By this I am sure he meant that the man was crazy to imagine that the spirit of Father Christmas would grace him at this incongruous time of the year.

Although Tilly always lays more stress on a doll's high chair than any of the other items on her present list, I notice that she has not played with her dolls nearly so much since starting school. Jack's list is invariably headed by a spaceship. He has no idea what a spaceship is, or rather he has a very clear idea, but it is nine-tenths fantasy. Indeed, most of his fantasies continue to centre around guns and powerful machines of transport – tractors, lorries, fire engines, combine harvesters, trains and so on. Spaceships belong to this category, but really the only thing he knows about them is that they are launched by counting down 'Three-two-one' as fast as possible and then shouting 'Blast-off' to the accompaniment of tremendous exploding noises.

Sunday, 14 November
I have just been reading a review of a book which evidently attempts to correct received psychological wisdom regarding siblings. Having studied forty firstborn children, the authors concluded that sibling relations were not by any means automatically fraught with jealousy and rivalry. For what it is worth, I can report evidence pointing both ways. For the last seven weeks I have worked as writer-in-residence at St Benedict's School in Bury St Edmunds, a most enjoyable experience, incidentally. During this time I read innumerable autobiographical essays, for the younger kids are asked to write, and do so with every appearance of willingness, at a level of personal intimacy which the rest of us would find intolerably intrusive. On the basis of these self-portraits, I can confirm that, apart from exceptional tragedies such as the death of a parent, the most commonly recorded trauma is the birth of a younger sibling. 'I lived in paradise,' these

accounts tend, in effect, to say, 'and then my little brother/sister was born, since when I have dwelt in exile.'

And yet, I do not believe Tilly will grow up to write this in her school essays. For one thing, the period of her solitary and, admittedly, gloriously despotic reign was comparatively short; furthermore, during the latter part of her monarchy the baby-to-be was a powerful presence, albeit an invisible one, impinging on all our lives. Because they are so close in age, it has been possible to treat them more or less equally, and whenever it has not been possible, the advantage has usually run her way.

They very seldom express jealousy overtly. I suppose their curious complaint about the other being first upstairs is a product of jealousy, deriving from the misconceived idea that they have been deliberately handicapped by us in order to favour the winner. Incidentally, a variant of this complaint has emerged lately, though it is only voiced by Tilly. She often has porridge for breakfast, which Jack does not like; he is therefore given his food first, simply because his cereal takes less time to pour out of the packet than Tilly's porridge takes to cook. Nonetheless, his primacy, which we now try to remember to avoid, gives rise to anguished protests by Tilly at the injustice of his privileged treatment. It is her gross overreaction to so trivial an accident that makes me think she is more sensitive than we generally realize to seeming differentials in our affection. But apart from these flash-points, neither seems to be afflicted by the idea of being ousted by the other, or of the other being preferred.

They are occasionally competitive, but never urgently so. For long stretches of time they will play together harmoniously and creatively. Tilly tends to dominate, but not destructively; on the contrary, she invariably gives the games a dimension Jack would not have thought up by himself. They very rarely get into full-blooded fights and, although they bicker, they do not keep up running arguments, nor do they persist with complaints against the other for more than a few minutes. I have often discovered her comforting him when he is crying and we have not been close by. More than once, I have been told that they look after each other when they are together, without us, in a strange house. In this context, I am sure the age ratio is mutually rewarding, for Jack gets the benefit of Tilly's protection and concern, while she, in her turn, enjoys the role of elder sister and, no doubt, draws some comfort too from having him to look after. All in all, I do not believe I am deceiving myself or being sentimental when I say that our children show considerable understanding of each other's needs, and are able and willing to empathize with each other. I also believe that they are not exceptional in this.

Monday, 15 November
As often happens on Mondays, Sally had to drive up to the field first thing in the morning to load the lambs which had grown fat enough to be slaughtered. I think the children have come to hate the job, and usually Sally does it on her own, but on this occasion she needed my help, so we all had to go. Once the lambs were packed into the back of the car and we were on the road, Tilly asked, in a very anxious voice, 'Do they kill them without hurting?'

'Yes,' said Sally.

'How?'

Sally tried to explain the technique of the stunner gun and how it killed them by putting them to sleep.

168

'Yes, but does it hurt?' asked Tilly again, very insistently.

The idea that children are too narcissistic, too absorbed in the business of their own survival and development, to concern themselves with the feelings of others seems to me quite wrong. Both our children, and I don't believe they are out of the ordinary in this respect, have always shown the most agitated regard for the fate of our lambs.

Thursday, 18 November

November gales are beating about the house, forcing the rain into our sitting-room and hurling the dustbin lids round the garden, like frisbees. Every day I forget to stock up the logs for our wood-burner in the sitting-room, and so every evening Jack and I march bravely into the darkness to make a sortie on the woodshed. He carries the torch, waving the beam in all directions, and he talks continually to keep up his courage, because, as he never fails to confide in me, he is 'a little bit frightened'.

Tilly now reads obsessively and is seldom to be seen without a book, especially in the early mornings after we have got up. She manages to read, muttering the words tonelessly to herself, while putting on her clothes and eating breakfast. She reads very resourcefully. If one of us is around, she will continually ask us to decipher difficult words, but if we are busy she will simply invent words to replace the unintelligible ones and press on. Without being proficient yet, she has improved by leaps and bounds since going to school. She soaks up praise addictively and, fortunately, her teachers seem to be very lavish with it; I am sure she earns it too, for she is very keen and appears, at least to me, to be bright.

Last night, still wearing her preposterous leotard after dancing class, she began to show us some of the steps she had learnt. We cast an indulgent eye over this writhing figure on the carpet, but it was not good enough. 'I want you *all* to look at me for a long time,' she demanded, and we did.

Sunday, 21 November

The goose is dead. A fox bit off its head one night last week and left it, decapitated but otherwise untouched, in the field among the lambs. Six other geese in the district were found that morning in the same state of wanton assassination.

This unexpected vacation of the goose's palatial quarters made room for Sally to move her hay out of the little pen where it had been stacked, thus enlarging what will be her lambing yard next spring. The hay, though of excellent quality and very dry despite the wet weather in August when it was cut, had collapsed out of its baler twine and was lying in a billowing mound. The only way to transport it was by the armful. The children became deeply engrossed in this task, especially in the last stage, which involved their jumping up and down on the new pile to compress it.

When we are working in the sheep pens, they will often stay in the car, looking out at our labours with refined disdain, or will find something of their own to do in the buildings. But on this occasion, they both decided to collaborate in their heartiest, most vociferous style, maintaining a state of hilarious morale throughout, together with a ceaseless commentary on their activities. They were quite undaunted by falls, thistles, hay dust, disintegrating bales and a dozen other misadventures, any one of which, on other days, would have been sufficient to render them *hors de combat.* Indeed, their irrepressible spirits became positively wearing.

Two little girls, for whom our children have whipped up a passionate liking, were expected, but towards the end of the afternoon a car drew up and their mother got out alone, saying the girls had gone somewhere else. 'Oh, bum!' said Tilly. Currently, this is her most feeling swear word.

It was dark by the time we had finished moving the hay. The children had immersed themselves in it so thoroughly they looked like effigies, with stalks sticking out of their joints and down their sleeves. They had also begun to itch, in Jack's case to the point of tearfulness, so we took them home for baths.

More rows with Sally today. Sometimes Tilly puts her hands over her ears, and sometimes she leaves the room. Usually, however, she just stares in that blank, expressionless, but actually all-absorbing way that children have when they are most anxious or disturbed. As it happened, today's row took place in front of Jack, who responded rather splendidly by shouting at us to stop in an avuncular tone, as if to say, 'Now, now, children; enough is enough.' We did as he told us.

I have been working very hard lately and, though I am in the house permanently, I hardly see the children. This makes me sad. But, at the same time, it also makes me impatient with them when I do see them, which I deeply regret. My work, or a significant part of it, consists in trying to bring order out of chaos – the chaos of researched material, the chaos of half-finished books and, most of all, the chaos of my thoughts. Writing does not come easily to me, and thinking even less so. Such order as I do manage to impose on the turmoil is the product of extended struggling, which is always out of all proportion to the economic reward and, sadly, even to the quality of the result.

Children, by contrast, are devoted, or ought to be, to bringing chaos to adult order – by turning neat sitting-rooms into spaceships, hospitals or trains, by building bridges out of carefully distributed cushions, by making nests out of books and picnicking in them. I am sure that conventional liberal thinking is right in this respect: children who are made to submit to adult schemes of orderliness gradually lose the faculty for spontaneous creativity, and perhaps for any kind of creativity at all. Indeed, one can see it already crushed and defunct in the very parents who institute regimes of strict tidiness.

But, lately, I have found myself shouting more and more at the children, and more often than not my anger is provoked by their unruliness. I emerge from my room and seem to plunge headlong into a maelstrom: all the fragile, laboriously built structures in my head are summarily torn down and hurled to the four winds as I try to deal with spilled drinks, infantile squabbles, lost shoes, skull-shattering squeals and all the other perfectly ordinary aspects of family life. I boil up in an apoplectic rage at the sight of the drifts of toys marking the tide of their games all over the house; I boil when they splash water out of the bath, when they drop their clothes in a trail down the stairs, crumble their biscuits in the carpets and push sweet-papers behind cushions. I boil when they importune me in their scratchy, relentless voices. I boil when they won't do what they are told; I boil when they do it, but don't do it fast enough. In short, I am intolerable.

And afterwards, I am of course miserable with remorse.

On Sunday evenings, by way of a treat, the children stay up late to watch the animal behaviour programme currently being serialized on BBC 1. Last night, however, they were mostly bored because the work of the early ethologists, Lorenz, Huxley and Tinbergen, was being discussed and this was almost entirely preoccupied with birds. They enjoyed the fluffy goslings tripping down to a lake, following an actor representing Lorenz, to have their first swim, but otherwise they kept asking for the monkeys and the bears. They had good cause, too, for last week's programme had included some remarkable footage of grizzly bears fishing for salmon in a river. The children still have not really grasped the fact that as viewers we have no control over what appears on the screen. They still think that I can somehow adjust the programmes to their liking, or conjure up topics at their request. Whenever I try to explain the logistics of television, which I do very ineptly, their faces take on that pitying, cynical look and I know that they are simply humouring what they take to be one of my crankish theories.

Among adults, by far the most popular category of wildlife would appear to be birds, if the astonishing increase in the membership figures of the Royal Society for the Protection of Birds is any indication, for they far outstrip those for any comparable body dedicated to mammals, fish and so on. Children, however, though indiscriminately fascinated by all kinds of creatures, respond most passionately to furriness or fluffiness, no matter what form it takes. The sight of any strokeable 'baby animal' is enough to elicit revoltingly mawkish sighs of endearment.

This, presumably, is what accounts in large measure for the lamb's very rich symbolic heritage, not least as the Lamb of God, which was the favoured Victorian image of Jesus. No young animal is more amenable to the affectionate attentions of children, or more satisfying to touch and stroke. Like the offspring of all grazing animals, it is capable of walking almost as soon as it has been born, and is therefore able to withstand children at a relatively earlier age than most. Though the epitome of innocence and meekness, it is in fact tough enough to be handled, not to say mauled, and will survive human adoption without too much difficulty, remaining closely attached to its foster parents well into adulthood.

Tuesday, 23 November
Yesterday evening, as Sally was getting Jack into his pyjamas after his bath, she discovered a tremendous erection.

'Don't put my trousers on,' he said, 'willy wouldn't like it.'

'Does he like being stiff?' Sally asked him.

'Oh, yes,' he replied, in an ecstatic tone.

Later, he asked Sally if she loved his willy. She told him she did.

'And do you love Daddy's willy?' he enquired.

In the afternoon he had come into my study dressed, so he told me, as a Roman soldier. His costume amounted to a long towel draped over his shoulders and trailing on the ground. He asked me to write him a message, so I scribbled some 'orders' on a piece of paper, folded it up, and despatched him to the front. Seconds later, Tilly appeared, demanding a message too. Without thinking about it, I instructed her to rehearse her best dance and have it ready for me in twenty minutes.

Sure enough, when I came out of my room twenty

minutes later, she was ready to perform. She danced a complete little ballet, which involved some delicate movements suggestive of flowers opening and closing, as well as the whole repertoire of formal movements and positions she has learnt at dancing class. I was surprised to see that she was clearly following a prepared scheme and not just making up the steps as she went along. Even more surprisingly, when she came to the end of her choreography, she stopped. Usually, she cannot bear to lose the attention of her audience and will continue to improvise until positively restrained, shamelessly milking our patience with cries of 'You haven't seen the best bit yet,' or 'Wait, I haven't begun properly.'

The Christmas pressure is beginning to tell. I took them into town and everywhere we went there were reminders of the great day. For a while they took this in their stride, shouting out 'Father Christmas' in a sing-song voice whenever they saw a picture of him, but at last Tilly broke down.

In Woolworth's she asked me, very petulantly, 'When is Christmas? How much longer?'

'About four weeks, but it's only two and a bit weeks until Granny and Grandpa come to stay,' I said, in an attempt to mollify her.

'I can't wait for Christmas,' she said. And then, beginning to look tearful, she shouted, 'I can't wait. I want it now! Now! Now!' stamping her foot each time.

'I want a pop-gun,' announced Jack, glumly.

Saturday, 27 November

I am between contracts at the moment, always a nerve-racking period. I am waiting for people to make decisions about no less than four projects for books which I have suggested. Having described these ideas as persuasively as I am able and having tried to make them look economically irresistible, I am now virtually powerless to influence the decisions, which could of course deeply affect my life, and I can do no more than languish here, waiting day by day for the post to bring news. Of all situations my job throws up, this helplessness is the one I most detest. Also, I am owed money by companies which are cynically withholding it for the sake of their cash flow, regardless of the effect on mine. These are merely everyday pinpricks, to which every self-employed person is subject, but they make me extremely short-tempered, and the children are the ones who suffer. I am peevish and my patience is as brittle as china. The fact that I am fully aware of all this, and brood on it continuously, only makes matters worse.

Their position is doubly unjust, because in moments of extreme despair I turn to them for comfort and reassurance, demanding from them their biggest hugs, which they always give unstintingly.

Tonight Jack asked if he could 'help' me wash up, but the thought of water swilling all over the floor and having to rewash everything after he had finished seemed unbearable, so I curtly told him to play somewhere else. This was brutal and quite unnecessary: he would have been quite happy with two or three plastic cups and he is much better about spilling the water than he used to be. In any case, it is the work of a moment to clear up after him and I had nothing else to do.

'I won't make a mess,' he whined.

'That's not the point,' I shouted back at him. 'I just don't want you near the sink. Find something else to do.'

Stubbornly, he dragged over a chair and climbed up to the sink.

'Get down, Jack,' I shouted again, in my most furious voice. He took no notice. I picked him up and thrust him, very forcefully, on to the floor.

He clutched his foot and howled, 'You've hurt me.'

Tilly came in to see what was happening.

'Daddy's being 'orrible to me,' he told her.

He got up and hit my legs as hard as he could with his clenched fist, swinging his arm in a mighty arc. I pushed him away. Snivelling, he joined Tilly in their playroom.

Five minutes later, perhaps even less, he ran in to show me how fast one of his cars could go: there was nothing in his manner, not the faintest hint or echo, to suggest that I had just been his mortal enemy.

I hate myself for these incidents. What they ask for is always so simple and small, so easily given. And by the same token, my reasons for refusing are so trivial, so mean. Usually, my reason simply amounts to not wanting to inconvenience myself or disrupt some pettifogging system I have set up. Not that I ever admit as much to them.

I hate the thought of slamming doors in their faces, closing down their world before they know how to explore it, instead of showing them new excitements, new marvels, which at their age can be done with next to no effort. They are of course splendidly resilient and shrug off my rebuffs to find some other amusement that does not require my permission or help. They accommodate, without much complaint, to whatever position they are faced with, no matter how unreasonable. Nonetheless, we are all impoverished by my small-mindedness.

Sunday, 28 November

This morning we woke to find the lawns crusted with frost. The children rushed out in their pyjamas to investigate, bringing back a thin disc of ice, about the size of a side-plate, which had formed over a puddle in the driveway and contained some shreds of vegetation. Crazily, they demanded a bowl of water in order to wash it clean. I pointed out the obvious, but they would not be deterred and did not seem at all disappointed when it melted as soon as it was immersed.

Sally spent the morning clearing up their playroom. Usually she does this surreptitiously while they are asleep, throwing out all their broken and discarded toys, which they never seem to miss, unless they happen to discover them in the dustbins. On this occasion, however, she did the job with their cooperation, which they gave willingly, even with a certain chilling heartiness. Tilly only balked once and that was when Sally was proposing to scrap Luby, an evil-smelling, revoltingly stained, shapeless creature, to whom Tilly had admittedly been devoted when she was much younger. Sally pointed out that they had tried to clean and deodorize her without success and that she was turning into a positive health hazard. Tilly conceded this, but as the doomed Luby was about to be dropped into the rubbish bin she suddenly intervened.

'She's nice, though, isn't she, Mummy?'

'Yes,' said Sally, seeing what she meant.

'She's *very* nice.' With that she turned her back on the victim and has not mentioned her since.

Far from being a sign of callousness, I think her remark showed feeling, as well as a nice discrimination between fantasy and reality. She was prepared to agree that as a toy it had reached the end of its practical life, but at the same time she was not content to betray her old affection for Luby as a doll. By putting her niceness on the record, as it were, she was saying that it was not Luby the doll's fault that Luby the toy was being rubbed out.

December

Wednesday, 1 December
When I was in London last week I bought Jack a little battery-driven police car, which flipped itself over every couple of feet by means of a sprung lever in its floor and drove off in a different direction. He was tremendously excited by it and told me it was just what he had wanted.

However, within half an hour, the wretched thing was no longer functioning properly. The batteries seemed to have been exhausted and it could only up-end itself, without completely overturning. Every time he set it off, it crept along the floor for an inch or two and then, with excruciating difficulty, sat up on its rear fender and froze. I had had the sense to buy a spare set of batteries, and for a blissful five minutes we thought we had cured the problem. But it soon failed again, and we knew that it was fundamentally flawed. No amount of gentle pushing by Jack would get it to somersault. He began to look very upset and ran into the sitting-room, where he lay in the dark, his head buried in cushions, quietly sobbing.

By sheer accident, I discovered that it would run backwards, though without turning over, if the batteries were put in the wrong way round. I opened the sitting-room door and released it. Obligingly, it drove smoothly to his very feet. He was delighted with this compromise; in fact, I think he preferred it. But by the following morning the car would not even go backwards; it was irreparably paralysed. By this time Jack was exhausted himself: his hopes had been raised and dashed too often, and when I told him I was going to put it away and buy him another when I was next in London he seemed glad to be rid of it and agreed straightaway.

As luck would have it, I had to go to London again yesterday. At three times the cost, I bought him a much superior kind of battery-driven car, a jeep which churned along with a pleasingly authentic noise until it met an obstacle, when it would also overturn, but by a far more sophisticated method, and set off again. He was doubly thrilled by this replacement and, to our mutual relief, it performed faultlessly all evening. He took it to bed with him and it was on the move as soon as he woke, chugging beneath our bed, to the accompaniment of exploding and driving noises. He took it to his nursery school and when Sally picked him up afterwards she had to buy fresh batteries.

I could not believe my ears, therefore, when he came into my room, just before lunch, to tell me that a wheel had broken off. He held out his hand and showed me. He was not distressed, for he had a touching confidence in my ability to mend it. I have applied superglue to the tiny bit of wheel hub remaining on the axle, but I do not think there is enough of it to secure the wheel and stand up to the strain. We shall see.

He has been at his most obstreperous today. During lunch he took to kicking me over and over again. He does this kind of thing in a spirit of provocative hilarity which is both infuriating and irresistibly comical, but in the end his sheer persistence always ensures that anger comes out on top, at least it does with me. I issued a series of final warnings and ultimata, all of which he jeered at and scorned. At last I warned him that if he did not stop we would not let him watch *Pigeon Street*, his favourite afternoon programme. Inevitably, he kicked me again.

'That's it,' I told him. 'No *Pigeon Street*.'

Something in my tone must have convinced him that I was finally in earnest, because he immediately began to cry and protest. But we had hardened our hearts and, after remonstrating bitterly, he fled the room.

Five minutes later I went to look for him and discovered a truly pathetic figure huddled outside the kitchen, sobbing and shivering. He had peed in his trousers too. Whether this was a gesture of defiance or a symptom of distress, I do not know. It was probably inadvertent, because he is generally in the habit of hanging on until the last possible moment, refusing to submit even when hopping and writhing in discomfort.

I took him inside, changed his clothes and diverted him during the period of his programme, so he never realized he had been deprived of it. Thus, the moral point of the incident was muffled, if not obliterated altogether, but he had suffered enough.

Or had he? Half an hour later, when I had returned to my room to work, I heard Sally telling him to get into the car. Next I heard the drumming of his footsteps as he ran to hide, one of his most aggravating tricks, and then Sally roaring after him, 'If you don't come now, you won't watch television again – *ever*.'

Friday, 3 December
The saga of the jeep continues. As I had feared, the glue did not hold and the wheel snapped off again as soon as he tried to play with it. I decided to take a risk, which to my considerable relief paid off, by jamming the

185

wheel as hard as I could on to the axle: it wedged tight and is now probably stronger than before. Joy was restored and another set of batteries has been worn out.

Yesterday morning, as we were getting breakfast, Tilly was having one of her rare turns with the sacred vehicle. Suddenly she let out a shriek of real pain and we heard the noise of the jeep's motor grinding against some obstacle and then choking to a halt. She had been leaning over it, watching it chug along the kitchen floor, when its front wheels had become enmeshed in her hair, coiling a huge clump round its axle, until it had finally rammed itself tightly against her skull. She sat crying on the floor, her head weighed down by this grotesque ornament. Sally was only able to disentangle it with the greatest difficulty and Tilly whimpered with pain throughout.

I took Jack to the dentist yesterday. We are fortunate in having Dave as our family dentist; he is not only very skilful and gentle, but a great friend too. He also has the distinction of being the father of Imogen, one of Tilly's admittedly numerous 'best friends'. When the four of us go, he sees us together and lets the children pump up the patient's chair, play with his equipment and generally turn the place into a play-school. I am delighted he has the patience to do this, because our children never associate his surgery with pain or fear, and they visit him quite willingly. I suppose it might be argued that their present trust and fearlessness will only make their disillusionment all the more shattering when, as must happen one day, he is unavoidably obliged to hurt them, but I do not think so. A large part of the terror one feels towards the dentist derives from the fact that he is usually a relative stranger, seen in no other context but his surgery, whom one is too embarrassed or frightened to ask what he is doing to the inside of one's head. Dave, however, is an agreeably familiar figure and he never fails to explain every detail of his treatment.

In fact, now I think about it, we have already witnessed an eloquent demonstration of the principle that trust goes a long way to minimizing pain. A year and a half ago, Tilly suffered a nasty accident. Despite being told more than once to get down, she was standing on the seat of a child's bicycle, eating a biscuit, when the wheels rolled from beneath her, causing her to smash her mouth against the edge of a kitchen table. This happened in someone else's house and she was rushed home, where as it happened I was on my own. She was bleeding horribly and I could not tell the full extent of the damage, though I could see that one of her front teeth had been pushed back at right angles to the rest. I rang Dave, who saw her as soon as I was able to drive her to his surgery.

Tilly was very shocked and hardly cried, although her teeth and lips must have been wretchedly sore. Without a word or sign of resistance, she sat in his chair and allowed him to examine her. He told us that in spite of the gore she was not seriously harmed because at that age their gums were so malleable that it was possible simply to manipulate the tooth back into place. This he proceeded to do, without inducing a single cry of pain from Tilly, who to her great credit was being outstandingly brave. He lined it up with the other tooth and warned us that it might turn black, but that her adult tooth would not be affected.

Her mouth was very swollen and tender for a while, and the damaged tooth whistled when she talked and wobbled while she ate, but in the event did not turn black, and has not even become discoloured.

The incident has entered the family folklore and 'the day I bashed my tooth in' is often referred to as a historical milestone, but as far as I can tell it has left no heritage of fear or mistrust of Dave.

An old schoolfriend of Sally's came to stay this weekend, with her husband and two children – Tom, who is four, and Amy, who is two.

What is expected socially of children in these situations is far more demanding than any of us could manage. Without knowing each other at all well, they were supposed to spend most of the day together playing peaceably, without calling for adult assistance. In fact, it worked out quite successfully. Tom led Jack on a series of looting and pillaging expeditions round the house, which vastly entertained him and, for some reason, reinforced his present identification with 'Mighty Mouse'. Tilly, meanwhile, had taken the most matronly interest in little Amy, and had virtually adopted her. At meals, for example, she spoke unanswerably for both of them, without consulting Amy.

'Amy and me'll have toast with lemon curd on and Sugar Puffs,' she announced, when her mother asked Amy what she wanted for breakfast.

'Amy and me want more milk in our favourite cup,' was another, typical official utterance.

Her unflagging solicitude became quite sickening after a while, though Amy herself appeared to have no objection to being confiscated like this.

In the afternoon they were all driven to Tostock church to take part in a Christingle service, something I had not heard of before. Evidently, it took the form of a conventional carol service, but with a procession added, for which each child was given a candle stuck in an orange. This church, incidentally, is most attractive

188

and possesses nearly as many animal carvings on its bench ends as our own.

I did not go to the service myself, but Sally reported that it was very charming, as expected, but also dangerous. Jack, like most of the children his age, had almost succumbed to sleep by the time he had to join the procession. Droopingly, he tottered along the aisle and contrived to get his candle under the coat of the child in front, who happened to be much taller than he. Tilly performed impeccably, but was in peril from the child behind, whose candle flame played among the tresses of her hair.

She is fascinated by the nativity story and comes from school each day with some new detail; Friday's concerned the shepherds, though only the part describing their visit to the stable. The appearance of the angels does not seem to have caught her imagination, but then it is 'baby-Jesus' who interests her, and nothing else.

She has developed a resourceful theological line to reconcile what she clearly understands at some level to be a contradiction between her professed atheism and her deep enthralment to Jesus and the Christmas legend.

'Jesus was a true person,' she will declare, 'but God isn't. He isn't real, but some people believe in him.'

Sylvia has a sophisticated version of this to offer. She uses the same formulation of Jesus being 'true', adding that he was also 'a good man', but she goes on to explain that God is not real and that he is not a spirit either.

Whatever her religious views, Tilly remains as sanguine as ever in her attitude to my departure.

'When Daddy's dead, can we go and visit his grave?' she said to Sally, out of the blue.

'I suppose so.'

'And can we play on those stone things dead people have?'

Thursday, 9 December
Yesterday Sally's father brought us a splendid Christmas tree, which we have stood in our hall in the stairwell; it must be twelve or more feet high, for its tip nearly rises to the landing above.

Over the years we have built up quite a collection of ornaments, and this afternoon, with the children's manic assistance, Sally loaded the lot on to the tree. The few remaining bare twigs were liberally squirted with plastic snow. Throughout, the children's excitement was intense, and very close to hysteria, their mood wobbling all the time between tears and a sort of ecstatic joy. When the tree was fully decorated, we put out all the lights in the house and with some pomp Tilly performed the switching-on ceremony.

The children literally gasped in delight and, indeed, the tree did look very beautiful, rather like a still-life firework. At the very top is a fairy Tilly made last year, which we had preserved; it is a whimsical creature with a piece of wallpaper for a skirt, a spoon handle for a spine and the bowl of the spoon for its face. She has drawn on it a smile of such beatification that were it used for any other occasion it would look childish and absurd, but this crazy, half-circle grin beaming down at us from the top of the stairs is somehow fitting for Christmas.

For an hour or so after we switched on the lights the children hardly moved. Despite the cold and the fact that the hall floor is tiled, they lay below the tree, their elbows on the floor, their chins cupped in their hands, staring up at the lights and branches in worshipful silence. A little later, I discovered they had ranged

their entire collection of dolls and soft toys, a formidable force when gathered together in one place, around
the tree, all facing the great totem. An eerie sight they
made too, as thirty or so pairs of button eyes goggled in
the half-dark.

Saturday, 11 December
My parents are here to stay and to have an advance
Christmas with the children. The days before their
visit were counted off with fervent anticipation,
though I don't think it is too cynical to suggest that
this was partly inspired by the thought of presents,
from which this Granny and Grandpa are inseparable.

This morning they were taken shopping and bought
more things than they could carry. In the past, they
have sometimes been overwhelmed by these showers
of generosity and have become upset, unable to enjoy
what they have been given, but still demanding more.
On this occasion, however, they took it in their stride
and appeared to be genuinely pleased with each toy
they had chosen.

My parents are very kind and the children are devoted to them. It is true they tend to appear out of the
sky, like gods, to dispense their gifts and then depart,
but I see nothing wrong with having grandparents who
seem a little magical, especially since the children are
lucky enough to have another set of grandparents
nearby, with whom they have a more realistic, but no
less enjoyable, relationship.

Talking to my parents last night, I found myself
describing Jack's outbursts of kicking, slapping and
spitting as if they were posing a real problem – as if we
were confessing our anxieties about an incorrigible
football hooligan or train wrecker. Admittedly, his
attacks have been growing more frequent, and I

suppose they have been worrying me more than I realized, otherwise I would not have laid such stress on them. On the other hand, I also realized how guilty I feel about them, because I know that although he is extremely irritating when he is overtaken by one of his fits, I am the one who allows them to reach a different plane of nastiness, and turns them into major confrontations, which can only be resolved by submission and tears on his part. This is very unfair, for whenever I do manage to summon the necessary patience and take the time to think up a way of diverting his aggression, his mood is snuffed out in a moment and is in fact often replaced by one of great sweetness.

Yesterday, however, his naughtiness took a really dangerous turn. I took Tilly and him for a ride on their bikes up the village street in the hope of meeting my parents. Suddenly, he decided to return home. He dropped his bike and ran off. I told him to come back, not wanting him to get too far away from me on such a busy road, and certainly not wanting him to reach the farm entrance where tractors and lorries are coming in and out all the time. He ignored me and only ran the faster, looking back over his shoulder, giggling and taunting me. I shouted again, not angrily, but I hoped in an unmistakably serious tone. He still took no notice and I discovered that there seemed to be no tone of voice I could use that he would automatically obey. In the event, he did appear to be persuaded by my insistent earnestness: he slowed down, and still giggling, began gradually to move towards me.

Later, in a very pointed manner, I told him a story about a very naughty little boy, called Jack, who went running down the road, looking over his shoulder and not coming back when his daddy told him.

'He just kept on running,' I told him, 'and suddenly a

big lorry drove round the corner and squashed him flat and killed him.'

He looked a little horrified at this fatal denouement, but then began to laugh at me.

I asked him to tell me a story.

'Once upon a time,' he said, 'there was a good little boy called Jack and a stupid old daddy and the little boy ran down the road and a tractor came but Mighty Mouse took him away.'

This was delivered at great speed and accompanied by a heavily moralizing expression.

I was very disturbed by his story, because it seemed to me not only to express a belief in his own immortality, which most little children probably share, but also a crazy belief in being invulnerable to danger. He has no road sense as it is, and only goes through the motions of looking left and right before crossing as an empty ritual performed to please me. When this cluelessness is compounded with wilful mischief and a lunatic illusion of inviolability it adds up to a lethal risk. I tried to explain to him how important it was for him to do as I said on the streets, but he only giggled. Even so, I think I made some impression on him.

The other day, I had an amusing example of Tilly's belief in her retrospective immortality.

I was telling them stories from the time when, more than twenty years ago, I went on a voyage to the west coast of Africa aboard a merchant ship. They were deeply impressed: to them Africa is a place of great romantic charisma, because it is where Sally spent her childhood. As soon as I had finished my traveller's tales, Tilly asked me,

'Where did Mummy sleep on the ship?'

I told her Sally wasn't on the ship.

'Did the ship go to Mummy's house?'

193

I explained that all this had happened a long time ago, many years before I had met Sally.

'Ah, yes,' she said airily. 'I was in Mummy's tummy then.'

Apart from the legendary period of 'when Mummy/Daddy was a little girl/boy', there is no phase in our lives, according to her, during which she did not exist. Jack has not yet become so adamant on this point, and perhaps he never will. No doubt, her sense of security in existence was given a severe jolt when he was born, for she had known the era before his entire history, even as an embryo. Perhaps to compensate for this alarming discovery of the fortuitousness of life, as it must have appeared to her, she always insists on the permanence of her presence throughout every stage of our lives.

Wednesday, 15 December

Tilly did something rather splendid today.

Last night, while they were having their baths, I told them that when they woke up they must remind me to put out the dustbins, which we had forgotten to do last Wednesday. Sure enough, we were shocked out of sleep this morning by the sound of Tilly's scratchy little voice yelling at top volume, 'DUSTBIN DAY,' just as we had rehearsed it in the bathroom.

As I write this, a gale-force wind is thudding against the house, and huge chains of clouds are barrelling across the sky like freight trains. I am worried because Sally and the children are driving home from Bury St Edmunds and the radio news has just reported that cars are being blown off roads all over the country.

They have been to visit the Mathesons, who only yesterday moved from Norton, the village next to ours. Their departure will make quite a difference to all of us, for Emily Matheson is as good a friend of Tilly's as Jenny is of Jack. In fact Jack will go on seeing Jenny at their nursery school, but Emily is being sent to a new school in Bury St Edmunds next term, and so Tilly will be without one of her best friends.

The dynamics of children's friendships are very difficult to grasp, partly because children comment so elliptically on their feelings, and partly because they have far less autonomy in their social relations than any adult. They are continually being thrust into the company of other children, whether they have expressed a preference or not, and are expected to play amicably – and without the assistance of alcohol, which for most of us is indispensable to our social life. Nonetheless, strong affections, and antipathies, do unmistakably emerge.

By the same token, it is one of the conditions of childhood that passionate intimacies and loyalties are formed and then abandoned, with what seems bewildering callousness, only to be replaced by a new set of equally powerful affinities. Earlier this year we had someone staying with us for nearly a month and the children gave every sign of having grown very fond of him, but within two or three days of his leaving they had forgotten him and have rarely mentioned him since.

But then childhood, as a process of learning, would be impossible without both these capacities. The ability to form strong commitments to people and activities in adulthood could never fully develop if these safe and essentially irresponsible experiments were not made first in childhood. Children who were made to bear the consequences of freely and spontaneously extending their affections would never be able to do so again; they would be crippled long before they had worked out any understanding of what friendship or any kind of loving relationship requires.

Friday, 17 December
For the last four nights in succession Jack has had
nightmares. Twice we heard his screams on the landing before we had gone to bed and discovered him
running about in a state of terrified frenzy. We brought
him down to the sitting-room, but it was a good ten
minutes before he could be consoled. He sobbed and
stared round the room as if demons were stalking him.

On Monday night I heard him crying much later.
When I picked him out of his bed he began to hit me,
swinging his arms in slow, sleep-laden punches. I
carried him into bed with us and he snuggled contentedly beside me, while still continuing to flail me,
though now with little, pulsing jerks of his arm beneath the blankets. Somehow, this duality of closeness
and aggression seemed to sum up our relationship at
the moment.

Because I am feeling guilty about getting cross with
him, I keep thinking that my temper is causing these
nightmares, but Sally reminded me that Tilly too
suffered from a bout of them at just this age. As it
happens, I have been much more patient with him
lately, and I am sure it is no coincidence that he has
been much less provocative.

Monday, 20 December
On Saturday afternoon we took the children to the
village Christmas party. This is an altogether splendid
institution, involving games, dances, a huge tea, and of
course a visitation by Father Christmas, a role played
with great kindliness by Vic, one of the retired farm
workers. Because of my no doubt neurotic aversion to
dressing up in women's underwear, I had to absent
myself hastily from the hall as soon as entrants to the
Dads' Obstacle Race began to be recruited, and unfor-

tunately I got back too late to see Father Christmas make his entrance. However, it was evidently staged with theatrical finesse and our children were certainly convinced that they were in the presence of a magical being.

When I did return, I found all the children clustered round him, anxiously waiting for him to pull out of his sack the present with their name on its label. Tilly and Jack had both received theirs – a doctor's bag for her and a plastic dinghy with a clockwork motor for him – but they stayed near him, occasionally touching his robe in a very tentative, primitive gesture, which was at once a way of confirming his reality and venerating him.

Once we were at home again, tragedy struck. To the disbelief of all of us, Jack's boat failed to work. No amount of tinkering by me could get its propeller to operate under water. Crassly, I suggested that I should ask the organizer of the party where she had bought the toys, so I could replace it.

'Father Christmas gave it to me,' he screamed through his tears.

Understandably, he could not credit the fact that Father Christmas had come all the way to Stowlangtoft to present him with a defective present, and he was very upset.

Sally then had a brainwave. She rang some number which played a recorded Christmas story, persuaded the children that she was speaking directly to Father Christmas's workshop and left a message to the effect that Jack's present was broken and he would be very grateful if Father Christmas could possibly find time to drop in a replacement. Though a little puzzled by all this, Jack was mollified and went to bed in reasonably good spirits.

When they were asleep we wrapped up two of the

197

presents we had bought for them and left them at the front door, with an apologetic note from Father Christmas to Jack. In the morning, after they had climbed into our bed, Jack's first words were,

'I haven't got nuffing.'

'Perhaps Father Christmas came in the night,' Sally said.

'You can share my doctor's bag, if you like,' said Tilly.

'Maybe Bill can mend my boat.'

Bill is due to stay over Christmas and is indeed very skilful at making and mending things.

'You can give half of Sylvia's present to her,' offered Tilly. This was a most generous offer, for Sylvia's present had been entrusted to her by Father Christmas himself, and was to be handed over when she came next to her cottage. Tilly had treated the parcel as her own.

'I haven't got nuffing,' Jack repeated.

'I heard a bang outside last night,' I told him. 'And I thought I heard a jingling sound.'

'That would be Father Christmas's reindeer,' said Tilly knowledgeably.

I got Jack to put on his dressing-gown and took him downstairs to investigate. In the cause of credibility, I took him first to our post box in the garage, which was empty since it was Sunday.

'That's odd,' I told him, 'I was sure I heard jingling in the night.'

'It must have been pigs,' said Jack miserably.

But at the front door was a parcel with his name on, which he joyfully seized. He ran upstairs to open it with Tilly. Inside was a fearsome-looking spacegun, which emits sparks and a form of white noise; it has hardly been out of his hands since. His faith in Father Christmas, to say nothing of his high spirits, was fully restored.

Tilly found a jigsaw puzzle in the parcel for her and she was pleased to have it, though she is much cooler about the Father Christmas cult and even about presents.

Sally made some reference to his clockwork dinghy, but Jack told her, 'Father Christmas has taken it away and broken it up in little pieces.'

This seemed to be a just fate for something that had caused such distress and disappointment and, surreptitiously, I buried it at the bottom of the kitchen wastebin.

Tuesday, 21 December
Another unfortunate chapter in the Father Christmas saga.

Arrangements had been made for Father Christmas (this time personified by Max, the owner of our local post office) to visit every house in the village with a child under the age of eight. We decided not to tell our children about his imminent appearance at their very front door, but leave it to be a surprise. We miscalculated. He arrived at seven-thirty, looking the part in a beautiful red coat, but for once the children were asleep, and we had been able to do nothing to keep them awake.

Tilly was easily woken and was quite bright during his visit; brighter in fact than we realized. Jack, however, was very bleary and could hardly lift his head off Sally's shoulder. Tilly dragged him off to admire our Christmas tree, something they automatically require of every visitor to the house at the moment; she chatted to him and fingered his red coat, while Jack stared at him glassily, his thumb in his mouth. Jack fell asleep almost as soon as he had gone, but Tilly stayed awake long enough to ask Sally,

'How many Father Christmases are there?'

'What do you mean?'

'Well, this one didn't have glasses on and the one at the party who gave us our presents did.'

'He needed his glasses then to read the labels on the presents,' said Sally with admirable presence of mind.

'But he had white hair and this one had black hair. I could see it under his hat.'

Sally wisely did not attempt to debate this irrefutable piece of observation.

Jack's belief in Father Christmas is unclouded by doubt and will accommodate all sorts of anomalies and contradictions. Of course, many of these difficulties do not strike him as such, because at his age his sense of time and space is so unformed that he will happily accept the most impossible propositions concerning Father Christmas's movements and schedules. The other day I took him shopping in Bury St Edmunds and when we went into the Eastern Electricity shop, which is rather large and lavishly appointed, he asked me, 'Is this Cambridge?' Clearly, someone who thinks Cambridge might be an Electricity showroom is going to have no difficulty coming to terms with the idea of Father Christmas travelling by sleigh to every child's house in the country and sliding down their chimneys.

Our chimney might be thought to present a problem insofar as we have a wood-burner in our sitting-room, where the children will hang up their stockings, and the aperture is blocked off by steel register plate, but they are both happy with the notion of Father Christmas making his way down the narrow, untouchably hot pipe that leads from the plate to the fire. In Jack's case, his belief in Father Christmas is bolstered by a fair amount of auto-suggestion; for instance, he told me that he had seen Father Christmas being driven away by his reindeer from the village party.

They talk about very little other than presents these days, except when they are asking how many days are left till Christmas. They spend hours in our arctic hall worshipping the tree and rearranging the parcels underneath. We have adamantly refused to let them open a single one before the official day and so far they have resisted doing so. Instead, they put all their own parcels in separate piles with compulsive repetitiveness in order to count them, shake them, stroke them and commune with them.

Although the Christmas ritual is very gratifying to the children, it is cruel too, for they are never allowed to forget the great day and yet they are driven mad by having to wait for it. Everyone who comes to the house seems to bring a fresh load of presents, which are of course gleefully piled up under the tree, but also add to the tension. They cannot switch on the television without seeing some reference to Christmas, and they cannot go into any shop, even our local garage, without being reminded. And, in any case, most of our own conversations at the moment are either about presents and food, or drift inexorably towards some other aspect of Christmas.

Monday, 27 December
During the three days immediately before Christmas Day I was afflicted with some viral condition reminiscent of the ague, whose symptoms included an extremely sore throat, producing the sensation of swallowing razor blades. Today is in fact the first time I have felt anything like well and I certainly hope to improve considerably on my present state. It is now poor Sally's turn, for she has spent the whole day in bed and is unlikely to leave it tomorrow. Though not laid low like us, the children have nonetheless been

the victims of chronic coughs, colds, flushes, shivers, and all the rest.

By Christmas Eve present-fever was of course at its height. However, the corollary of this was that they were very willing to go to bed, and to sleep, on the dot of seven-thirty once it had been pointed out to them that the sooner they were asleep, the sooner Father Christmas would climb down the chimney.

'Go away, Mummy. Go away, quickly,' Tilly told Sal after she had read them only one story.

They hung up their stockings in the sitting-room, leaving a mince pie each and a glass of sherry, or in Jack's case Coca Cola, for Father Christmas, and every-thing seemed to be gathering smoothly towards the grand climax as we put out the lights at midnight and said goodnight to our great friend Bill, who had astounded those less familiar with his prowess by cycling from Croydon to join us.

But we were wrong. During the night, Jack woke again and again in a state of hysterical anticipation.

'Is it Christmas Day now?' he would moan de-liriously. Or, 'Has Father Christmas come? Where are my presents? I want my toys.'

Apart from Tilly, none of us slept more than fitfully and, in the event, neither of the children woke before eight o'clock. Even then, it was some minutes before they remembered what day it was.

Soon enough, however, the sitting-room was knee deep in wrapping paper. Jack seemed most pleased with his space capsule, which my parents had left for him. The combined ingenuity of Bill and ourselves was required to assemble it, but despite its appearance of complexity, once in operation it proved to be a kind of boys' miniature dolls' house, at least that was the way Jack received it. He spent much of the morning happily putting his spacemen to bed, getting them dressed and

202

giving them breakfast; perhaps because he was so tired, he only let off the occasional intergalactic detonation.

Tilly was most pleased with her desk, a wooden, double-lidded affair, which we had bought from a local school. Though it was supposed to be a joint present, she seems to have appropriated it for the time being, without complaint from him. She spent the morning sorting out her office, stacking up her considerable collection of pens, notebooks, diaries, colouring books and so on into the same kind of fastidious little piles as I have deployed on my own desk. She was also extremely pleased with the doll's high chair we gave her. We could hardly have avoided giving her one, since it had been her official request to Father Christmas, without variation, since well before August, but I had feared that it would not be a success since she appears to play less and less with her dolls these days. However, so far it has been put to extensive use and is always brought out first to impress visitors.

After the presents had been opened I took Jack up to the loo. As he was sitting there his face took on the special, lugubrious look he reserves for denouncing great injustices that have been done to him.

'When's it going to be Christmas?' he asked me.

This seemed an extraordinarily crass question.

'What do you mean?'

'We haven't got no dec'rations here,' he said gloomily, pointing to the bathroom wall, which is possibly the only surface in the entire house that does not in some way register the time of the year.

We all went to Sally's parents for a splendid Christmas lunch. Her sister and her two boys were staying, so the children were immediately plunged into another orgy of present-opening. We should have been fourteen round the table, but just before we were due to take our seats Jack fell into a deep sleep, making it thirteen, and did not wake until the late afternoon when I took him on a long walk to work off the lunch he had missed. Tilly stayed behind to watch *International Velvet* with Sally, but evidently she soon grew bored and left Sally to snivel over it alone.

I, meanwhile, was feeling more and more ill and had by then virtually lost my voice. When we came to leave, we were all coughing, each at a different pitch; with a bit of practice, we could probably have coughed out, 'God Rest You, Merry Gentlemen'.

Thursday, 30 December
Much worse has followed.

Sally spent the last three days in bed and only got up today for the first time, feeling very frail. On Tuesday night I woke at four o'clock to find her in tears: her headache was so painful she could not lift her head from the pillow, far less blow her nose or sit up to take a drink of water. This was distressing enough in itself, but the situation was rendered bizarre as well by the fact that all the lights were blazing and a radio was playing somewhere. The explanation was simple enough. That evening we had suffered a power cut, incidentally depriving Tilly of the ending of *The Wizard of Oz* and ourselves of the whole of *Anyone for Dennis?*, and we had gone to bed by candle-light, forgetting of course to turn off the inoperative lights. Nonetheless, I felt very disoriented for a moment when I woke in the middle of an apparently fully functioning household.

I rang the doctor first thing in the morning and when he saw Sally he diagnosed mild inflammation of the lungs, together with encephalitis, which sounds dreadful, but is in fact inflammation of the brain.

While being very painful, it is evidently just one of the many, nasty side-effects accompanying a virus that has struck down most of the county over Christmas.

The only good thing to be said for this virus is that children seem to be relatively immune to it. Ours have had chronic coughs and colds, but have not been really ill.

Tuesday found us at our lowest ebb. Sally could not move from her bed, and I was not feeling much better. The house was still littered with the trash of Christmas Day: a nearly impassable drift of dirty washing had accumulated on the landing, the kitchen was clogged with unwashed dishes and there were toys everywhere which had hardly been taken out of their boxes, but were already trampled and broken. I only had the strength to dress and feed the children and sit with them while they watched television, so it was hardly surprising that they soon grew bored and began to squabble. To be precise, Jack behaved abominably. Despite being fascinated by matches, candles and fire generally, even the power cut failed to cheer him up.

A typical scene went as follows. I decided to give them a bath as usual, calculating that a candle-lit session would amuse them. Tilly asked if she could carry one of the oil lamps upstairs. Remembering that Jack had carried it on the previous two expeditions we had made, I agreed. Jack immediately shrieked in protest.

'Tilly will let you carry it when we get half-way up the stairs.' I made this offer without consulting Tilly, for I could be sure she would cooperate.

However, he shrieked again and fell to the floor, thrashing his legs viciously at our ankles.

I dragged him to the stairs. At the bottom, without being asked, Tilly held out the lamp to him, but he only screamed all the louder and pulled himself out of my grasp.

As patiently as I could, I tried to persuade him to take the lamp. I did not succeed and so returned the lamp to Tilly. This of course provoked the loudest shrieking fit so far.

And so it went throughout the evening.

Peter suggested that he was probably angry with Sally for being ill, a theory that appeared to be substantiated this morning, because when Sally got up and got dressed, for the first time in three days, he followed her around like a dog, cuddling up to her whenever he could and displaying his most amiable side.

The worse he behaves, the sweeter Tilly becomes. This is, I suppose, partly because she is astute enough to recognize a good opportunity to shine by comparison, and partly because she wants to protect herself from the bad feelings that threaten – or so she must fear – to bombard her during these incidents. But there is a positive aspect too, for Jack's generally combative and confrontational style is quite opposed to her own, which is flexible and creative. While his whole mode of behaviour at the moment is one of challenge and provocation, she will never take on a fight with us unless the issue is extremely important to her. As often as not, her bouts of rage are aimed against some fix in which she has trapped herself, and are not couched in terms of personal antagonism; his, by contrast, invariably are.

January

Monday, 3 January
I have been trying to think back to this time last year and remember Tilly and Jack as they were then, but even with the help of my diary I cannot really recreate them convincingly. The year that has just finished represented roughly a quarter of Jack's entire existence and a fifth of Tilly's, but nonetheless in many ways they do not seem to have changed at all. Like plants, they grow imperceptibly most of the time, with occasional bursts of sudden and extraordinary transformation.

In Tilly, the biggest, or at least most obvious, changes have taken place during the last third of the year, that is while she has been at school. Whereas before, when she was at Charlotte Mummery's nursery school, despite the excellent teaching she received there, each holiday saw an almost complete regression in her reading and writing, but I have noticed that during this holiday she has lost none of her skills. She can now read most children's books to her own satisfaction and writes very legibly, if with an erratic use of upper- and lower-case letters.

She has started a diary. Its first entry reads:

I went to watch ET
It was frightening
I cuddled my Daddy
                    Tilly
                        3 January

This is accompanied by a vivid drawing of ET itself. (We went to see the film on Boxing Day and, unusually, Tilly has continued to mention it on and off ever since.)

Peter suggested to her that she should keep a diary about me, recording my funny ways and the stages of my senility, but though she is interested in my diary she did not get the joke. I remember when I was thinking of starting this I asked her if I should write a book about her.

'No!' she scoffed. 'Everyone knows me.'

She has grown tall and slender this year, although she is still much slighter than her contemporaries. Jack is still at the age when a winter coat renders him the shape of a hamburger bun, but Tilly's legs are now long enough for her to retain something of her coltish daintiness in even the thickest overcoat. She has become even more sweet-tempered than she was, and only very rarely has one of her tantrums, which punctuated the previous year. These can be spectacular and carry an explosive tonnage that Jack's have never rivalled. They may lack the dimension of physical violence that makes his outbursts impressive, but they achieve an emotional impact quite beyond his present powers. Sally and I will never forget an occasion when she became cross with a drawing and suddenly hurled everything – paper, felt-tip pens, ruler, scissors, Sellotape and rubber – on to the floor with a single, convulsive lunge, and ran out of the kitchen, shrieking, 'It won't come right, it won't come right.'

Sally told her not to be silly and, with some difficulty, persuaded her to try again. Within seconds, however, she was on the rampage once more.

We tried to soothe her, but to no avail. We attempted to restrain her by telling her that the drawing was not that important, and that she was being childish (!). But

Tilly, her pigtails streaming and her face purple with fury, bellowed back at us, 'You don't know what it feels like to be me. You just don't know.'

This devastating utterance crushed us, and we left her temper to blow itself out.

As far as Jack is concerned, last year saw him change decisively from being a baby to being a little boy. It was not long after his third birthday, early in the year (4 February), that he at last no longer required nappies at night, and there is no more definitive sign of having left infanthood behind than that, at least in the eyes of all parents. Tilly, incidentally, had dispensed with them well before her third birthday; in fact, as is supposed to be the way with girls, she was quicker than he to walk and talk, and in most other respects too.

It was during this year that all his current obsessions with soldiers, explosions, slaughter and heavy-duty vehicles first emerged, together with his generally combative approach to his immediate family.

He has recently become very interested in writing and can make a passably recognizable attempt at his own name. In this last week, he has developed the knack of writing quite plausible, though meaningless, characters, which he studiously grinds out in large quantities and then comes to us to demand what they mean. This poses something of a problem, since the letters themselves are entirely enigmatic and yet he becomes very angry if you fail to decipher them correctly.

I suppose it is predictable that one's measure of their development should be their increasing proficiency in reading and writing. There are so many other achievements and milestones of maturity, but none have the same concrete, publicly demonstrable quality as reading and writing, especially the former.

211

Tilly went back to school on Wednesday with every appearance of enthusiasm, but yesterday she cried wretchedly when it was time to go. In the afternoon I asked her how she had got on at school.

'I was very helpful,' she told me.

'What did you do?'

'I handed out the books, and put out the chairs, and tidied up and put everything away after class.'

'Do all the children help?'

'Naah! Some boys don't. They throw everything on the floor and make Miss Blunden cross. They're stupid.'

Winning the teacher's approval seems to be important to her, but I think she also finds these activities reassuring when she is feeling anxious or homesick: not only do they involve a rewarding identification with the teacher, but they are familiar too and reminiscent of being at home.

Even if her enthusiasm for school has cooled for the moment, it has not affected her productivity: we continue to be recipients of a ceaseless flow of messages, letters, notes and drawings. She has developed her own shorthand iconography: for example, she always represents herself as having an upturned, perfectly semicircular, madly happy smile, set in a round face, from the top of which a pair of thick, black pigtails reach down, like snakes, to well below her waist. I am always recognizable by the mass of tightly scribbled curls on top of my head, which are drawn in pencil to indicate their greyness.

Sunday, 9 January

For the last ten days or so we had a dog staying with us: an enormous, rather handsome Labrador bitch. For the most part, she displayed a docile and affable tempera-

212

ment, but occasionally and unpredictably she became fearsomely aggressive, snarling and barking at certain people who came to the door. Her choice of victims could not have been more unfortunate: a neighbour, who is notoriously nervous of dogs, a visitor in a wheelchair, and a friend whose terror of dogs we have always scoffed at and dismissed as irrational cowardice.

With the children, at least, the dog was a model of tolerance. Each morning, as soon as they woke, they rushed to see her, and by the time we came down she would be draped in fancy dress, with a hat stuck on her head, and both children would be hanging round her neck, hugging and kissing her in the most disgusting way. All of this she put up with, and did not even stir from her blanket.

When we first came to live here, seven years ago, my idea of my new country life was inseparable from that of owning a dog. I fantasized about whistling up my faithful little terrier as he scurried in the hedgerows and I strolled the leafy lanes. Accordingly, we acquired not one, but two dogs, neither of which remotely lived up to my modest little dream.

One was adorable and whimsical, but quite untrainable, at any rate by me. Furthermore, as she grew older, she developed killer tendencies towards strangers who came to the gate. The other was contemptibly craven at the gate, and grovelled in terror at the sight of a stranger, but she became increasingly menacing inside the house. In the end, they both had to be taken to the vet and killed.

Later, we bought a Jack Russell, called Tom, who was very endearing as a puppy. Alas, when he matured, he proved to be incorrigibly lecherous and, as the cliché has it, began to treat his home as a hotel. By way of taking the boredom out of his long forays in search

213

of mates, he took up sheep-harrying. Fortunately, he was far too randy to allow this to turn into a serious occupation, but he too had to go. In his case, being sent to a better place was no mere euphemism, for we were able to find him a new home on a grand estate in Norfolk where, by all accounts, he leads a life of rare canine fulfilment. We sent him there with great misgivings, because the children had become very attached to him and even now, two years later, they still speak of him wistfully.

Since then, however, my own taste for dogs has atrophied; indeed, I find myself feeling more and more repelled by the dogs with which I come into close contact. Of course, I have real children now, who love me, who run beside me when I go for walks, and chase balls when I throw them, so I have no need for a dog.

On the other hand, the children, I know, would like us to have a pet. One of Tilly's regular speeches, delivered in a tone of heart-breaking poignancy, which she has perfected, goes as follows:

'I'd love, I really would love a puppy dog of my very own to look after and care for.'

Towards the Labrador, they showed a spontaneous and unashamedly sensual affection. Jack, in particular, never failed to drape himself round her, kissing and nuzzling her, murmuring throatily into her ear, 'My darling, my darling dog.'

I am glad to say they show the same spontaneous sensuality in their affection for us and each other. When they get into bed in the mornings, they snuggle and wriggle with delicious abandon, which I confess is entirely reciprocated. Towards each other, they show a hearty and usually hilarious interest in what Jack nowadays calls their 'rude' parts. Many a happy hour is passed in the bath pinching bottoms and grabbing willies. I can only think that all this is laying the foundations of a gratifying sex life in adulthood.

Monday, 10 January

We made a great mistake yesterday night.

We put the children to bed and then settled down to watch *Jaws 2*. Half an hour later we heard footsteps along the landing and two impish faces appeared at the little window in our hall that looks in on the sitting-room. They insisted they could not get to sleep and so, rather than miss the film by fighting them, we agreed they could stay with us for a little while. Knowing this was a most exceptional treat, they were happy to sit quietly on our laps.

Suddenly the film got nasty as the shark began to munch its way through a gang of teenagers. As our mordant friend Den pointed out later, the only pleasure to be had out of the film was seeing how many spoilt kids the shark would chew up. But both our children shrieked and buried their heads. I asked them if they wanted to go back to bed, and of course they said no.

After a respite, the tension was screwed up again. Jack became very agitated, running from me to Sally, and back, and looking truly frightened. Tilly was not so affected.

'Will it eat the girls next?' she asked, after the shark had dragged a boy into the deep. Her tone conveyed no more than curiosity, though she seemed to think the girls deserved their fate less than the boys.

The shark lunged out of the water and devoured another victim. This was too much for Jack. He rushed to the television and turned it off. We both shouted at him to turn it on, telling him again that he could go to bed if he didn't want to watch. We made him turn it on. He had no choice, because by now he was too wound up by the shark to get any sleep, even if he had been prepared to go back to his room.

The shark attacked once more. Jack ran to the middle of the room, crying hysterically.

We turned it off at last.

Sally took them to bed and was not able to soothe him for a long time. Predictably, he woke later out of a bad dream, crying and shouting. We both feel guilty about all this; in fact, I have been castigating myself ever since. The children should never have been exposed to such a film, which was not worth watching in any case. I am angry too because my pride is stung: my only New Year resolution, which I have not begun to keep, was to watch less trash on television. In effect, we punished them for interrupting our evening's viewing.

Their world is already alive with monsters and ogres of their own imagining. Jack, being the younger, senses menacing presences everywhere, as Tilly used to do. His nights are haunted by 'wolvers' and there is a room in the attic he would not enter at any price, for he is quite convinced it is full of pigs. As well as being terrified of these creatures, which seem to dominate their dreams, they are fascinated by them, or their equivalents, when they read about them or see them in films. Stories featuring witches, giants, hobgoblins and savage animals of all kinds, whether real or mythological (not that they know the difference, or care), are always among their favourites. At the moment Jack regularly asks for *Jack and the Beanstalk* as his bedtime story, and this is not just because the hero is his namesake. He likes to hear about the giant, especially his famous 'Fee Fi Fo Fum', which I pronounce in my most blood-curdling tone.

They both enjoyed *King Kong* (the original version) when they saw it on television. These huge, semi-mythical beasts offer them an excitingly ambiguous promise of protectiveness and aggression. Once they were persuaded that Kong was essentially amiable and vulnerable, they loved him and were deeply saddened

216

by his death at the end. Thereafter, they adopted him and for a while he became a constant member of their family, which always contains some shadowy figures, like him, among the tangible dolls and teddies; ET currently enjoys this honour.

More than terror, it is tension which agitates Jack and makes him run round in circles, clutching his penis. The shark can hardly have been too realistic for him, since he has no idea what a real shark looks like, but presumably it conformed too closely to the monsters that infest his nightmares, the nameless, shapeless things that rush out of the dark at him, threatening to overpower and engulf him.

Wednesday, 12 January

For Christmas Jack had been given a cardboard rocket, a six-sided affair with a pointed roof to simulate the rocket's nose, which is big enough for him to crawl inside. It had been badly scribbled over and this afternoon Sally suggested to him that he paint it. He took up the idea with great gusto. She fitted him out with an old vest of mine, which fell to his ankles, and he voluntarily put on a pair of her wellington boots, giving himself the grotesque appearance of a troll.

Equipped with a pot of cornflower-blue emulsion and a large brush, he slapped on the paint with a will and had soon covered every square inch with a thick layer. When he had finished his boots and vest were spotless, but he had managed to land a broad streak of cornflower across the top of his head, the only unprotected area.

I stood in the kitchen looking out on to our little back yard where he was working, thinking how inapplicable the word 'work' was to the activities of children; or rather that the way they throw themselves into their projects epitomizes William Morris's idea of 'joy in labour', something that is not associated by most people with their experience of working. An idle child, at least of this age, is virtually a contradiction in terms; a lazy four-year-old would either be sick or very disturbed. Children bring to whatever they do an astonishing industriousness, but then they are also able to break off as soon as it ceases to give them pleasure or fails to satisfy their imaginations. Yet this combination of unstinting energy and creative fulfilment, which is the hallmark of children's play, is surely the rehearsal for an adult potentiality, which under a system of divided labour is only realized by an exceptional few.

Sunday, 16 January
On Friday Sally found one of her older ewes dead in the field. It had been a very cold and wet night, so we presumed that the sudden change in the weather had killed her, but we subsequently found out that she had in fact died of a ruptured kidney. Only extreme exertion could have caused that, which suggests she was worried by a dog.

Sally brought the body home and together we hauled it into our back scullery. This breed, Border Leicester, is distinguished by its large, white head standing smoothly above a ruff of wool, and its long, curved Roman nose. As we dragged her in, I found myself trying to manipulate her in ways that would not have hurt her had she been alive. Her legs had already stiffened, and when we hauled on them to pull her considerable bulk they cracked ominously. Only her neck still seemed pliable and it allowed her head to drag backwards and bounce on the cobbles. Her eyes were shut, but her bottom lip caught on the stones to reveal the splayed teeth along the front of her bottom jaw.

Lying on the floor, the body looked enormous with her belly standing in a great swollen mound like a barrow. Of course, it did literally resemble a barrow because it was itself full of dead bodies – two fully formed, healthy lambs.

Later, when Jack had returned from his playschool, the man from the local hunt called to collect the body, which was to be fed to the hounds. Jack had not seen it before, but I took him into the scullery while the man was backing up his van. I told him that she had died in the night and that she was old, though she had lambs inside her. I bent down to touch her, telling him she was cold.

'Don't touch her, you'll get dirty,' he said, pulling back my arm.

The place I was about to feel was not noticeably dirty, and I think his reaction was prompted by some primitive association of pollution with death.

The man then pushed a long, double-ended butcher's hook into the ewe's mouth and twisted it so that one point pierced the floor of her bottom jaw. By tugging on the other end he was able to pull her up a ramp into his van. I hastily told Jack that because she was dead she could not feel anything, and he nodded silently in reply.

Apart from his remark about the dirty wool, he watched the whole operation in silence, staring at everything in that all-absorbing, unshielded way that children have, especially when they are confronting some new and disturbing phenomenon. They seem unable to protect themselves, as adults do, by filtering and screening the information their senses bring them; yet, by the same token, they are perhaps able to suck some purer extract from their experiences than adults.

219

Afterwards, he made no mention of the incident, except to get me to reassure him that the sheep really was dead and could not feel the hook. I do not think he was distressed by what he saw, which after all was not so horrific; on the contrary, I think he was interested.

In principle, and providing no real unhappiness is caused, I believe children should be exposed to every event in the life cycle of animals, death no less than birth. The great horror of our own version of civilization is that we have thrust biological process so far away from our own everyday view that each individual faces the prospect of his own death, undergoes illness and physical deterioration, and indeed comes to terms with his own sexual needs, as if these were unique events, uniquely affecting him. Of course, in one sense, subjective experience of this order is unique, and by no means all of it tragic or painful. However, its terror can be alleviated a little, and its pleasures considerably heightened, through a developed awareness of nature. A positive familiarity with life and death in animals, which is not available to most people, is, I feel certain, indispensable at some level to our species' wellbeing.

Tuesday, 18 January
During the last three of four days both the children have been in the grip of a most remarkable spasm of creativity.

Sylvia stayed the night with them on Friday and they were all awake very early on Saturday morning; by the time we got up they had completely taken over one of the spare bedrooms and had filled every corner with little communities of dolls and other toys. They moved on to other rooms, their playroom, the sitting-room, an unobtrusive niche in the kitchen, and then into the corridors and doorways, and finally out into the garage, which proved to be the site of their most spectacular establishment. Using pieces of firewood and cardboard boxes, they equipped the place with an entire set of furniture – beds, tables, row upon row of chairs and assorted, though mostly unidentifiable, domestic appliances. At the moment one side of the garage is occupied by a bank of paper sacks of sugar-beet pulp, which Sally feeds to her sheep, and these they had turned into sets of galleries for their dolls to sit in and look down on the dramas below. In the best seats I noticed Jack and Tilly's ET dolls, which they were given a week ago, and have remained passionately attached to ever since.

By the end of the day there was hardly any part of the house or garden that did not bear some trace of this ruthlessly expansive colonization. We are still coming across forgotten dolls propped up in unexpected niches to stare at games long since abandoned. I have to confess that as the day wore on I found myself becoming irritated by the never-ending spread of their activities. It was not only that I could see hours of clearing away opening up before us, but I was disturbed by the relentlessness of their advance. They reminded me of an army of ants on the march, inexorably overwhelming every obstacle in their way. In the event, my apprehensions were shown to be quite ungrounded, for they were very good about helping us tidy up, and by the time it was dark most of their settlements had been dispersed. They did not seem to resent this; indeed, they entered into the business of dismantling their games with the same zest they had brought to putting them up.

Sylvia certainly played a large part in galvanizing their games, which always take on a noticeably more expansive quality when she joins in, but this intensely creative phase has continued now for three days, with and without her. For example, this morning, after Tilly had left for school, Jack chalked out on the kitchen floor a vast network of roads, parking areas, garages, bridges, roundabouts and sinister areas of no-man's-land, on which it was death to tread. And this evening, as soon as Tilly was back, they plunged into yet another community-building programme.

Their role in these fantasy worlds is mostly that of being the Great Architect, but occasionally they decide to descend from Olympus, taking on the form of toys themselves, and play happily among their families of dolls and bears. Of course, like gods, they can turn themselves into any shape they please, though this may sometimes give rise to confusion. A moment ago, I heard Tilly telling Jack, in a very firm tone, 'I'm not a mole, I'm a baby horse.'

I have another, thoroughly ignoble reaction to these completely absorbing games: I find myself resenting them because Tilly becomes very distant and only responds with annoyance to anything I say to her. In turn, I become infuriatingly insistent. On Sunday, when she was playing with Sylvia and some other, older girls, and was thoroughly involved, I interrupted their game to make a quite unnecessary issue out of a dustbin lid which Tilly had knocked over and left on the ground. I asked her to put it back and she took no notice. I asked her again. She refused and rushed off. In the end, I became unpleasant about it. Wearily and with many exchanges of glances confirming the universal tiresomeness of fathers, one of the bigger girls helped Tilly bang the lid down on its bin.

In truth, I could not have cared less about the wretched lid – the garden is littered with rubbish, which I myself have failed to clear up all winter. And I knew that it was unfair, and unrealistic, to expect her to break off from an exciting game in order to humour me over what was clearly a matter of principle. No, I was annoyed because she had no time for me; in a word, I was jealous. What a fool!

Saturday, 22 January
I have embarked on a rigorous programme of self-improvement.

In recent months I have been growing more and more gross and I have also begun to feel faint whenever I attempt the lightest physical task – getting out of my chair too quickly has been enough to bring on the vapours. And so, in an effort to become thin and fit, I now spend an hour a day in the garden, tackling jobs that require the most strenuous effort.

I no longer feel faint, but my weight has if anything increased, for there is nothing like an hour's heavy digging to give one a fine appetite.

Apart from feeling much healthier, I find this work deeply satisfying for another reason. Most of my life I have been haunted by the sensation of things turning to dust as soon as I touch them – a sort of Midas complex in reverse. Things that seemed solid and colourful from a distance tend to disintegrate, like mummified bodies exposed to the air, when I reach out for them. The garden, however, has not shrivelled and died under my hands; on the contrary, not only is my labour unmistakably recorded in the soil, for all to see, but I am also bringing forth new life. Despite having lived here for seven years, this trite realization has never really occurred to me before.

In fact, since the birth of the children, my sense of the ghostliness of reality has not impinged on me nearly as sharply as in the past. Children seize hold of reality like bulldogs. In their hands, things glow more brightly and throb with a secret energy only they seem able to galvanize. For me, one of the greatest joys of having children is being able to identify vicariously with the wonderful intensity and excitement they bring simply to being.

Tuesday, 25 January

This afternoon, as soon as Tilly was home from school, we took the children and Sally's father up to the Hall to see the shepherd's lambing yard, if that is not too lowly a term to apply to the palatial encampment he has designed and built.

He has sited his maternity village at the back of the Hall, just beyond a line of magnificent old beeches and under the protection of two huge walls of straw bales. Round a circus ring of straw he has erected fifty or so pens made out of hurdles, with planks and bales for their roofs, each intended to shelter a ewe and her lambs immediately after they are born. He has more than five hundred ewes in his flock and expects a hundred to lamb during the next three days. They are waiting in a fold next to the pens, their barrel bellies and swollen udders making their condition unmistakable. The shepherd spends most of his time here at the moment and he has the use of a little green hut on wheels, where he sleeps and makes his tea. As we walked past the beeches towards his sheep, a corkscrew of smoke was winding out of his stovepipe chimney and we could hear the ewes muttering and grumbling in the special guttural bleat they use when they feel their lambs stirring inside them.

Most of his flock are Suffolks, which have black faces and creamy bodies. At birth their lambs' colouring ranges from white to a pure charcoal black, with every kind of speckled, mottled and spotted combination between. The shepherd was very kind with the children and gave Tilly a two-day-old lamb to hold. Jack asked to have one of his own, but when Tilly dumped hers in his arms he clutched it woodenly and was obviously relieved to have it taken away. Nevertheless, he was as intrigued as Tilly by the sight of so many lambs, and they both released their melting, sickly sighs whenever they saw a particularly small or appealing one. Rather perversely, Jack was even more interested in the 'poorly' ewes, which had been isolated in a separate pen. He had apparently heard that their bottoms had been sewn up by the shepherd with string. For many minutes we peered into the recesses of the sick-bay, facing the indignant stares of the patients, but we saw no string.

Wednesday, 26 January
I do my hour's gardening before lunch and if he is at home Jack is always very keen to help me. This largely consists of my giving him rides in the wheelbarrow and listening to him invent persuasive reasons why we should light a bonfire.

Neither of them has yet grasped the fact that growing plants is not just a question of pushing stalks into the soil and waiting for the flowers to appear. Jack's 'garden', which to my shame has once more reverted to a state of wilderness, boasts a long stick, standing at a drunken angle among the docks. While this is in fact a small branch that blew off our syca-more in a recent gale, to Jack it is a 'tree' and he proudly points it out to anyone who will look. I have tried to tell him that it will not grow, but he only replies, in a heart-breakingly earnest voice, 'No, I planted it.'

They have discovered the snowdrops which at the

moment are blooming in profusion along the many wild edges of the garden. These they ruthlessly pick and bring into the house in great sheaves.

'Please don't pick any more.'

'It's all right, Dad. We're growing them.'

Tilly showed me a small box filled with earth and stiff with snowdrop stems.

'Well, leave some. They don't really like being moved, and they won't live without their roots.'

'It's all right,' she repeated impatiently, and danced off before the discussion could continue.

There is a difference, however, in their attitudes: she is playing at gardening and does not want the game spoilt by tiresome horticulture, whereas he, poor fellow, really believes his tree will flourish in the spring.

Thursday, 27 January

This afternoon we went to Tilly's school to discuss her work with Miss Blunden. We both felt intensely proud to be told that she is doing 'exceptionally well'. Miss Blunden has undoubtedly played a significant part in Tilly's current appetite for reading and writing, a fact that seemed to be borne out by Tilly's giving her a kiss as we left. The idea of my kissing my primary school teacher, a stimulating but formidable dame, aptly named Miss Stone, would have been unthinkable to either party.

Afterwards Sally took them to see *ET* for the second time, though the first for her. Apparently, Tilly told her teacher that her eyes had 'filled up with water' when she last saw *ET*. This rather odd formulation, in place of simply saying 'I cried', reminded me that she had used exactly those words at the cinema, and in tones of slight shock. It must have been the first occasion she had been induced to cry by the sufferings of a character in a story (ET appeared to be dying) and she was surprised by her own emotions, even wondering whether her response was appropriate.

Though they are capable of showing great concern over our unhappinesses, they never cry except on their own account. Tilly may have cried at the death of Sparkle, our orphan lamb, but if so it was quite exceptional.

Jack, incidentally, bears some small resemblance to ET, which both of us and Peter have independently observed. Of course, I am not suggesting he has a leathery skin or tortoise-like head. On the other hand, he is roughly the same size as ET and sometimes walks with a shuffling, rolling gait, reminiscent of ET's, which is caused by the same shortness of leg in relation to his torso. He also has a similar way of walking with his head thrust forward.

But then these likenesses only go to confirm the cleverness of the people who designed the little creature, for his apparently grotesque shape is in fact made up of many irresistible infantile features. For example, at first sight his reptilian skin seems an odd choice, and much less attractive than a furry or woolly exterior might have been. Yet his wrinkly hide only emphasizes his hairlessness and thus his affinity with human beings. A furry pelt would have made him strokeable, and therefore like an animal, but his nakedness makes him vulnerable, which is exactly the quality little children have. I believe ET's enormous eyes were designed on the basis of behavioural research; his skin, however, must have been the result of intuitive genius.

Monday, 31 January

Both Sally and I have noticed that Jack has seemed much calmer lately. His violent attacks and tornadoes of rage have given way to a new serenity. However, his preoccupations have not altered. Today he spent hours in his version of a Roman soldier's costume. This consists of a bath towel draped round his shoulders and secured by his army brooch, one of Tilly's head-bands worn low over his eyebrows and a piece of elastic tied round his waist to hold his scabbard. For his birthday, which is on Friday, he has requested a cake in the shape of four soldiers and a cannon, which should test Sally's modelling powers. Nonetheless, despite the endurance of these old fantasies, his behaviour is entering a fresh phase.

He does not seem to have grasped the fact that his birthday is imminent. I even think that if we just ignored it he would not notice. He looks forward passionately to next Christmas, and often makes references to Father Christmas, but for some reason his own birthday has not registered as a great event to be longed for and counted down.

Tilly too seems to have made one of their sudden, unpredictable but unmistakable leaps towards maturity. One sign of this is a new cynicism. Yesterday, as I was driving them and Sylvia up the lane to Peter's cottage, I said in an unctuous tone, 'Look at the little lambs, children.'

'What's so exciting about lambs?' came Tilly's sardonic reply.

February

Tuesday, 1 February

Today provided another sign of Jack's increasing maturity – and my own juvenility.

As a treat they were allowed to take their supper through to the sitting-room and eat it while watching television. Jack, however, got bored with the programme and embarked on a routine which he must know by now is guaranteed to drive me into an ungovernable fury. Looking at me tauntingly, he began to throw his food bit by bit on to the carpet.

'Please don't do that,' I said, 'it only makes me cross.'

He threw a piece of cheese on the floor. I snatched up his plate and took it out to the kitchen. When I came back he picked a felt-tip pen out of their pencil box and in his most provoking manner dangled it for a moment, then threw it into the fireplace. I grabbed him and thrust him violently out of the room, which only made him giggle.

I paced the room, breathing heavily and trying to contain the apoplexy of rage which had exploded inside me, like a grenade.

The door opened and his grinning face appeared. Usually he cannot resist taking these situations to the point of cataclysm and I felt myself puffing up in angry anticipation. But on this occasion he just rushed past me cheerily, all his taunting gone, and took up some game with Tilly.

In reality, I was the one spoiling for a fight, because I discovered I was a little disappointed by his unexpected switch of manner.

Wednesday, 2 February
This new ripeness of Jack's has not affected his ordinary, day-to-day mode of grappling with existence, I am glad to say. He goes nowhere without running, and generally emits mechanical or explosive noises. For him, entering a room involves bursting through the door, so that it smashes back against the wall, and roaring heartily at anyone who happens to be inside. He cannot put his hand into a coat sleeve without plunging it in, as if stabbing to death something inside. He takes off his shoes by kicking them as high in the air as they will fly. He eats, when he eats, by cramming as much food into his mouth as it will hold. And his way of conveying affection, which he does very freely, is to 'bonk' one on the head and grasp one's neck in a suffocating hug.

Sally told me a very sweet thing he said yesterday. A friend of ours asked him where Tilly was.

'I haven't seen her for ages,' she said. 'What does she look like these days?'

After some serious thought, he answered, 'She has black hair, a pretty face, pretty eyes and *very* pretty titties.'

Tilly herself, as part of her new maturity, has taken to arranging the contents of her desk with a fastidious tidiness bordering on the obsessive. She has a little shelf by her bed where she keeps her china figures and other treasures, and these are also lined up with mathematical precision. Fortunately, however, the rest of her behaviour is not cramped with orderliness and she shares with Jack a jovial spontaneity.

Friday, 4 February
Jack's birthday.

By yesterday evening he was at last fully aware of what the next day held for him. We let him carry his parcels upstairs to put under his bed, and they both went to sleep very early without a word of protest, but in a state of rare excitement, which was ominously reminiscent of Christmas. As we feared, he woke again and again during the night, asking if it was morning yet. In the end they both came into our bed and we told them they had to lie quietly until they heard the tractor coming to feed the pigs. This usually happens around seven o'clock, but by that time they had so exhausted themselves that they were in a deep sleep and did not wake for half an hour. Even then, it took Jack some moments to recall what day it was.

He rushed off to look under his bed. This is always a difficult moment for the other child, but Tilly compensated by helping him rip open his presents and seemed no less excited than he. My parents had sent him a remote-control car, which he played with almost continuously through the day and still amazes him. They had also sent Tilly a necklace, which pleased her greatly.

Later, at breakfast, poor Tilly suddenly broke into tears and said she did not want to go to school. She complained of feeling ill, having a stomach ache, a head ache, and other familiar symptoms, which she announces whenever she needs an excuse for getting out of something. She cried incommunicably for ten minutes. Finally I managed to say to her that I thought she was upset because she was afraid we were all going to have a good time with Jack in her absence. She did not deny this. I told her that in fact Jack was going to playschool.

Suddenly, she gulped out, in tragic tones, 'You're going to lay the table for Jack's party while I'm at school.'

I took her to Sally and extracted a promise that the table would not be touched until she was home. She still did not stop crying, though she was a little mollified by this assurance.

'I'm too ill to do any work. I feel ill when I have to work at school.'

This again was a well-known complaint, and one we now know to be quite untrue, because when we saw her teacher the other day she told us that Tilly positively asked for work. However, I offered to take her to school and explain how she felt; she accepted and stopped crying immediately.

When we got to school I made a speech on Tilly's behalf along the agreed lines. The admirable Miss Blunden promptly replied that she did not feel like working either and led Tilly away, but she came running back to give me a kiss.

Needless to say, when she returned in the afternoon, she showed not the slightest interest in laying the table.

Twenty children – perhaps even more, I lost count – assembled and we drove to our local fire station. Here we were met by a teacher friend of ours who is also a volunteer fireman and had kindly agreed to show the children round the station. This had been planned as a surprise for Jack, though Tilly had known about it all week. In the teeth of constant temptation, she had managed to keep the secret, but at the last moment one of the other children blurted out our destination. Jack was nevertheless very excited.

Our friend put on an excellent show: he climbed into his uniform, strapped on his breathing apparatus, let the children wear his yellow helmet and encouraged them to stamp on his toes, which were protected by steel caps. For some reason Jack became very reserved, clinging to me and insisting that I carried him. However, he soon jumped down when they were allowed into the cab of the fire engine. This of course was what they had all been waiting for and twenty minutes later they were still happily crawling over it.

When we got home Sally unveiled a magnificent cake in the shape of four soldiers, as ordered, each with a red coat and blue trousers. The cannon had defeated her, but fortunately Jack appeared to have forgotten that detail. Indeed, he was so overwhelmed by his cake that for a moment or two could only gasp, 'That's lovely, that's lovely.' Without exception, every one of the children also ate a substantial plate of shepherd's pie, which Sally, rather originally, had provided instead of the customary sausage rolls and crisps.

Although it is one of the great conventions that the child for whom the birthday party is being given either cries throughout or behaves unforgivably towards one of his little guests, on this occasion Jack only cried once and then briefly.

Sunday, 6 February
Yesterday Tilly maintained a campaign of resistance over the party she was supposed to attend in the afternoon. She would not say why she did not want to go, but adamantly refused every inducement and compromise. Both Sally and I were insistent that she should go, on the grounds that it was hurtful to accept an invitation and then not turn up. This made no impression on her.

On our way home from Sally's parents, where we had had lunch, she mounted a continual barrage of tears and shrieking, knowing that the moment for getting changed was coming nearer and nearer.

Suddenly, she proposed what seemed to me a most ingenious solution, which also had its own Marx Brothers logic.

'If I don't have to put on my party dress, I'll go. Or, I'll put on my party dress and won't go.'

I immediately agreed to this deal. Sally objected to her looking so scruffy, but I did get her to the party without any further fuss.

We never did discover why she did not want to go, or if there was a reason at all. Often these clashes are really trials of will, which can only be resolved by diplomatic concessions on both sides. They may not even be relevant to the ostensible issue, but naturally they must not involve too much loss of face. Tilly is usually the first to propose some slight but significant shift in her terms, which she manages to effect without apparently having changed her basic position.

A footnote to ET: Peter and I were talking about ET, which seems to fascinate both of us, but we agreed that its skin is its oddest feature. He pointed out that wrinkled skin is generally associated with old age and I said that this only added to its appeal, because little children and old people have in common a vulnerability, which arouses protectiveness in the rest of us. However, today I saw a newborn baby, or at least one that was less than a week old, and I realized I had forgotten how wrinkled babies are at that age. Of course, very soon they become plump and ripe, but at first their skin is puckered and crumpled. This makes more sense, for clearly ET is much closer to being fetal than senile.

With this in mind, I was discussing old age with the children while they were in their bath tonight. I asked them who was the oldest person they knew. Tilly immediately named someone who is in her seventies.

'How do you know she's old?'

'Because she's crinkly.'

'Grandpa's the oldest,' said Jack, 'because he's got a thing in his ear and he whistles when he speaks.'

He was referring to my father who wears a hearing aid and has a way of sounding his *S*s so that they whistle, though he is in no respect physically decrepit.

We then turned to the ever-popular topic of when Daddy will be dead.

'They'll put you in a hole,' said Jack.

'In the church, with your name on a stone, and 31083.' This is our telephone number.

'Wizards don't die,' said Jack. 'They have potions.'

Tuesday, 8 February

When they come into my room they often ask to look at a picture book and yesterday Jack discovered a collection of photographs by Bill Brandt. These were all nude women, most of them photographed to resemble pebbles on the seashore. Jack was thrilled and showed it to Tilly.

'Look, botties,' he announced.

They pored over the pictures for some time.

'Lovely titties to bite,' said Jack gleefully.

They looked carefully at every page and then asked for another 'bottie book', which at the time I was unable to find for them. This morning Jack came into my room, wearing on his face the expression he reserves for matters of the deepest seriousness, and without a trace of archness asked me again. I searched my shelves once more and was able to give him another collection of photographs, though only a few of them were nudes. He was nonetheless delighted and rushed off to show the book to Sally. She told me later that he studied it diligently and crowed with pleasure at every breast and bottom.

I do not really know why these pictures please him so much; I can only say that they do. His response to them does, however, have the same slightly hysterical and emphatically aggressive quality as his reaction to Sally's naked body. Just as Tilly makes playful, but forceful grabs for my penis whenever she sees it, Jack pinches and snatches at Sally's breasts, generally shouting 'tittie' and hallooing as if he were on some kind of hunt.

They are both becoming more self-conscious about their own bodies, especially Tilly, who I am sure picks up her notions of 'rudeness' from school. Yesterday, after they had finished with the photographs, they began to turn somersaults. Tilly was in her nightdress and suddenly told me to get her some pants so that 'people' would not be able to see her bottom. The only people present were Jack and myself, who were hardly strangers to her bottom, but I did as she asked.

This afternoon, as I was typing this, Jack ran in to say that the pigs had escaped and Mummy was chasing them. I grabbed him and dashed outside.

It was getting dark and a desultory snow shower was drifting across the farmyard. I discovered Tilly cheerfully hanging on a five-bar gate, craning over it to get a better view of what proved to be a spectacular sight. Looming out of the twilight were a dozen or so amiable, bustling spectres of pigs, their customary bulk made quite ethereal by their whiteness seemingly floating among the snow flakes. Behind them, like devils hurrying the damned down to hell, came Sally and the shepherd, shaking sticks and uttering brutal cries.

'I'm frightened,' Jack told me. 'Them pigs are going to eat me all up.'

'They won't eat me,' said Tilly. 'They don't like little girls' bones. And they wouldn't eat my shoes.'

Jack clung tightly to me, and would not climb on the gate with Tilly. He was clearly very relieved when the pigs were finally chased into their pens and locked up.

But then I think pigs still haunt his dreams, while for Tilly they are no longer objects of terror.

Saturday, 12 February
A fiendish virus is circulating round the district at the moment, which inflicts prolonged bouts of vomiting on children and adults alike, laying them low for as long as a week. Jack is the first to fall victim in this house and it seems certain that the rest of us will follow in due course.

Last night, around ten o'clock, one of the most dreaded of all announcements rang out upstairs – 'I've been sick.'

I ran up and found poor Jack sitting up in his bed, crying and staring in horrified disgust at his pillow, where he had indeed been sick. We changed his bed, but he would not go back to sleep. In the end he went to bed with Sally, and I slept in another room.

He was sick another dozen times through the night, growing paler and paler, but never crying or whining once.

In the morning I went in to find them both asleep at last. Tilly came downstairs with me and we made some tea. By the time we took it up, Sally and Jack were both awake and we learnt that Jack had not stopped vomiting until five o'clock. Within minutes of waking he was sucking a discarded sweet he had found and was bouncing on our bed with Tilly. Such are their almost miraculous powers of recuperation.

He has eaten nothing else today, but for once we have let him have his way. Next to getting children to bed, getting them to eat and to 'behave' at table must be the source of conflict that most preoccupies parents. Despite our best efforts and direst threats, our children seem to eat next to nothing. As converters of fuel into energy they are wonderfully economic. A half-eaten piece of toast, a bag of crisps, a packet of sweets, a sausage and a handful of chips is more than enough to keep a four-year-old in perpetual, vigorous motion for more than twelve hours. They do, however, have a lion-like tendency to gorge themselves, relatively speaking, every three or four days. Sweets and, to a lesser degree, crisps are the only forms of food for which they show real enthusiasm, though they are prepared to eat a very narrow selection of other things – 'bang' (boiled) eggs, corn flakes, porridge, toast, biscuits and, most popular of all, sausages and chips. Jack invariably asks for sausages and chips, whatever the meal in question.

This indifference to food surprises me, because they indulge all their other senses so freely: without hesitation, they will touch, smell and look at anything new, providing it is not frightening.

Their refusal to eat does worry us, but we do not make a big issue out of it. If we do, meals become intolerable, and I am always frightened that we are laying the foundations of anorexia nervosa in Tilly when we force food on her. In any case, though they are both small, they are hardly listless or etiolated.

As to 'manners', I have to admit that our approach is sporadic, arbitrary and, for the most part, ineffectual. We tend to round on the children suddenly and out of the blue, insisting that they say 'please' and 'thank you' for every mouthful, and then we forget so that by the next meal they will have lapsed back into their old, casual way – which, if the truth be told, I really prefer. A meal punctuated by continual politenesses soon becomes a nightmare, especially in the company of small children being conspicuously good.

In itself, the absence of 'please' and 'thank you' never bothers me too much. After all, it is quite possible to ask for something and receive it without using the magic spell, but in a way that nevertheless conveys a sense of request and appreciation. Politeness is much more a matter of gesture, eye contact, tone of voice and all the rest than strict observance of form. What does annoy me, however, is when the children make their demands imperiously, as if to servants, or rather slaves. This invariably provokes a short, sharp shock of table discipline.

The time-honoured phrase, 'What do you say?' following a failure to use 'please', is not one that features much in these occasional programmes of improvement, for on a famous occasion Tilly gave it a truly crushing retort, which disposed of it forever, as far as I was concerned.

'I want a drink of milk,' she announced to the world at large, in her most queenly manner.

'What do you say?' I yelled back.

'I want it *now*,' she said patiently, but firmly, in the kind of tone suitable for making oneself understood to a particularly thick waiter.

I also well remember a meal during our summer holiday at Burnham Market when the four adults put the children through an especially gruelling course of good manners. After it was over the children were sent out to play, leaving the adults to eat their meal. We set to like pigs. I have forgotten what we ate, but it involved much passing of butter, salt, jugs, plates, bottles and so on. For a solid ten minutes of concentrated self-gratification not one of these sticklers for politeness uttered so much as a single 'please' or 'thank you'.

Some months ago a friend of ours asked me what I thought of the idea of a story magazine for children combined with a tape-cassette, which would allow them to listen to the story while following the text at the same time. I scoffed, saying that I was sure that children, of Tilly's age at any rate, lacked the necessary patience and application to make real use of such a package. All of which shows how much I know about these things, because the magazine, now published as *Storyteller*, has proved a tremendous success. Furthermore, both our children have become addicted to it and sit for hours listening again and again to their two tapes. Tilly follows the words magnetically with her finger. They have both mastered the technology and can insert the cassettes, set them going and turn them over. Tilly has even learnt how to run the tape backwards and forwards to select her favourite bits.

My only objection to this splendid innovation is that, like all games based on electronics, it involves a profound loss in terms of human exchange. To get the best from their tapes the children have to cut themselves off and positively repel adult intrusion, which amounts to a reversal, in fact a negation of the story-telling tradition.

It is true that we did not read to the children as often as they now listen to their tapes; nor are we able to read as expressively as the actors and actresses who have been commissioned to perform the stories. But, no matter how well they have done their job, these professionals can never be any more to the children than anonymous voices, mechanically reproduced. On the other hand, the most inept, monotone parent, simply by virtue of being who he is, creates a uniquely rich interaction between his children, the story and himself as soon as he begins to read to them. He cannot help but bring out all sorts of allusions, jokes and explanations, which are peculiar to his family and which make the story the basis of an exclusive experience, leading to feelings and imaginative connections a taped version could not possibly stimulate.

This may sound highfaluting. Coming from me, it may even sound hypocritical, since I have perfected a special bedtime reading tone, of irresistible dullness, designed to drone Jack to sleep. But that is the point: if he were tired, the tape would probably put him to sleep too, but it could hardly wrap him in a blanket, tell him to shut up and listen, cuddle him as he got drowsy, and let him snore on its paunch for a couple of minutes before tucking him into bed.

By the same token, a tape cannot provide the protection in which children can give themselves up to the ambivalent pleasure of being terrified; a tape can never be the camp fire whose flames light up the trees where the wolves lurk, but whose warmth makes it safe to contemplate them.

Of course, children whose parents regularly read to them are getting the best of both worlds if they also have the tapes, but Peter told me that some survey has revealed that the bedtime story is not a national institution. Contrary to what we assumed, only a relatively small minority of children are read to when they go to bed.

Friday, 18 February
Sally's ewes are due to lamb tomorrow, and as if out of deference to tradition the weather has turned bitingly cold. We have had a few light snow storms, generally during the night, but the afternoons have been sunny and the ground has usually cleared by sunset. Each morning the children have rushed out to make their

pathetic little snowmen, which by the time Tilly gets home from school have melted to shapeless heaps of snow, bizarrely topped off with assorted organs – potato-eyes, carrot-noses, banana-mouths and so on.

As I thought might happen, the children's interest in the sheep has revived now that the lambs are imminent. Sadly, over the year, they have learnt to associate the sheep operation only with sinister and unpleasant practices. I feel sure that the reason they find the smell of sheep dung in the car so intolerable – to my nose it is rather sweet, if pungent – is because it reminds them of our trips to the abattoir, which by the end of the season they were refusing to go on.

It is always difficult to tell precisely what impact these significant experiences have had on them; they say so little, and even when their feelings are acted out, which they almost always are, I still find them opaque. When, for example, Sparkle, the hand-fed orphan lamb, died last April they did not seem too upset, although they had been intimately involved with her nurture from the hour of her birth; they did not appear to react at all, except to take a keen interest in the business of her burial. But they have mentioned her on and off ever since, and along with Tom, the Jack Russell who promoted himself to an estate in Norfolk, she dominates the great pantheon of never-to-be-forgotten pets and other animal friends and acquaintances.

Lately, Tilly has more than once asked, 'When did Sparkle die?'

'Last year, a few weeks after she was born.'

'She was nice, wasn't she?'

This last question is always asked earnestly and requires positive confirmation. I take it to be more than just a banal gesture of respect to the dead: she seems to want to be reassured that Sparkle was not nasty, that is deserving of punishment.

In fact, the wretched Sparkle died of human neglect and not some unavoidable natural cause. Sally had weaned her off the bottle, but she would still come up to us and nuzzle our legs very insistently. Tragically, what we took to be an irritating habit left over from her hand-feeding days was in reality a desperate demand for food. Sally had weaned her too early, before she was capable of digesting grass, and she died of enteritis. The children were never told the exact cause of her death, but I think they got some inkling of the fact that she died unnecessarily.

I am sure that death is an ever-present factor in their thinking. I suppose it is in everyone's, but adults tend to confine themselves to talking about specific instances of death, rather than the phenomenon itself. This taboo leaves all of us so much the less prepared for our own individual fate and forces us to brood on it in secretive isolation. Children, however, meditate freely on death and often discuss it, trying to probe the mystery. The idea of their own extinction is far-fetched and remote, but their fantasies are fraught with violence and murder.

The other morning, after Jack had climbed into our bed, I could feel him ruminating, and at last, in the particular, lugubrious tone he reserves for topics of the utmost seriousness, he asked,

'Can optocuses [sic] kill you?'

'Yes,' I told him, 'they can put their arms round people and squeeze them, but they won't get you because they live in the sea.'

He looked at me, quite unconvinced. Clearly, they had been wrapping their tentacles round him night after night. The bestiary of his dreams is made up of ravening creatures, seeking to chase and kill him. But it is not only in dreams that he confronts death; his everyday conversation, and Tilly's for that matter, is peppered with references to killers and killing.

I began to read a novelized version of *Peter Pan* this evening. When I reached the bit that explained the dynamics of fairy population growth (a new fairy is born whenever a baby laughs for the first time, but a fairy dies every time a child says, 'I don't believe in fairies') I asked our children where they stood on this issue.

'Do you believe in fairies, Tilly?'

'Yes,' she replied, fervently.

'Do you, Jack?'

'Naah.'

It is now easy to tell when he is engrossed by a story or television programme, because he has taken to cramming his entire hand into his mouth at moments of tension. At moments of extreme tension, when he is close to running away, he pushes both his hands down his gullet.

Earlier in the evening he had wanted to watch a film about King Arthur and his knights during supper, and I agreed on condition that he finished his yoghurt while he watched. He stuck to the terms of our agreement, though I wish he had not, for he kept one hand permanently lodged in his mouth while pushing spoonfuls of yoghurt past it with the other.

Sunday, 20 February

This morning Sally got up at six to check her ewes and when she came back for breakfast she told us that Carpet, so called because of the smooth, even pile of her fleece, had produced triplets without any difficulty.

Later, we all went up to see them. Sally has the use of a perfectly suited yard, owned by our friends the Clarkes. It contains a pair of little sheds where she has set up her delivery suite and maternity ward. She decided that the time had come to move Carpet from one to the other and told the children they could carry a lamb each. Tilly held hers with professional panache, but Jack quailed when he was handed his. I think he was put off by the sight of the yellow, waxy substance which coats them when they are born and was still clinging to his lamb; he blanched too at its dangling, bloody cord, which Sally had knotted and sprayed with purple antiseptic. However, he did enter into the spirit of the operation by bleating vigorously, as Sally had told him to do, to encourage the ewe to follow her lambs across the yard. In the event, she needed no urging and chased after us in great anxiety.

It was extremely cold and the children soon became bored. Although they always want to see the newborn ones, they are understandably blasé about lambs and lambing in general. They were diverted for a moment by the discovery of a bantam's nest among some straw bales: nine miniature, perfectly clean eggs lay in a deserted clutch. They were given one each and brought them home in their coat pockets, miraculously without accident. Tilly has laid hers on a nest of paper in a tiny straw basket, and has put one of her glass birds to sit on it.

The day turned out to be very hectic. Apart from the almost continual flow of people coming to see Sally and her animals, a man drove down from London to see me and talk about the possibility of making a television film about my book *Strange Land*. (A long shot, alas, but nonetheless very exciting.) Naturally, I devoted most of my attention to him and the children proceeded to behave abominably. Deserted by their mother, neglected by their father, they started a campaign of subversion, using every trick they knew to make conversation impossible. My guest took a kindly and patient view of their hooliganism, but this did not stop Tilly from saying to him after lunch, 'You're going home now, aren't you?'

Her tone was unmistakably dismissive.

Thursday, 24 February
Half-term this week. The children spent Monday and Tuesday nights with Sally's parents and thoroughly enjoyed themselves by all accounts: they were taken on special expeditions in both the morning and the afternoon, with lunch between at a Chinese restaurant, where they staunchly ordered sausages and chips. Tonight they are staying with friends.

And so, for the second time this week, Sally and I are alone in what seems a very empty house. Although it is nice not to have to do the evening routine, neither of us relishes their absence. I have been trying to reconstruct in my mind the feel of this house before Tilly's birth, which was almost exactly two years after we moved here, but I find it very difficult.

During the evening of the first day we brought Tilly home from the hospital I remember we took her outside to look at the harvest moon, which seemed to be floating only a few feet above our heads, like a huge, orange hot-air balloon. In one of the barns across the yard the farm was holding its harvest supper and they must have finished their meal because we could hear the men and their wives singing. We stood listening to them, holding Tilly in her shawl. Her eyes swam in her head as she looked upwards and her funny little crest of black hair ruffled in the wind. Suddenly we heard the strains of 'Waltzing Matilda' wafting from the party. This was pure coincidence, for nobody then knew what name we had finally chosen for her, and we took it to be the best possible omen and welcome.

All yesterday Sally was at her lambing yard. On Tuesday the second of her ewes to lamb, called Maggot because of her vulnerability to the blow-fly, had had quadruplets, as she did last year, and Sally was hoping that the next most expectant, Miss Piggy, would also produce. Despite her record-breaking fertility, Maggot was only able to feed a pair of her quartet and so the others must be fostered on quickly to avoid having to bottle-feed them. In the event, Miss Piggy failed to deliver, but nonetheless I had to entertain the children.

Fortunately, I had Peter's help. He and Sylvia are staying at their cottage for some of the holiday and the two girls have been playing with their usual absorption. Generally, Jack is able to join or destroy their games, but at any rate involve himself; however, for once he made no effort to play with them and pestered me instead. Wherever we went, he insisted on my carrying him, and whatever we did, he clung to me.

For one brief spell he did leave me to go upstairs and find the girls. Soon after they came running down. In enraged tones, Tilly told us, 'Jack's chasing after us and trying to look at our dollies' tits.'

This morning I took them up to Sylvia's cottage, but Jack would not stay, despite being offered a special 'boy's treat' by Peter. I brought him home and left him to play in the kitchen while Sally did the washing up. An hour later he came into my room and asked to be taken back to the cottage. An hour with Sally on his own was all it had taken to reassure him he was not being usurped in her affections by the lambs.

Monday, 28 February
Yesterday morning Tilly got into bed with me and lay musing, as she often does, on the story of her life.

'When did you first come to live here?' she asked me,

a question which took me by surprise because her use of 'you', as opposed to 'we', implied that for the first time in my hearing she was willing to acknowledge an era of history prior to her own existence.

'Two years before you were born.' I expected her to make some mention of her having been in Mummy's tummy then, but she did not.

'When did you meet Mummy?'

'Two years before that.'

'You were married before, weren't you?' This was said with sly coyness. She does not really know what to make of my first marriage, though it fascinates her, for both she and Jack cannot conceive of people as single, disconnected units.

Later in the day we went to visit a friend who lives alone here in the village. After examining his sitting-room with great curiosity, Jack asked, in a tone of considerable astonishment, 'Where's his mummy [i.e. wife] and children?'

Tilly asked the same kind of question about another unmarried friend who came to visit us a couple of days ago. We took her home and as soon as we were in the car again, Tilly asked me, 'Is she going to have a baby?'

I am sure this was not the result of a mistaken inference on her part; she simply assumes that everyone must live within a family structure, as in fact almost everyone she knows does, and it puzzles her to meet people who are not visibly attached.

'Has she got a husband?' she asked next.

'No, but she's got a boyfriend.'

'I haven't got a boyfriend.'

'Would you like one?'

'No,' she said, without hesitation. 'I want a baby, but I don't want to live with a boyfriend.'

After we got up this morning I gave the children a notebook each – Sally was once more awaiting the arrival of Miss Piggy's lambs, in vain as it turned out — and I asked them to write and draw their own stories. Tilly immediately launched into an adventure featuring a mouse called Jeremy. She consulted me about the spelling of most words, but the story was entirely of her own invention. It was written in her microscopic 'best' writing, the beginning of each line jammed against the very edge of the page.

I remembered that when she was first old enough to hold a paint brush she would invariably start a picture by placing a broad, sweeping border round the perimeter of the paper, as though she were appropriating the space within. Everything she drew in those days was on a mighty and heroic scale, in comic contrast with her own dwarfish size. She was often to be seen stretching across the table, struggling to reach the far corner of some epic work. Incidentally, I notice that her recent drawings of herself have become taller, in proportion with her own increasing height.

She sustained the plot of Jeremy's story for three pages, which included illustrations, and then lapsed into copying from a book. Jack, meanwhile, had been filling page after page with his 'writing', which thankfully he did not ask me to decipher. He numbered the pages, following a list I wrote out for him. Inevitably, he made a mistake. He called for my liquid Tipp-Ex, which I gave him, and though he applied it very liberally he could not completely eradicate a badly deformed '5'. He became upset and nothing I could say dissuaded him from ripping out all the pages he had written and crumpling them up.

It was a common complaint among the kids at the school where I worked last year that writing was difficult because you could not help making mistakes which spoilt the look of what you had done; they were quite unconcerned about the meaning of what they had put down. They too were lavish users of Tipp-Ex.

Sadly, Jack is far less able than Tilly to get pleasure from his writing and drawing; more often than not he ends up destroying his work. I hope for his sake this is only a phase. For myself, I can only say that, apart from my family, nothing gives me so much real pleasure as completing a piece of writing to my own satisfaction.

March

Tuesday, 1 March
This evening we went to Tilly's school to watch a video made of the children in their classes. We joined the throng of doting parents and watched shot after shot of children happily weighing, measuring, reading, drawing, counting and so on. Everyone seemed to be having a thoroughly stimulating and enjoyable time. We were therefore very disconcerted suddenly to see a shot of a little girl with pigtails sitting alone in a corner in front of a piece of equipment crying her heart out and rubbing her eyes with her sleeve. This scene was all the more poignant for being silent. The little girl was none other than Tilly, who, it was hastily explained to us, had 'got stuck' using one of the self-teaching spelling tapes. She told us later that she had not been able to get the earphones to work.

Tilly herself had urged us to watch the film and had given us the impression that she had taken a starring role. In fact, I think this shows her basic confidence: while she only had a dim memory of the incident with the tape machine, she clearly remembered the camera being in her classroom and had simply assumed that she would look splendid.

Wednesday, 2 March
I forgot to mention an amusing remark Jack made when we went to see Den recently. The whole episode was very fascinating to them, because Den used to be an

antique dealer and his house is full of curios and old-fashioned toys. Soon after we arrived he hurried out of the sitting-room, saying he had to get his crumpets out of the oven before they burnt.

Jack stared at him in wonderment. When he had gone, he whispered to me, 'Why is he eating trumpets?'

We now have two lambs in the house. One is suffering from a nasty disease which affects lambs' joints and prevents them from standing up. The other is perfectly healthy, but has been taken from Maggot to give her other two lambs a chance to feed properly.

Sally has rigged up a splendid creche for them by turning an old wardrobe on its side, filling it with straw and hot-water bottles and hanging a heater bulb above. The lambs lie in there quite contentedly, only bleating when they get hungry.

At first the children leaned over the side of the wardrobe, but now they take every opportunity to get in with the lambs and cuddle them, wearing the most maudlin looks on their faces. Jack occasionally gives way to bouts of whooping, but Tilly is unfailingly solicitous. They take it in turns to feed the sick lamb, which seems to be growing stronger.

Tilly appears to be reconciled to Sally's preoccupation with her sheep. Yesterday she wrote Sally one of her letters, which was a classic of its kind.

'To Mummy,' it read. 'I hope you like the lamps [sic]. I like them very much.' And it was grandly signed, 'Love, Matilda K. Harrison, Street Farm, Stowlangtoft.'

Below was a vivid drawing of a sheep with three lambs suckling at nipples that were placed, like humans', on its chest behind its front legs.

Jack, however, is by no means reconciled, and he continues to show signs of disturbance whenever Sally attends her lambs for long stretches, or is particularly agitated about them.

Friday, 4 March

Yesterday evening we saw another instance of poor Jack's inability to be pleased with his own work. The children had equipped themselves with paper and envelopes, and were writing letters. Typically, Tilly soon prepared a prodigious load of post, having written to all her friends and both sets of grandparents. The letters themselves were, admittedly, not much more than token squiggles, for it was sealing up and addressing the envelopes that interested her most. Jack, meanwhile, had laboriously drawn and written a letter for Sally incorporating all our names, which I had written out for him to copy. As we were admiring Tilly's mail-mountain, he brought his piece of paper to show me.

'I've gone wrong,' he said grimly. I knew from his tone and expression that he was on the brink of crying. He had in fact transcribed only half my name, though it was quite clear what he meant.

'That's splendid,' I said, but with a false ring to my heartiness which I knew he picked up.

'Don't show Mummy,' he told me, now glowering.

'I won't. Why don't you finish it and we'll put it in an envelope for her to get in the morning. Don't worry about the mistake.'

If only I had refrained from confirming that he had made a mistake, all might have been well. As it was, he immediately hurled himself into a chair, raging and crying.

'Don't cry,' I said. 'Look, let's make another one for Mummy.'

He snatched the piece of paper and crumpled it up. Then he tore it into shreds, shouting, 'It's no good, it's no good.'

It was impossible to console him or to make any positive suggestion to him; we could only wait until the storm passed. I found the incident so sad, because as far as I could tell his condemnation of his own efforts was entirely self-induced. I suppose he must feel that we judge his work unfavourably next to Tilly's, though it is not true. What is true is that Tilly has always had a deeply enviable gift for being able to turn out drawings, and now pieces of writing, with spontaneous panache, whereas he tends to struggle for a standard of perfection he cannot reach.

Perhaps because of this incident, he was restless during the night and ended up with me in our bed, while Sally went to sleep in his. This, incidentally, she never resents because she likes his trench-shaped mattress, which allows one to sink in so deeply the edges almost close over one's head.

Very early this morning, long before it was light, I was woken by his kicking me in the ribs.

'You're lazy,' he told me angrily.

'What?' I moaned.

'I want you to get up and go to the shops straight now and buy my torch. A red one. You promised.'

I had indeed promised.

'The shops aren't open yet. Go to sleep.'

Without another word or movement he plunged directly into his deepest sleep, and snored resonantly with his first breath. I was not so lucky.

Monday, 7 March

Tilly was very upset this morning, saying she did not want to go to school. This sometimes happens on a Monday and we did not take it too seriously at first. Also, apart from her customary disquiet about school, there were other factors at work. We had just taken Sylvia and Peter to the station to catch the train back to London after the weekend at their cottage. She and

Sylvia had spent nearly every waking and sleeping hour together since Friday. I assumed that, as often happens following a weekend of very intensive playing, she was both exhausted and unhappy at being parted.

Crying wretchedly, she told us over and over again that she wanted a packed lunch, something she had not had all this term. I did not understand why she was suddenly refusing school lunches, but thought she had perhaps fixed on this issue as a way of protesting about school generally; I thought too that perhaps she was insisting on a packed lunch because it made a link with home during what, as usual, she complained was too long a day.

I was quite wrong. She finally confided to Sally that she did not want school lunch because we were not sending her with her lunch money. It was true; for some reason, we never seem to have the necessary three pounds in cash to send with her on Monday mornings, as we are supposed to do. She has never mentioned it before, although it has happened often enough, but obviously it has been worrying her dreadfully. We rustled up half the money and wrote a note to go with it. However, she was not much consoled and went off crying and pleading. Of course, we will never do this to her again, but I have been cursing myself all day.

It is especially sad to think of her being distressed on a day like this, which is sharp and sunny. Surely the first of spring. 'I love fresh days,' announced Jack, as we walked out into the garden to collect bits of kindling that had blown down from the trees overnight. (He, incidentally, uses the word 'boiling' to mean 'extremely'. So he will say, 'I'm boiling cold,' when he is freezing.)

Much of the weekend was devoted to setting up a museum in Sylvia's cottage. The core of their display was a heap of glass, china and pottery shards that were dug up during the summer when Peter's as yet unfinished goldfish pond was being excavated. Apparently, his house is built on the site of an old clay pit which was later used as the village tip.

The girls laid out their items in different categories and placed a large notice near the cottage door, which read, 'Do not touch. If you want to, see the Boss, Tilly and Sylvia.' Below, they had listed their various collections: 'china, glass, nature, children's centre, faraway countries'.

Having set up this institution, they then spent the remainder of the weekend ruthlessly scouring the house for additional items. Nothing was safe. If some object caught their fancy they grabbed it and bore it away, their eyes glazed with monomaniacal lust. If it did not fit into any of their classifications, they merely invented a new one to suit it.

Later we all went to tea with someone who is herself a keen collector and whose house is virtually a museum. On the way there she had indulgently told the girls she would find them something to take away. She did not realize whom she was dealing with. No sooner were they inside the place than they fell on her possessions like thieves, filling their pockets and the bags they had brought for the purpose. They did not get away with their haul, though they did receive some generous donations.

Meanwhile, Jack, who had not come with us to tea, had started his own collection of treasures at home. With a sound instinct for security he has, however, kept his display covered by a tea towel.

Tuesday, 8 March

Tonight, while watching *Dr Who* on my knee, Tilly took off her blouse and pinched up her nipple.

'What are you doing?' I asked her.

'I do it every night.'

'Are you seeing if there's any milk there?'

'Yes.'

'You won't get any milk until you're much bigger.'

'I know. You've got to wait until they're . . .' She gestured roundly and hugely. 'Mary [a pubescent friend] is going to have milk soon.'

Thursday, 10 March

Last night Tilly was at her most affectionate. When Sally brought her home around five o'clock I was peeling potatoes and cutting up kidneys for our supper. She was still dressed for dancing in her touching and ridiculous leotard. She drew up a chair and stood beside me at the sink, hugging me or hanging on to my arm.

'I love you, Daddy,' she said, squeezing me. 'I don't want you to die.'

She was nevertheless disgusted by the kidneys, which she would not touch. She asked me where they came from and was fascinated, if faintly incredulous, to hear that I carried a card saying that if I died I was willing to let someone else have my kidneys, or any other bit of me that was useful.

Sally thought that her outburst of affection – not that she is ever reserved or withdrawn – was prompted by her being alone in the house with us for once. Jack was having tea elsewhere at the time, and it is certainly more unusual for her to be on her own with us than him. Sally's theory seemed to be borne out when she suddenly said to the both of us, 'I love it here in this house,' and twirled round, hugging herself.

Jack, on the other hand, does not seem very happy at the moment. He continues to be obsessed with buying things. 'I wanna buy somefink,' he dolefully reiterates hour after hour.

Yesterday, as a result of a day-long campaign throughout Tuesday, Sally took him to a toy shop after she had picked him up from his nursery school and he bought himself a soldier – a splendid Confederate infantryman, holding a flag and firing a pistol. In the evening he set out all his soldiers on a table in the sitting-room and called us to look at his 'battle', which was a glorious mélange of cowboys, knights, modern soldiers and a lone spaceman. Suddenly, he knocked over his new flagbearer and told us he didn't like it.

'What's wrong with it? He's magnificent,' I said.

'He's 'orrible. I only like the flag.'

'It's a beautiful flag. Pick him up so all the other soldiers can see it.'

Instead he threw it on the floor and began to cry. 'I want a crocodile,' he sobbed.

He cried for a long time and was not easily comforted, for he was very angry as well as dissatisfied. Thereafter, 'crocodile' was his constant refrain for the rest of the evening and it was his first word this morning. The whole situation is complicated by the ambiguous factor of his having his own money saved in his money box. Of course, these 'savings' came from us in the first place and he often asks for money, which we give him on an erratic basis. The time has clearly come for them to receive regular pocket money. But this would not altogether solve his problem.

Yesterday he told Sally, 'When I want something, I want it so badly I can't think about anything else.'

I recognize that feeling all too well, for it has haunted me all my adult life, but it depresses me terribly to hear Jack express it. Presumably, he feels an emptiness and is trying to fill it with these toys, for which he longs so passionately, and which in the end bring him no comfort or, worse, make his sense of emptiness seem bigger. All this must tie in with his inability to be pleased with his own work: it does not bring him any satisfaction and when it fails him, that is, when he makes a mistake, he is overwhelmed with bad feelings.

It was decided that Sally would buy him the crocodile while she was in Bury St Edmunds this morning, but to her horror she found the shop closed, and none of the others she tried had crocodiles in stock. I gave him a plastic beetle, which I happened to have in my secret supply of treats, but although it was horrifically realistic and under other circumstances he would have loved it, he would not look at it and shrieked 'crocodile' all the louder. Sally held him and tried to comfort him, promising that we would get his crocodile as soon as possible. In time, he fell asleep, something he has not done in the middle of the afternoon for many months.

He slept for more than two hours and was on excellent form when he woke. Some other children were here and he immediately joined in their games in his heartiest manner, even leading an expedition across the road that runs beside our garden. This is a great local crime, and he would not have committed it if he had not been in the best of moods.

To divert the children, Sally released into the garden the two lambs she has been keeping here in our woodshed. The 'poorly' lamb (Jack's description), which could not stand up a week ago, tottered about gamely, while the fit one gambolled and frolicked like a cliché.

In the evening Sally drove off to a jumble sale in the next village and Jack became very distressed again,

263

shouting after her, 'Buy me something, buy me something.'

I took him inside and told him that we were going to try to make things instead of thinking about buying them. They had been doing some writing and, to my surprise, he returned to it with new gusto. Soon enough, however, he made a mistake — a perfectly formed letter fractionally out of alignment — and screwed up the paper, throwing it on the floor in a rage.

'That makes me very sad,' I told him. 'That was one of your best pieces of writing and I wanted to keep it. Now you've spoiled it.'

He listened to me in amazement. When I had finished my speech, he grabbed a fresh piece of paper and feverishly began to rewrite what he had destroyed. I showed him some of my own work, pointed out that it was full of errors, corrections and blemishes.

Tilly wrote a story, keeping the plot going for over three pages, which is her longest unaided effort. Jack completed two entire pages of letters and figures copied out from my crippled calligraphy. I made these into little versions of my typescripts, punching holes in the pages and holding them together with treasury tags. These 'books' were shown with great pride to Sally on her return.

They went to bed much later than usual. Tilly, who had not had the benefit of an afternoon nap, was very tired and fell asleep almost immediately, but we left Jack continuing to write and draw. At half past ten we could still hear footsteps above. We came up ourselves an hour later and had to put him in his bed wide awake. The last thing I remember is hearing a low 'toot-toot' from his plastic trumpet, which he was playing in the dark — though quietly, lest he woke Tilly.

The end of the crocodile saga was quite predictable. It finally came into his possession on Friday evening and was rapturously received. He played with it almost continually until bedtime, when of course he took it to bed with him. By the morning, however, its lustre was dimming; by Sunday it was hardly worth looking at; and today I should think he would be very hard pressed to say exactly where it is to be found.

We are nonetheless making progress.

On and off throughout the day he muttered about buying things and whined for his pocket money, which he had been promised for Friday, but apart from a couple of minor incidents we managed to divert him before his importuning became desperate. For instance, Sally took him on a long bike ride, which he always enjoys – more than Tilly. And this evening, following my resolution, I offered to play a game with them the minute he began to complain about having less money than Tilly. (True, incidentally, for despite his great preoccupation with spending, he is absurdly careless with his actual cash, which lies scattered about the house. Tilly, by contrast, scrupulously hoards her savings.) I suggested dominoes, but they chose musical statues. And then, taking up my idea of the other night, Jack asked if we could make something. With no urging from me, they both began to make books again, this time out of tiny leaves of paper, hardly bigger than postage stamps, which they cut out and had me staple together.

Tilly wrote a delightful story about herself and a rabbit going for a picnic, which she illustrated on the same miniature scale as the text. Jack asked me to write out, 'The pig butted the little boy over' for him to copy, which he did with laborious care and impressive accuracy.

His words referred to an attack made on him in the morning by one of Sally's ewes – Carpet – which chased him into a corner of its pen while Sally was attending to its lambs and attempted to butt him. Fortunately, he was able to escape easily and the experience did not appear to have upset him, but for all that it was obviously still on his mind by this evening. Though it seems surprising, as far as I can recall, Tilly has never made a direct allusion like this in her writing to an experience of hers; nor has Jack done so before.

As they were working I introduced them to a few new tricks of the trade, such as insertion marks to deal with omitted letters and words, and hyphens to carry words over from the end of one line to the beginning of the next. Once grasped, these were used with great enthusiasm. For the first time, Jack was content to cross out mistakes and make corrections without calling for the Tipp-Ex whitewash, and without losing his temper.

Wednesday, 16 March
We are going through a very difficult patch at the moment: we have no money and I am still waiting on publishers' decisions.

I wonder to what degree Jack's current pre-occupation with money is an echo of my own. We do sometimes talk about money in front of them, or rather we do not, as I suspect my parents did, have a positive policy of censoring such discussions in their hearing. On the other hand, I am always careful to keep out of my voice, as far as possible, any note of panic or anxiety I may be feeling.

Disappointment and frustration are, alas, the order of the day with my professional work, and have been for some months now. These are both very destructive emotions and, ironically, they tend to compound the very situation that caused them in the first place. I am conscious of having to guard against venting my feelings on the children, but in fact they are my most reliable consolation. As a certain Hamilton Fyfe, author of *Good Words*, a Victorian book of advice to parents, wrote, the society of children is 'a fine moral shower-bath, into which one might go jaded, chilly and torpid, but from which one is sure to come out refreshed and glowing, with brisker circulation and a lighter heart'. Though I would not have chosen his watery metaphor, I endorse his sentiments. No matter how bad things may look when I am in here, in my room, once I step outside into their world I am immediately restored to confidence and hope. Far from taking it out on them, I look to them to take me out of it.

Thursday, 17 March
Last night, while we were all watching television together, we saw a shot of some people sitting round a swimming pool and for a moment it appeared that one of the girls was naked. I could feel Jack's interest quickening with my own. Then she turned round and we could see that she was wearing a bikini top.

'We can't see her titties,' said Jack, disappointedly.

Their response to what they now call the 'rude' bits of the body is usually one of hilarity: nothing is funnier to them than the sight of a bare bottom. Tilly told me the other day that certain boys at her school chase certain girls, herself included, into a corner of the playground and attempt to kiss them and pinch their bottoms. She seemed to regard this as a perfectly natural, if irritating practice and was not worried by it, except when they kept her 'in prison' for too long. Indeed, she now reproduces their behaviour whenever she sees me dressing or undressing by snatching at my penis and squeezing it viciously if she catches hold. I am often reduced to the ridiculous position of having to hop round the bedroom, one foot in my pants and one out, in order to fend off two pairs of grabbing hands, for Jack joins in the hunt with equal ferocity. They will chase Sally with the same aggression, trying to pinch her bottom. Why our bodies should attract these sadistic onslaughts, I really don't know.

Certainly, their response is by no means confined to projecting their newly discovered shame. They appear to derive guiltless pleasure from their bodies and to understand that other people do the same. It is exposure, not self-awareness, that is shameful and laughable.

I remember Sally telling me recently that she had been with Jack when, for some reason, he wanted to make a special gesture of affection to Tilly and had deliberated for a moment before finally deciding to reach out and give her vagina a playful tickle. By the same token, if I interpret his tone of disappointment correctly, he had wanted to look at the girl's breasts for the sake of his own pleasure and curiosity, and not in order to ridicule her. His eagerness to see her breasts uncovered was quite different from his usual infantile guffawing at nakedness, and I believe this must have a bearing on the fact that men do seem to get more enjoyment than women from pornography and nude pictures.

Saturday, 19 March
On Thursday evening Sally went to inspect her sheep and I played with the children in the kitchen; they were making frottage images of leaves with crayons.

Suddenly Jack got up and told me not to come and look at what he was going to do. I agreed and he hurried out of the room. A minute or two later I saw him staggering past the window, struggling to carry a one-and-a-half-litre bottle of my homemade wine (a very successful plum, incidentally). I ran out to help him and save the wine before he dropped it. He was upset at my not trusting him, but after crying and rolling on the carpet for a while, he gulped, touchingly, that the wine was for Father Christmas to thank him for their presents.

He made me wrap up the bottle in pieces of paper decorated with his leaf rubbings and then sat down to write a letter to Father Christmas. At his dictation, I wrote out, 'Thank you for my lorry, love from Jack,' which he carefully copied.

Tilly joined in and wrote to Father Christmas as well, though her letter was a list of requests. For a while I washed up and tidied the kitchen in a silence that was only punctuated by Tilly rapping out words for me to spell – 'wheelbarrow', 'Santa Claus', 'present' and so on, all of which made for a lunatic-sounding conversation.

I do not know what prompted Jack to thank Father Christmas, nor what motivated him. Presents have certainly formed a dominant theme in his thinking over the last few weeks and perhaps his idea was to take out some insurance against possible disappointment next Christmas. But, as is no doubt common with second children, he is also much more prone to making ingratiatory and deferential gestures.

Tilly looked up from her work and said, 'Father Christmas isn't real, is he? He's a person dressed up. I know, because one Father Christmas we saw had a beard and the other one didn't.'

I was just going out of the room and I attempted to

put the door between myself and Jack, while signalling to her that she was right. I thought it only fair to encourage her faith in her reasoning powers, but at the same time I did not want to disillusion Jack. Tilly did not pick up my hint, and made her speech again. I was nodding at her vigorously when Jack put his head round the door, obviously interested in my reply to Tilly's heresy.

'What do you think?' I said to him.

'Real,' he said shortly, in the tone of one who has decided as a matter of policy to remain deaf to his doubts.

In spite of her atheism, Tilly entered enthusiastically into the business of leaving their letters and presents on the doorstep for Father Christmas to collect during the night. When she returned, Sally was required to telephone her secret number to Father Christmas's workshop (actually the Puffin Storyline) and inform his chief dwarf about these offerings. Jack seemed to believe implicitly in this part of the arrangements, for the next day he told everybody about the 'stupid dorf' (i.e. the recorded voice) that would not stop talking.

Throughout the rest of the evening they kept opening the door to see if their presents were still there. They continued to play in this same expansive way, their fantasies switching to 'Lord Henry', a frightening, though basically benign, personage who has his being in the back-stairs that lead to our attic.

Predictably, I suppose, they were very difficult to get to bed that night and at nine o'clock I found myself reading to them. In fact I finished one of my own stories, concerning a character called Jim, which I had begun the night before. The story intrigued Tilly, I think, but Jack had already told me that he did not like it because it was 'nasty'. His last words before falling asleep on my lap were, 'Bloomin' ole Jim.'

After he fell asleep I told Tilly that she was right about Father Christmas, but that she must not spoil it for Jack. Then I asked her if she liked my story. She said it was 'nice'.

'Do you think I should try to get it published?'

'No,' she said firmly and to my surprise.

'Why not?'

'It's got too many scribblings out.'

Monday, 21 March

At some point on Saturday Jack, unnoticed by me, must have gone into my room and started experimenting with my paper punch. It has a badly designed, loose back which falls off very easily, as I know to my cost, and inevitably it came apart while he was playing with it, releasing a thousand spots of paper on to the carpet. Evidently, he tried to sweep them up with my hearth brush but made no progress, for despite being lighter than snow flakes they stick to the carpet as if gummed. In the end he admitted defeat and confided in Sally. He told her that he wanted me to help him hoover them up, but that he wanted her to ask me on his behalf.

I know exactly how he must have felt when the spots exploded in front of him, turning what had been an amusing game into a nightmare.

When I was a child my parents and I used to spend almost every holiday on my grandfather's farm in what was then Pembrokeshire. Indeed, I was born there. In the summer holidays, when I was old enough to wander round the place on my own, nothing gave me greater pleasure than to play in the farmyard during the men's lunch hour, which seemed timeless to me, like summer itself. I would throw stones, look into the black hole of the smithy to see if there was any life in

271

the coals on the forge; I would let the calves suck my hands with their Velcro tongues and surf down the great heaps of grain drying in the barns. Best of all, however, I would sit on the tractors, or, greatly daring, on the combine harvester, that used to be lined up in an open-fronted shed. I would spin the wheel as if negotiating Alpine hairpins, pump the pedals and shift gears continually, while making suitable engine noises. I was not at all mechanically inclined, but the sheer size of these toys and the sense of power they conferred made them very exciting.

One sultry, silent, dusty day the tractor I was playing on suddenly began to move. This brusque intrusion of reality on my careless game was at the time as shattering to me as it would be to Jack if somebody fell dead at his feet after he had 'killed' him with one of his explosions. The tractor rolled forward into the sunlight and, following a curving course, inexorably crossed the considerable expanse of the yard until, with a jarring crunch, it was halted by the stone wall of a cowshed.

I jumped down and ran. Nobody saw me, as far as I know. I told nobody about what had happened and nobody spoke to me. Unlike Jack, I was not eager to put right what I had done; I simply wanted the incident erased from history, which it had been – up to now.

Tuesday, 22 March
Yesterday was extremely cold. A flurry of hail in the afternoon brought Jack running into the garden, yelling, 'Snow. Yahoo! Yahoo!' – his current cry of jubilation. He dashed about, being pounded mercilessly by large lumps of hail from which he contrived to make a tiny snowball, no bigger than a large

272

marble, before the sun appeared and the whole salvo liquified.

I hate snow, probably because it always evokes childhood memories of extreme discomfort, but my children get so much pleasure from it I almost wish we had had a proper fall this winter. Almost.

Thursday, 24 March
On Tuesday night, for the first time in many weeks, I lost my temper with Jack while putting them to bed. He put himself entirely in the wrong, but my behaviour was inexcusable.

He chose as his bedtime story the book of *ET*, however Tilly objected, saying it was too sad. He would not choose an alternative, so it was agreed that I would read a few pages of *ET* and then a few of *The Wind in the Willows*, Tilly's current favourite. Even though, by dint of ruthless skipping, we have now reached the most exciting part, Toad's picaresque adventures on the road, Jack does not like the book. Usually this has the happy result of putting him to sleep out of sheer boredom, but on this occasion he obstructed my reading by emitting his own form of white noise and bouncing mischievously on my knee. I reminded him of our agreement. He only turned up the volume and put his fingers in his ears.

At this point I could feel a bore tide of anger surging through me and I hurled down the book, dimly hoping to stem my feelings. He slid off my knee, darting towards the door.

'Don't, Jack,' I shouted, grabbing him and very forcefully planting him back in my lap. 'It's not fair to Tilly or me if you don't stick to what you said.'

'That's right,' Tilly said feelingly from the depths of her bed.

He was quite indifferent to this appeal to his finer self and sense of justice; in fact, he laughed his most clownish laugh and began his screeching once more.

'Jack, shut up and listen.'

I hoped to sound menacing, but my gritted teeth and the glottal way I have of talking when I am only just able to restrain my anger had the effect of reducing him to hysterical laughter. He was a little frightened, but mostly he was feeling provocative. His giggling in my face was too much for me and I threw him into his bed.

'I won't read now. You can go to sleep without a story.'

'Not fair,' whined Tilly. 'He's had his story,' she said, with a relentless logic, 'but I haven't had mine yet.'

By way of demonstrating that I had not weakened and lost, I picked him out, shoved him on my knee again, and began reading in a fierce, staccato voice. After much more shouting and manhandling I finally subdued him and was able to read a few lines in relative tranquillity.

They then went to sleep peacefully enough, but downstairs I was stabbed by guilt over and over throughout the evening. I could not forgive myself for having reacted so horribly to his playfulness, nor for having countered his lack of principle with nothing more elevating than a tantrum. I thought over the resolutions I had made never again to lose my temper and realized with horror they probably number as many as a hundred.

Having resolved for the hundred and first time not to give way to rage, the very next evening I found myself holding Jack in mid-air by his pyjama jacket and threatening to stop his pocket money if he did not get into bed NOW.

Watching the television later, though hardly able to concentrate on it for brooding on my petulance, I did hear a telling remark made during an adaptation of Virginia Woolf's *To the Lighthouse*. James, the little boy who is always begging to go to the lighthouse, is bowled out by his first ball in a game of beach cricket. He demands another turn and there is some discussion for and against among his brothers and sisters. This is cut short by their father, who utters the immortal words, 'Out is out, James,' with all the unanswerable authority of a Victorian paterfamilias.

As a generation of parents, we have no such authority; it is simply not available to us.

Monday, 28 March
On Saturday, after lunch, Jack began to whine for 'paper money'. Although he does not have a clue about the value of money, or about the relative value of coins, he has at least grasped that it is better to get hold of notes than coins. However, much to my delight, he quickly stopped asking and, without my suggesting it, he set about drawing his own money. He collected together scissors, paper and a green pen, and cut out a blank strip, instructing me to write out 'fifty-four pounds' for him to copy.

I was very pleased with this development, because I thought he was learning to come to terms with reality by means of fantasy, which after all is the only way of evading madness.

'What can you buy for fifty-four pounds?' he asked me.

I had to think for a while, which shows what a low ebb my fantasies have fallen to.

'A first-class radio.'

'Yahoo!'

He immediately sat down to manufacture more currency. After he had drawn a couple more notes of relatively trivial denominations, I told him that if he made himself a million-pound note he would be able to buy himself anything and everything he wanted. With considerable excitement he copied out the figures and instantly showed a hundredfold increment by writing '£1,0000,0000'.

Defying monetarism with laudable extravagance, he continued to print his own money until it was time for us to go out.

I had already planned with Peter to take Sylvia and our children to Stowmarket for the afternoon. It had been agreed that we would go to a tea shop and then to see *ET*, for the third time. I added further lustre to the trip by reminding them that it was pocket money day and handing them their twenty pences.

Jack looked at his rather disdainfully.

'I'm going to spend my million pounds,' he announced.

I was a little shocked to hear him say this, but he was very insistent and our laughter began to upset him. Of course he knew that he could not really use his money in shops, but the prospect of boundless consuming had gone to his head.

In any event, our visit to Stowmarket was very enjoyable. They were as raptly absorbed in *ET* as before. They both sat on my knee throughout and I could feel that their interest never slackened once. Indeed, during the bicycle chase that brings the film to a close, Jack whispered to me, 'Can we go to *ET* at Easter?'

One of the reasons, I am sure, they enjoy seeing films they like over and over again is that the first time they only understand a small part of what is going on, and each new viewing produces a wealth of revelations. Of course, having next to no history of their own, they are also very quick to establish traditions and make agreeable experiences into institutions.

The Easter holidays have begun.

Yesterday Tilly said, out of the blue, 'Everybody loves me.'

'What?'

'All the boys at school love me. They try to kiss me.'

During the weekend I overheard her discussing this feature of school life with Sylvia, who receives the same attentions from the boys at her school. Neither seemed to relish being 'loved', but both were resigned to putting up with it as an occupational hazard. It certainly had not crossed their minds to chase the boys and inflict some kind of redress; far less take the initiative with kissing.

As we were driving home from Bury St Edmunds this morning, Jack, who is evidently a kisser in the making, asked me if I liked 'titties'. I told him I did, and he told me that he did too.

'Why?'

'I like to pinch them,' he said fiendishly, but piously adding, 'I don't pinch Mummy's.'

'Why do you like pinching them?'

'Because they're nice to suck. They're all milky.' This was said in a much softer tone. Then, waxing positively mournful, he said, 'I'm not allowed to have milk.'

This is true, for he has a mild allergy to milk, which brings his face out in a rash.

Poor Tilly does not seem very well: Sally is giving her a bath at the moment and talking of putting her to bed, though it is only five o'clock. She was sick last night and has been very subdued all day. More than anything I put this down to end-of-term fatigue. Sylvia was in just the same state of debility over the weekend. I am certain we underestimate the toll taken on their resources by school; nor do they seem to have learnt yet how to measure their own powers and to know when they are tired. They stoically press on, unaware of approaching their limits.

On Sunday night, when their friend Emily was staying, a terrible row broke out between Tilly and Jack. The girls had been putting the dominoes back into their box and I made them leave out the last layer for Jack. Taking great pains, he proceeded to lay them down, but in a different pattern from Tilly's. She objected, he persisted, and this profound issue then provoked a bitter and violent row. I intervened and made things a thousand times worse by losing my temper and shouting far louder than they had been.

Tilly clearly felt that I had been taking Jack's side and refused to make peace with me. Every overture I offered was spurned with a vicious, 'Leave me alone.' Spitting and pleading, we struggled upstairs to bed. Emily watched all this with the glum detachment of a bored, but anxious outsider. I took Tilly into a room on our own and asked her to be my friend again. She refused to listen, sticking her fingers in her ears and shrieking, 'I'm always last.' And indeed she was, for the other two had by then got into their beds. I tried again to mollify her and this time succeeded: she suddenly became calm and almost instantly cheered up.

I am always much more distressed by my fights with Tilly than those with Jack. For some reason, I am frightened she will withdraw her love, whereas even my most terrible and regrettable confrontations with Jack never, for a moment, make me think that his love is at risk. Not that Tilly's really is, of course. I know that. On the other hand, our clashes, which thankfully are as rare as my battles with Jack are common, seem to arouse a very deep fear of rejection. I am as sure as one can be about such things that this fear originated with my being sent to prep school, but in any event it has been a potent, and sometimes paralysing force in all my serious relationships with women.

Wednesday, 30 March
I must find out what BANA (Bury Against Nuclear Arms) has arranged for this coming weekend. Two Easters ago, when Tilly and Jack were only three and two, I took them both in our big push-chair on a march round Bury on the Saturday. They thought it was all splendid.

By accident, we took our position immediately below the local Labour Party's banner, a magnificent crimson and gold affair, with coloured ropes and tassels, supported by two long poles. We were preceded by a man, who solemnly and inexhaustibly pounded a big brass drum. The children were given balloons, bearing the CND symbol, and we tied them to the chair. Anything that involves uniforms or smacks of military ceremonial greatly appeals to them, and so they threw themselves into the spirit of the occasion, shouting, 'Bang the bomb' with uninhibited zest.

The march turned out to be very orderly and sedate. We wound our way through the main shopping streets and people respectfully stood back to let us pass. The atmosphere will be very different this time, I am sure. Indeed, everything went off so innocuously that one marcher was driven to shout at a particularly bovine knot of people, 'Come on, you bums, heckle!' He was not rewarded with a reply.

April

Friday, 1 April
Good Friday.

A miserable wet day and very cold too. However, we have contrived to import our spring indoors, for Sally has brought home another lamb to be fed, this time the progeny of Brian, the Hampshire ram, and a Greyface ewe. The lamb, named Vic by Tilly for no fathomable reason, has a big wedge-shaped face covered with blotched charcoal markings, and his rear legs are encased below the knee in what appear to be thick, curly warmers – the height of fashion. He has been installed in our capsized wardrobe, which has been brought into the kitchen to stand beside the Aga. To fend off any boredom or sadness his solitariness might bring, the children have loaded his straw nest with toys and dolls, including a pair of appropriate lambs.

I have read that lambs tend to suckle between sixty and seventy times during their first twenty-four hours of life, and that the duration of their sucking is between one and three minutes. This means they are continually topping up with relatively small quantities of milk. Under the human timetable imposed on orphan lambs, things are very different: they are fed only once every five hours, give or take a few bungled alarm clock settings, and they are of course ravenous when the time comes. Even though a mere two days old, Vic will reliably empty a baby's half-pint bottle in a hundred seconds flat, during which his stomach visibly swells as if being inflated with a bicycle pump.

The children are now old hands at lambing, having watched no less than five being born on Tuesday afternoon, but they are still very excited at having one to live in the kitchen. This morning, I heard Tilly giving Sylvia a lecture on how lambs are born, as they were hanging over the edge of the cupboard, playing with Vic.

'Well, first a bag comes out of the mummy's vagina, and then the lamb's head, and then – whoosh! – there it is.'

'It's the same with horses,' said Sylvia knowledgeably. 'They come in bags too. But no one puts the bag in the horse.'

This last comment was made in a very confused tone, but Tilly did not offer an explanation to the mystery of how the bag, which they both seemed to think of as plastic, got inside these animals.

The lamb itself suddenly performed a series of characteristic leaps, jumping vertically on four stiff legs, its head momentarily popping over the side of the cupboard. It is no wonder lambs are the archetypal symbols of spring. Despite the absurdly artificial context of this display, it was still intoxicating. Nothing could be more expressive of sap rising, growth bursting forth, new life defying the death of winter, the triumph of joy over despair, and so on, than these spontaneous outbursts of sheer vitality.

Sunday, 3 April
Last night, around two or three o'clock, I went to the loo and looked out of the window to find that everything appeared to be incandescent. At first I assumed there must be an unusually strong moon, but it was

really too bright. Next I wondered if I had left on the lights downstairs, and it was only after thoroughly waking myself up to think properly about it that I realized what I was looking at was snow. A freak storm had left a fall of a couple of inches, though it was already thawing.

When we woke up this morning the sun was shining, but the farm and the parkland round our house were still thickly covered in sparkling snow and everything looked very beautiful. The children immediately rushed out to make a snowman. By lunchtime the snow had completely cleared, leaving deep pools of water along Kiln Lane, which leads to Peter's cottage.

The children also searched the snow for the Easter Bunny's footprints. This being, in whom they all claim to believe, though with varying degrees of self-interest, is a recent innovation and appears to have been invented by children themselves solely for the purpose of dispensing presents. As it happened, their faith was vindicated, for he had indeed left them an Easter egg each to discover in the herb garden.

I asked Jack what he thought Easter was all about.

'Chickens,' he said firmly.

This afternoon it was suggested that as an Easter gesture we walk down to the church. The idea was canvassed among the children: ours were keen to go, but Sylvia was not. In an effort to sell the expedition to her, Tilly said, 'When we get there, you can go up into that place [i.e. the pulpit] and talk like the Prime Minister.'

A fearful virus is going round at the moment, which mostly affects children and whose nastiest symptom is chronic vomiting. Tilly was afflicted three nights ago and although she managed to get herself to the loo, her aim was not so impressive. She was sick again the following night, when unluckily she was staying with Sylvia at her cottage. Peter reported that she had not been at all upset and had in fact surveyed the mess with quiet pride when he came to clear it up.

Two nights ago it was Jack's turn. He was sick four or five times, but always got himself to the loo, where he stood heroically over the bowl, his hands firmly grasping the sides and his head stuck well down.

I thought he had recovered, but at lunch today he suddenly disappeared and we heard his footsteps above in the bathroom. After a while, I went up to help him, but found that he was sitting on the floor, equipped with paper and pencil, studiously copying out the lavatory's trademark, which is grandiosely printed in blue letters below the rim and reads: 'The Maxim'. I cannot think how this resounding epithet came to be chosen, except that it dates from a period of flamboyant brand names. A friend's house in Cambridge, for example, boasted a fine old machine, complete with polished wooden seat, which bore the daunting title of 'The Storm King'. Our own 'Maxim' can hardly be a reference to the Parisian restaurateur, and it seems altogether too bizarre that it should be named after the gun, though my dictionary does define this as obsolete and water-cooled. In any event, it inspired a page of Jack's most legible writing to date.

This morning Tim and Polly Brooks came here to play. Tim is Tilly's age, but is a great favourite with Jack because of his unfailing appetite for homicide and mayhem.

The girls settled into some game upstairs, while the boys resorted to making repeated raids on them, armed with Jack's guns, a pop-gun and a death-ray which produces a teeth-gritting noise when wielded by a merciless child. They were beaten off again and again, but to no avail until at last they were confronted with a threat to which they had no reply and no deterrent.

'If you don't go away and leave us alone,' I heard Tilly shout in her most determined tone, 'we'll *lick* you.'

The boys ran screaming down the stairs and did not return.

Wednesday, 6 April
Tilly has now lost two teeth, the front ones from her bottom jaw. These were left under her pillow and the fairies exchanged them for twenty pence apiece, the going rate round here.

Losing them has been a source of great pride to her. The first one to fall out was taken to school for exhibition in her class, among whom she is the youngest to have gaps in her mouth. As adults, we of course fear change taking place in our bodies, for it usually involves deterioration or some kind of loss. Pregnancy is, I suppose, the great exception to this rule. But with children, change is achievement. Their bodies are in a continual state of flux and fermentation; nothing is permanent or even stable. Some part of them is always being enlarged and strengthened at a faster rate than the rest. But growth brings loss as well as gain: although their teeth are the only bits of themselves they shed, they are constantly discarding other aspects of their being, notably clothes. This extreme volatility helps to explain why they are so eager to have pleasurable things repeated and turned into fixed routines.

Tuesday, 12 April
We have been travelling – in Sal's case, for the first time since February last year. We had arranged that I should take the children to stay with my parents, who

live near Chester, while Sally went to help her cousin in Warwickshire with his lambing. He has a flock of eight hundred ewes and his system involves a daily round of inspections on foot over a distance of twenty-five miles or more. Thus, for her, the world beyond Stowlangtoft turned out to be just the same, only on a larger scale, an impression reinforced by the fact that our first stop on the way was at Reading where we spent the night with some friends who have children named Tilly and Jack. This extraordinary coincidence was enough to turn our children into besotted disciples of their slightly older namesakes.

The next morning (Friday) Sally took us to Reading station to catch our train for Crewe, where my parents were to pick us up. Tilly and I had made the journey before, but apart from a short trip to Stowmarket on our little local train, this was Jack's first railway ride. As the train pulled in, Sally leapt aboard and secured us three seats on either side of a table, and once she had waved us off the children settled down like seasoned travellers. Of course, in a sense they do not 'travel' at all, but simply rebuild their own world wherever they find themselves. With hardly a glance out of the window, they spread out their books and toys and began to play as they do every day on our kitchen table at home. But having set up their stronghold, they then felt confident enough, I suppose, to accommodate the flow of strange, new experiences, whose input they could also control.

Perhaps inevitably, it was the toilets, which we visited many times, that proved the most interesting feature of the train. They competed each time to press the stud on the floor which operated the flush mechanism, but even their combined weight, the application of all four feet at once and much jumping up and down failed to activate it.

The next most interesting object was the sailor occupying the seat next to Jack. He had just come off his ship and looked exhausted, which presumably was why he slept throughout most of the journey, though the children regarded this as very eccentric behaviour. He was awake when we boarded and I noticed that he had a Falklands campaign medal. I asked him if he would show it to Jack, saying that he would be thrilled to see it. However, when the obliging sailor held it out for his inspection that notorious militarist and butcher of men was too shy to look.

At some point during the journey I noticed Jack picking his nose and, thinking that it was time he became aware of the impact his behaviour made on other people, I asked him to stop. Tilly then said, 'He eats his bogies. I tried them once,' she added thoughtfully, 'but I didn't like them.'

Although I may well be quite wrong, I have the impression that nose-picking is more common among boys than girls, or at least conspicuous nose-picking. I don't imagine there is any scientific evidence to prove it one way or the other. However, Jack, for one, has discovered the pleasures of this least attractive, but most gratifying habit and indulges in them freely, though not chronically.

The weekend with my parents passed off very smoothly and enjoyably. Only on Sunday did the children's behaviour reach a level of manic boisterousness that threatened to test everybody's temper. The day was spoilt by continuous rain and by lunchtime prolonged confinement was beginning to tell. My mother cooked a piece of exquisite beef, but Jack disdained it entirely, while Tilly would only toy with a couple of tiny slices as thin and pink as rose petals. They left the table and began to run in and out of the kitchen, giggling and wrestling in the doorway.

To break the tension I took them off to a little motor-car museum nearby where they played riotously with a broken-down child's electric car for nearly half an hour, after which they were restored to something like tranquillity.

We drove on to visit some friends of Sally's, who live on a beautiful Cheshire farm. Sadly, they were out, but we walked round the yard to look at some heifers, who peered back at us through the rain with bovine hauteur. As we drove home we came to a Little Chef and when I asked the children if they wanted to stop for tea they roared, 'Yes.' The inevitable sausages and chips were ordered, together with milk shakes, and everything was consumed at ulcerous speed. The cashier honoured the Little Chef 'pledge' with a pair of lollies and ten minutes later we were out in the rain again. Back at my parents' house they then settled into an extended bout of drawing, letter-writing and so on.

On the way to the station on Monday morning, Jack rather sweetly announced, 'I've forgotten what Mummy looks like.'

Throughout the whole weekend he only cried for her once, and that was following a nasty incident in the middle of our first night away. I heard crying and went into their room to find that he had fallen out of bed and was stuck, head-first, between his mattress and a wardrobe. His pyjama trousers, which were far too large for him, had fallen off and all I could see of him in the half-light was his lunar bottom. I released him and took him into my bed, but it was a long time before I could soothe him.

Tilly never cried for Sally; instead, she made her the target of quantities of letters and drawings.

On the way home we had lunch with our great friends the Thomases and felt sad that we only see them so rarely. This, however, is entirely because we

290

hardly ever leave Stowlangtoft, never mind Suffolk, for reasons which pressed themselves on us very affectingly the moment we stepped inside our house again on Monday night. Even ET himself (itself?) never said 'home' as feelingly as we did then.

Friday, 15 April
Tilly started school on Wednesday. She makes token protests each morning, but goes without putting up any serious resistance.

I myself went to school yesterday. For the next five weeks or so I am to be the so-called writer-in-residence at King Edward's in Bury St Edmunds. As part of my introduction I was invited by Ed Hills to sit in during his drama class for third-year kids. They were told to divide into groups of two and three and, inevitably, the segregation between the boys and girls was complete. At one point they were asked to make up playlets, using chairs. One of the girls' groups turned three chairs into a pram and devised a sketch involving a baby, which fell out. Giggling prevented them from acting out this drama to its conclusion. One of the boys' groups, no less predictably, turned a chair upside-down and made its legs represent 'a turbojet, fully automated, four-way nose-picker', which they proceeded to utilize with disgustingly energetic enjoyment.

Part of Tilly's reluctance to go to school is owing to the fact that neither Sylvia nor Jack go back until next week. In Tilly's enforced absence, these two have been thrown together and, somewhat to our surprise, have got on extremely well. At first, as the elder one tends to do, Sylvia mothered him with almost sickly solicitude, but now that they have had two long stretches in each other's company they seem to have settled into a more equitable relationship.

They spent all this morning out in the garden and only came into the house for drinks and to requisition teaspoons, of which we now have none. The sun has shone with nearly summery force for the first time this month. I have even seen a couple of butterflies cavorting above the lawn outside my window. We have also seen another less welcome reminder of summer, for the windows of the bathroom, which faces south, were fizzing with newly woken flies, their chitinous jackets gleaming greenly and evilly in the sunlight.

Since Wednesday Sylvia and Jack have been working on and off to construct a house in the garden. So far they have only laid the foundations, but they have done so with impressive thoroughness. First, they dug a considerable hole, which they lined with bricks and stones, and now they are putting down the first layer of bricks. Each one is liberally buttered with 'cement' – a sloppy mixture of water and ash from the Aga – and it is this process which is proving so expensive to our teaspoons.

Sunday, 17 April
Jack spent all Friday afternoon and much of yesterday in the garden building a 'mouse hole'. This was intended to be a combination of trap and home, into which he hoped to tempt a wild mouse. He distributed little bits of biscuit all round it and laid a long trail of biscuit into some nearby long grass. When he had finished, his hole was big enough to accommodate a badger, never mind a mouse.

At his request, I came to inspect it.

'The mouse will go in there,' he said, pointing down into the yawning pit he had dug.

'What are you going to do with it?'

'I want a pet.'

'What for?'

'To stroke.'

I agreed that in the morning, as soon as I woke, I would go on tiptoe to find out if a mouse had been caught, but as we stood looking at his laborious earthworks, he said forlornly, 'No mouse is going to come, is it?'

This did not stop his being disappointed in the morning. However, I have made a loose promise that I will research the possibility of buying him a pet mouse. In fact, although he does not know it, I have to go to Bury St Edmunds tomorrow and will put my promise into action then.

He has two distinctive modes of behaviour at the moment – the manic and the lugubrious. The latter is most strikingly expressed in his manner of walking, which is ploddingly dogged and gives the illusion he is wading knee-deep through a quagmire, but resolutely pressing forward. When in his lugubrious vein, his manner of talking is wretchedly doleful, as if he were resigned to making the best of a hopeless situation. This mood most often gives rise to the double-binds, which are so typical of him and which Tilly never makes for herself.

This morning, for example, he climbed into my bed and sank down beside me with the air of one who had just journeyed through inpenetrable jungle and across burning desert.

'I'm hungry,' he announced in his melancholy tone.

'Go downstairs and Mummy will make you some breakfast.'

'I don't want no breakfast.'

On the other hand, he wears a gloomy look when he is simply being thoughtful. This afternoon we watched *The Charge of the Light Brigade* (Errol Flynn version) and throughout he was at his most serious. His interest in the 'bakkles' was by no means bloodthirsty: he was fascinated by the fighting, but also repelled. During the charge itself, as a British lancer impaled a Russian gunner, he said, 'That man isn't being very kind.'

After more carnage he said, 'It isn't very good to shoot guns, is it?'

'No.'

The question hardly needed answering, since there were dead and dying bodies piled up everywhere.

However, a little later he added, 'But it's all right to shoot pretend guns.'

In contrast with his trudging pensiveness, Tilly grows more sprightly and impish every day. She darts about like a dragonfly, or perhaps I should say, like a damselfly. She never lolls or slumps, but always seems to hover, shimmering with a kind of dainty radiance, before hopping away to vibrate somewhere else.

I know that throughout this diary I have probably written about her less than Jack, but that is because in some ways Jack is easier to write about. For obvious reasons, I find myself quicker to identify with his boyishness, and I have no doubt that by the same token if Sally were keeping this journal she would give more space to Tilly. His plodding earnestness, his preposterous obsessions and outbursts are readily translated, by me at least, into vivid anecdotes, which are of course the stuff and essence of diaries. Where she is witty and subtle, he is clownish and vulgar, and this too makes for effortless copy.

But it was Tilly who first roused in me the fiercest, deepest feeling of love I have ever experienced and to some extent Jack simply inherited these. Before she was born, I was unfulfilled, an emotionally smaller person. She brought about this new growth in me more by being our firstborn than by being a girl. Nevertheless, our relationship has always been tinged with romance, just as my relationship with Jack is inflected by a special kind of comradeship. These may be clichés, but I am not ashamed of them, for they do authentically reflect the differing qualities of my feelings for the two of them.

Monday, 18 April
In the event, I was unable to get to Bury today, so the children's mice will have to wait until tomorrow. Jack still knows nothing of my plans, but this afternoon he got out his plasticine and made some miniature furniture, which he assured Sally was to furnish the 'upstairs' of his new mouse-house.

Wednesday, 20 April
Yesterday I went to one of the pet shops in Bury, and bought two white mice, both females. At this experimental stage, it seemed folly to invite multiplication. I was glad to see that, contrary to what I had expected, they did not have pink eyes. One is flawlessly white, but the other shows signs of reversion and has a slightly dusty complexion. At staggering expense, I also bought a tiny wooden hutch. This contains an upper chamber, approached by a ramp, and it has a sheet of glass at the front, which gives it the look of a television. Finally, I bought some wood shavings for their bedding and a bag of specially prepared mouse food, which appears to be a kind of high-octane muesli. The mice themselves were picked up with brisk professionalism by their tails, which are neon pink, and popped into cardboard travelling boxes, complete with air-holes.

Their surprise arrival naturally caused intense excitement. I immediately set up their new home, giving them a liberal supply of food to create a welcoming atmosphere. Their journey must have hungered them, because they both made directly for the heap of food and picked up a nut each, holding it in their fore-paws and chewing it with little drilling movements of their jaws. The children were entranced, though Sally looked on very doubtfully.

Tilly was quick to choose the all-white mouse and announced that it was to be called Perky.

'Mine's called Posy Posy Jack Harrison,' said Jack.

They could not wait to get them out of the hutch and stroke them.

'Come here, you little rascal,' Tilly said over and over again as she winkled hers out of the shavings, hauled it out by the tail and let it run inside again. The mice did not seem to mind being handled, but they soon grew adventurous. Jack's suddenly ran along his arm and escaped on to the floor. He screamed, Tilly lunged at it with a grab that would certainly have crushed it to pulp if she had made contact, and I attempted to keep calm while sprinting after it on my knees.

We caught it at last and I then put the hutch inside a bigger box – a long ammunition box which used to hold the logs for my fire – in the hope that the children would be able to watch the mice moving about without too much risk of tragic defections. However, this did not prove successful, for the children could not stop the mice running up their arms when they reached down to catch and stroke them. More hysterical chases ensued and I still have to devise a means of keeping their run secure.

Small, strokeable animals hold a profound fascination for children. Like all compelling relationships, it is made up of a mixture of sensuality and power: the children long to fondle and caress the mice, but their appeal also lies in their being too small to resist.

Tilly and Jack are at school as I write this; I have just been to look at their 'mouses', as Jack inevitably calls them, and found them asleep, buried in their shavings. They have curled themselves up in little balls, only distinguishable from ping-pong balls by the hectic trembling of their breathing.

Friday, 22 April
The last few weeks have been record-breakingly cold and wet, threatening the lives of everyone's lambs, which can withstand almost any extreme of weather, except prolonged damp. But at last the weather has broken, as it was bound to do, I suppose, on the very day I resigned myself to the cold continuing and ordered an extra load of logs.

Nevertheless, it is a welcome sight to discover the children playing in the garden while I type this at a quarter to seven in the evening. They are not wearing coats, and Jack has kicked off his wellingtons long ago.

Playing is too benign a word to describe what they are doing, which is one of their favourite and incurable summer occupations – stripping the garden of every bloom foolish enough to show its head. Not a single daffodil or narcissus is now to be seen and, despite my plea for clemency, the first of the tulips have been razed too.

Their ruthlessness appears to be the result of that peculiar combination of opposites which goes to make up the sportsman-naturalist, the big-game hunter who genuinely loves animals. They are not content simply to look at the flowers and admire them; nor are they satisfied with picking one or two. Unless restrained, they will not rest until they have completed a total wipeout. On the other hand, there is no question that they appreciate them and want to possess them for the sake of their beauty. Of course, it is true that their open-ended view of time does not help them realize that the life of a cut flower in a vase is considerably shorter than that of a growing flower, but all the same their predatoriness does seem to confirm Wilde's belief that 'All men kill the thing they love' (*The Ballad of Reading Gaol*).

Jack, the great white hunter, has now abandoned flower-collecting in favour of mole-trapping. Last year our lawn was reduced to a no-man's-land of little slag-heaps erupted by what appeared to be a whole regiment of moles. The grass was so thoroughly riddled with tunnels it was hardly safe to walk on. By some miracle, however, they have suddenly disappeared. The old mole hills, all of which used to show fresh soil at least twice a week, have subsided and are just flat patches of bald soil. In fact, the damage was probably done by a single mole, or at most a pair, for I believe they need to consume an astonishing quantity of earthworms merely to keep alive. Indeed, their appetite is so demanding they cannot sleep like other animals, but have to snatch naps during their unending quest for food. At all events, our mole or moles have either died or abandoned this network of tunnels. I am most relieved, because I no longer have to wriggle, as I did all last summer, on the dilemma of whether to save the lawns from the moles, or the moles from being trapped.

Jack is excavating one of these deserted tunnels with a screwdriver and muttering about keeping a mole in his bedroom as a pet.

Sally told Jack that he was going to go to Tilly's school once a week during the next term to prepare him for the following term, when he goes full-time. In his most despondent tone, he asked her, 'What do them men want with me?'

This was a projection of fear born entirely of fantasy: he has quite often been to school and on every occasion, apart from myself, there has never been a man in sight, for the staff consists only of women. Nor has he previously expressed anything but eagerness to join Tilly there; he has even complained about his playschool on the grounds that he is not allowed to work like Tilly does at her school.

However, on Friday Sally took him to meet Tilly out of school and they all attended a jumble sale (to raise money for textbooks, among other essentials!). By this time he had acquired, from another jumble sale, a splendid old-fashioned, all-leather school satchel, of which he is rightly very proud. Before leaving, he strapped on this unmistakable symbol of education and it seemed to fill him with new confidence. As it happened, he need not have worried because he was immediately taken off by Tilly and her friends to be entertained. Sally told me that soon enough he was to be seen clowning in one of the classrooms, falling over 'accidentally on purpose' and performing the rest of his repertoire of finely honed gags and tricks.

On Friday night they both stayed with Sally's parents, who in their generous way had given them a good time. This was nearly spoilt by Jack when we came to pick them up, for he was tearful and difficult, which was no doubt a punitive reaction to our leaving him. I began to kick a football in the garden with them, but Jack persistently ran away with the ball and then complained that we would not play with him. This all too typical no-win ploy finally exasperated me and I left him to Tilly. Somewhat to my surprise, she restored his good spirits within less than five minutes. Looking through the window, I could see them contentedly playing in their 'secret places' among the shrubs.

This is by no means the first occasion on which she has succeeded when we have failed. Although her method of re-engaging him in her games contains echoes of our own, it is essentially different. It appears to involve a combination of patience and ruthless self-interest, but the real point is, I suppose, that she needs him as a partner, whereas we aim to soothe him in order to recover our peace of mind and leave ourselves free to carry on with our own activities – in this case, drinking gin and tonic with Sally's parents.

On the same theme, Tilly made a very touching remark this morning.

Our friend, the great actor Ian Redford, asked Jack if he would like to join a party of small boys he was taking to Bury St Edmunds to watch a grand parade through the town of Boy Scouts, Girl Guides and other uniformed bodies. Jack does not know Ian well and in any case usually says no in the first instance to any invitation, but the lure of a parade proved to be irresistible and he accepted without hesitating. It was arranged that he would be picked up after lunch.

Out of his hearing, but in Tilly's, Sally and I discussed whether he would really be willing to go on the expedition when it came to the crunch. Tilly suddenly intervened.

'If it makes it any easier,' she said, 'I'll go with him, but I don't really want to. I'll go if he asks me,' she added.

In the event, he left us without a backward glance, returning many hours later, thrilled with what he had seen: 'Flags, drums, trumpets and spears.' The last item, which seemed an unlikely piece of equipment for Boy Scouts to be brandishing, turned out to be the pointed poles used for displaying their banners.

Sadly, the white mice have been more or less forgotten. This is not the result of the children being fickle, but rather the fact that they cannot play with them, as they wish to, without running the risk of letting them escape.

I must build them a high-security hutch.

Wednesday, 27 April
A very positive sign from Jack today.

After lunch he watched a programme on television about Red Indians, in which the principles of erecting a tepee were explained. For some reason, he was enormously interested, and as soon as the programme finished he asked if we could build our own tepee in the garden. Sally explained that we did not have the necessary poles, but promised that she would see if Granny (her mother, who is an expert gardener) would give us some bamboos. Instead of crying and making a scene, as he often does when frustrated, he immediately set about constructing his version of a tepee. He used little strips of paper, laboriously cut out, for the poles, and cones of card for the walls, and stapled them all together with what he calls my 'stabilizer'.

In this case art has not only substituted for reality, but improved on it, for he now has a whole encampment of tepees inhabited by his toy Red Indians. However, this community leads an unenviable existence, being under perpetual siege from a bizarre army of cowboys, modern soldiers, knights on chargers and assorted aliens.

For some reason, houses have been on his mind lately. As I drove him home from his nursery school

301

this morning, out of the blue he announced, 'I'm going to live in my own little house, with my own bed, my own cooker, my own table, my own roof, my own chairs.'

He elaborated on this list in a sing-song voice.

'Are you going to live on your own?' I interrupted him to ask.

'Yes,' he said, very emphatically, 'but people can come and see me.'

But as we came closer to home the fantasy began to lose some of its heroic independence and when he told Sally about his plans, he began, 'I'm going to get Daddy's saw and cut a hole in the wall of the kitchen and build my own little house, with my own little . . .' etc.

More often than not, their drawings are of houses, or rather houses and their families, who are usually shown lined up outside, as if parading for a friendly inspection. The most striking feature of these line-ups is that no distinction of size is made between adults and children, except that, in the case of Tilly's drawings, her own figure is always a little larger than the rest. This, presumably, indicates that they perceive themselves as equal partners in the family, and not as juniors or subordinates.

Saturday, 30 April
I was in London on Thursday and Friday.

My excitement at the prospect of a trip to London is, thankfully, always replaced by a no less intense feeling of relief when I am on my way home. I never leave London with regret.

After our disastrous experiences in December when I last went to London, I was determined that this time I would make no mistakes over the children's presents. I bought Tilly an exquisite Chinese doll, made mostly of coloured paper, which sits cross-legged at a little table painting a scroll. She seemed very pleased with it and this morning I noticed it had been put in a place of honour among her collection of ornaments and treasures which she keeps beside her bed. For Jack I had bought a US police helicopter; its blades go round, it has a winch mechanism beneath, and in the cockpit are a couple of removable officers, one of whom is in the act of spraying the ground with bullets. To my immense relief, he was very pleased as well, and even though the winch has proved too finicky for him to work he has continued to play with it and show it off to all visitors; indeed, it has hardly been out of his hands since I gave it to him.

Sally reported an amusing thing he said to her today.

He asked her why men's voices were different from women's and she told him about boy's voices breaking when they get older. He looked at her incredulously, but also anxiously.

'Do they mend again?' he asked.

May

Monday, 2 May
The May Day bank holiday.

It has rained most of the day, and it rained most of yesterday. Perhaps nature really has failed this time. As I write this, my fire is crackling cheerfully and I feel snug in my heaviest sweater. The children have just come in from the garden and have thrown down their boots and coats in the hall. Sally is about to give them a warming tea. However, these infallible signs of winter are set against a surreal background of bursting buds, nesting birds. fields jaundiced with oil-seed rape flowers and trees already blurred with greenery.

Tilly has spent almost every waking and sleeping minute of this long weekend with Sylvia. They seem to have been even more encapsulated in their own portable world than usual. It is often impossible to get their attention, even by shouting at them, when they are talking or playing together. Of course, Jack is the victim of their mutual absorption, but in fairness to them I think this points to his lack of a regular boy companion rather than their exclusivity. It is sheer bad luck that there is a dearth of boys his age round here.

As far as I can remember, Tilly and Sylvia have never had a tiff, far less a serious fight. On the very few occasions when they do get a little bored with each other's company, they vent their irritation on other people, usually an adult, but never become unpleasant to one another. It sometimes worries me, and I know it worries Peter too, that we do not play with them enough or provide them with enough stimulating entertainment; on the other hand, children who are capable of amusing themselves, with almost no adult intervention, for three successive days and nights can hardly be described as stultified or without imaginative resources.

This morning Sally and I laid a new carpet in the bathroom and very splendid and luxurious it looks too. Tilly evidently thought so as well, for as soon as she had the opportunity she took off all her clothes and was to be found rolling on it in ecstasies of shameless sensuality.

'Come on, Daddy. Take your clothes off,' she urged me, wriggling and squirming. 'Please do, Daddy, please.'

She was quite annoyed with me when I refused.

The priceless sight of her skinny fish of a body shimmying on our green carpet reminded me that, apart from a single reel of black and white prints, we have not taken a single photograph of the children since I started this diary. Like everybody else, we took innumerable pictures of our firstborn and rather fewer of our second child, but even so there is hardly a month of the five years preceding the start of the diary which is not represented by a snap of some kind. I am not sure why I stopped so abruptly. It certainly was not the result of any deliberate policy. I suppose throughout the year I have been inhibited by the fear that I am already exposing the children too much by writing about them; after all, I have had publication in mind since the beginning. To take photographs of them as well has always seemed an excessive abuse of their privacy. I admit the distinction is probably irrational and serves more to salve my queasy conscience than to protect the children, but nevertheless I am glad we have no photographs of this last year.

Photographs disclose nothing of their author, but at least this written account of the children reveals me to some degree and makes me vulnerable too.

The children have just had their bath. A minute ago Tilly ran into my room in her nightdress.

'Do you want a flash, Dad?' she asked me, somewhat to my surprise.

'Yes, all right.'

I looked round from my desk, not knowing what to expect.

She lifted her nightdress up to her waist, wiggled her bottom for a moment and then ran out, giggling.

Presumably, this extraordinary display was an echo of what the headmaster of my primary school used to refer to, with a shiver of disgust, as 'playground smut'.

Wednesday, 4 May
Yesterday the children came back from Tilly's school with a new book each. Jack had chosen a splendid anthology of jokes for kids, called *The Ha Ha Bonk Book* (What goes ha ha bonk? A man laughing his head off).

After they had had their tea, we all went into the sitting-room and Tilly proceeded to read out jokes to us.

'What do you give a sick pig?'

'I don't know. What do you give a sick pig?'

'Oinkment.'

Her punch-lines were mostly read out in a solemn voice, for she was concentrating on getting the words right rather than on her delivery.

'Why can't you play cards in the jungle?'

'I don't know. Why can't you play cards in the jungle?'

'Too many cheetahs.'

This line lodged itself in Jack's mind and for a while he shouted it out in reply to every joke Tilly read to us. As she ground through the book, he gradually extended his repertoire of killing punch-lines, throwing in some of his own invention. 'Elephant!' he would shout, or 'Because it's a big fat poo-poo!' or just 'Ha ha bonk!'

For him the joy of a joke is still the blissful release of laughter and the merging of his hilarity with someone else's. He is perfectly happy to go through the ritual, understanding nothing, but dissolving into hysterical laughter as soon as the punch-line is signalled. For Tilly, however, the meaning has now become all-important and she will not laugh unless she completely grasps the joke.

Friday, 6 May

I have been making all sorts of plans for the summer, if it ever comes, most of them concerning the garden. (Despite the prevailing monsoon, summer must be imminent, for I have just seen my first greenfinch and goldfinch of the year. I can never believe in the goldfinch as a native bird: it always looks so exotically tropical and makes even the tits seem drab.)

For once, the children's little patches are tidy and free of weeds and ready to be planted out. In fact, Jack has already planted an apple pip in his garden, which he inspects every day for signs of growth.

Instead of their gardens I now have their mice on my conscience. It seems that guilt is a constant and inescapable condition of being a parent. I still have not built a safe hutch and the children have lost interest. In the space of only two weeks the mice have gone

310

from being quite amenable to handling to being terrified of even the sight of humans; they have reverted to being 'wild'. Our shadows are enough to send them diving beneath their bedding and this puts off the children still more, since their only ambition is to get their hands on the mice and 'pet' them.

These last few days Jack has taken to intoning certain catch phrases of his own in a mechanical, repetitive style, reminiscent of ET. As we were driving to the station a week ago he began to chant, 'Daddy, don't go . . . Daddy, don't go . . .' in exactly the same rhythm used by ET to say 'ET go home' – his most poignant line, of course.

He is also in the habit of interminably droning ''appy . . . 'appy . . .'appy . . .' whenever he is in a good mood, which I am glad to say has been much more the case than not recently.

A new tranquillity has been settling on both of them during these last months since Christmas. Their lives seem to have taken on a steadier pace and their perspectives in time have lengthened; they are able to think of the immediate present as part of a far richer and more complex fabric of experience than they could have conceived of a year ago. Obviously, this is a capacity that develops naturally with age, but I think their new stability is also the result of Tilly's having finally resigned herself to school and settling into its more measured rhythms.

As adults we are very careful to pace ourselves through time, coming to terms with the present only by means of elaborate references to our future and past. Existence would be intolerable otherwise. But little children have no faculty for long-range anticipation and next to no personal history on which to draw. This is what makes them so exhausting to be with, especially for those unused to their very shallow im-

311

mersion in time. They treat everything that happens to them as an isolated and unique incident, committing themselves to it with indiscriminate intensity. For an adult, to live like that would be a short-cut to madness.

Jack has just told Sally a riveting piece of information.

'My willy hangs down when he's sad,' he confided in her, 'but when he's happy he stands up. And when he's very happy, he sometimes squirts.'

Sunday, 8 May
Another day of deluge and brilliant summer sunshine.

Everywhere is green and lush and spilling with sap. Our lawnmower is being serviced for the season, but we have arranged it a fortnight too late because the grass has suddenly sprung up, turning our already shaggy lawn into a little jungle.

This morning I found a bedraggled fledgling blackbird hopping among the logs near our back door. It was too soon out of the nest: its tail feathers had not grown and it could do no more than flutter just above the ground for a foot or so. Mostly it stood and cheeped. I showed it to the children, whose immediate reaction was to look for a suitable box in order to set it up in a home of its own. Their scheme was a typical mixture of care and possessiveness. The wretched creature was certainly doomed to die in the jaws of a cat, but it would probably have suffered more at their loving hands, so I persuaded them to feed it some bread and let it go.

An hour ago, on the strength of an especially plausible burst of sunshine, Sally took the children for a walk up Kiln Lane, which is looking even more beautiful than usual. As soon as they were out of sight, the clouds closed in and the sky turned black. It began to rain fiercely. However, Sally forced them to march on and they have just returned, drenched but in the highest spirits. To show me how wet they were, they danced about in front of my window, spinning round to make the water spray off their coats.

'Look, Dad. We're thirsty!'

They are standing in the driving rain with their heads thrown back and their mouths wide open.